TRANSCULTURAL
LITERACIES

TRANSCULTURAL
LITERACIES

RE-VISIONING RELATIONSHIPS IN TEACHING
AND LEARNING

Edited by Karen M. Magro and Michelle A. Honeyford

CANADIAN
SCHOLARS

Toronto | Vancouver

Transcultural Literacies: Re-Visioning Relationships in Teaching and Learning
Edited by Karen M. Magro and Michelle A. Honeyford

First published in 2019 by
Canadian Scholars, an imprint of CSP Books Inc.
425 Adelaide Street West, Suite 200
Toronto, Ontario
M5V 3C1

www.canadianscholars.ca

Library and Archives Canada Cataloguing in Publication

Title: Transcultural literacies : re-visioning relationships in teaching and learning / edited by Karen M. Magro and Michelle A. Honeyford.
Names: Magro, Karen M., 1972- editor. | Honeyford, Michelle A., 1956- editor.
Description: Includes bibliographical references.
Identifiers: Canadiana (print) 20190121424 | Canadiana (ebook) 2019012153X | ISBN 9781773381275 (softcover) | ISBN 9781773381282 (PDF) | ISBN 9781773381299 (EPUB)
Subjects: LCSH: Literacy—Study and teaching—Canada. | LCSH: Literacy—Social aspects—Canada. | LCSH: Minorities—Education—Canada. | LCSH: Critical pedagogy—Canada.
Classification: LCC LC149 .T73 2019 | DDC 302.2/244—dc23

Page layout by S4Carlisle Publishing Services
Cover design by Lauren Wickware
Cover artwork by Christi Belcourt, "Bear Lodge"

Printed and bound in Ontario, Canada

Canadä

Teaching, research, and writing are nurtured in communities. We dedicate this book to the transcultural communities of students, teachers, colleagues, scholars, storytellers, and knowledge keepers who have taught us and changed us; who inhabit our words and work; and who continue to inspire and move us in re-envisioning what is possible.

Table of Contents

Foreword

These are perilous times. But despite or even because of the social, cultural, political, economic, and ecological problems that abound around the world, possibilities are emerging that could move us beyond paralysis and polarization toward a profound social transformation. This is most evident in what we might call the "trans" movement, encapsulated in words like *transgender*, *transnational*, *translingual*, and *transcultural*: a converging set of processes that seek to transcend conceptual, political, and ideological boundaries that have long divided people, nations, languages, and cultures. We are being propelled by the energy of opposition into a new "beyond"—something that we perhaps cannot quite fully understand yet.

There are those who will surely critique these words, seeing them as blind to relations of power that are entrenching the very borders I see being erased. Certainly, we are living in a time when walls are being erected even as others are torn down. The quest to cross borders is being met with brutal backlash: the murder and detention of transgender and transmigrant people, and vicious re-assertions of racist, xenophobic, and transphobic discourses and policies.

Yet while bodies can be punished and held within borders, minds are harder to contain. Words are not restrained by walls. I can hit "send" and these words will go flying through the ethernet, crossing mountains, oceans, and multiple time zones in an instant. And words can sometimes transcend the biggest wall of all: the one that humans so often erect between our minds and our hearts.

Thus literacy is fundamental for furthering the processes of transcendence that are already taking form. Transgressive, critical, and compassionate literacy education is our best possible tool for forging a truly transcultural world. The authors in this book point the way. They reveal what is possible when educators build a literacy curriculum that makes reading basic: not simply to decode the word, and not even just to critically analyze the world (though that is important), but to engage deeply with the lives and experiences of those we might otherwise see as "other," and to break down the barriers around our own hearts.

The authors of this volume show us literacies of compassion, empathy, joy, playfulness, healing, and restoration. They describe curricula that lift the human spirit and that support students in rising to become their best selves. They show schools as sites of possibility and spaces for transforming the world—not reproducing it as it has been, but imagining how it could be. They do this with full awareness of the structural, institutional, political, and ideological forces that can lock learning into drudgery and pain. The authors show us how to break the locks.

At the time I write this, school children all around the UK just walked out of school in protest of government inaction around climate change. Another worldwide walkout is scheduled for next month. Young people are saying, effectively, that schools are not places to prepare for the future if the future is so perilous and at risk. Perhaps we should break all the locks, and abandon schools altogether. But there is another option, one that the authors of this volume make visible: to use schools as sites for transforming the future, preserving the planet, learning how to interrelate with others in new ways, and envisioning the world we want to live in and bequeath to future generations.

Marjorie E. Laine[1]
(formerly Marjorie Faulstich Orellana)

NOTE

1. This is my first publication under the new name that I am transitioning into, one that I assert as a kind of dialectical resolution of the tensions I have lived with post-divorce. I had thought my choices were to continue to walk the world as Marjorie Orellana or to revert to the name I abandoned 36 years ago. But this left me feeling tugged between two poles of patriarchy that no longer served my life. So, inspired by the "trans" movement and work such as that presented in this book, I have chosen to move forward with a new identity marker—one that holds some continuity with my past but that is also fresh, new, and full of possibility.

Preface

Insight and Imagination: Transcultural Literacies for Teaching and Learning

Karen M. Magro

Transcultural literacies have the potential to advance the discussion for meaningful teaching and learning in an increasingly cosmopolitan world. Pennycook (2010) defines transculturalism as the "fluidity of cultural relations across global contexts" (p. 27). Collectively, the authors in this volume view literacy as multimodal, lifelong, and evolving. Literacy is interconnected to the imaginal, rational, creative, intuitive, and analytical dimensions of learning. Literary and non-fiction texts created by students reflect their dreams, aspirations, conflicts, and needs. A deeper connection between literacy learning and being fully present in the world is encouraged (Freire, 1993). This creative journey involves an understanding, critical analysis, and exploration of how our social, cultural, historical, and geographic contexts continue to shape the way we think of and perceive words and worlds (Freire, 1993; Orellana, 2016).

What kind of a world might be created if individuals were more open to new cultural, linguistic, and philosophical paradigms? How might individual creativity and confidence be encouraged, and how might societies be improved if we encouraged our youth to develop their own literacies? Dagnino (2012) writes that "in this liquid age, patterns of mobility affect cultural orientations and sensibilities" and that "interactive and dialogic dynamics between and across cultures" can open up new understandings. Creative expressions can emerge that can remove barriers, borders, and binary ways of thinking (p. 1). Drawing from the work of Gloria Anzaldúa, Orellana (2016) writes that borders have served only to reinforce cultural stereotypes and misconceptions; borders have narrowed our understanding of interdisciplinary connections, different cultural ways of knowing, and the ability to value ideas that are different. In contrast, transcultural literacies encourage "animating hearts and minds, imagining possibilities, and finding our connections to the local community and to the world" (Orellana, 2016, p. 1). Epstein (2009) notes that youth are more inclined to confront social injustices when they read and write about current events, teen issues, and politics: "Their social critique can then stimulate their 'social imaginations,' or capacities to picture their streets, schools, and communities as different" (p. 61). Students can create visual and dramatic texts that communicate their ideas to the community at large when given the opportunity.

Linguistic diversity, global awareness, ethnographic skills, and emotional intelligence qualities such as self-awareness, empathy, resilience, learner empowerment, and significant personal and social change are themes that surface in the literature of transcultural literacies. Grounded in both theory and practice, the authors in this book address these themes in relation to key variables in the teaching/learning enterprise: the values, beliefs, and ideals that educators hold; learning processes; teaching/learning strategies; approaches to assessment; and the philosophical orientation of educational institutions.

The image of a prism (a triangular shape with refracting surfaces that separate white light into a spectrum of rainbow colours) can be used to describe the different dimensions of transcultural literacies. Each chapter in this book reflects a different light in this spectrum in examining approaches to decolonizing and re-envisioning education; positioning professional knowledge in relationship to theory and practice; the significance of transcultural texts and literature; global citizenship and transformational learning experiences; and the necessity of risk, vulnerability, and wholeness.

The teacher's ability to listen to their students' experiences and perspectives is a first step to ensure that the student no longer remains a passive bystander; when students create their own texts as an expression of their feelings, insights, and observations about their worlds, new understandings and solutions to problems can emerge. Reading and writing are interconnected with complex ways of being in the world. In chapter 1, George Sefa Dei advocates for a transformative vision of education that "is about the pursuit of decolonial resistance in everyday life" (Dei, this volume). He explains that teachers have their work cut out and a careful analysis is needed regarding the aims of education, the role of educators, teacher preparation, and the changing demographics of students in our classrooms. Too often, marginalized groups such as newcomer and refugee youth, older learners, individuals with mental health challenges, and First Nations, Métis, and Inuit learners continue to deal with social alienation and a devaluation of their histories, memories, experiences, and languages. "For Indigenous peoples who have been dispossessed of their Lands, the legacies of cultural genocide, residential schooling, and colonial settlerhood are yet to be fully addressed" (Dei, this volume). Literacy learning, from Dei's perspective, has the potential to correct misconceptions and racial stereotypes.

It is through "listening—reaching out from one human heart to another" that we can begin, as Richard Wagamese (2011) writes, to heal trauma and restore the human spirit (p. 81). In chapter 2, Marc Kuly's work with youth in the inner city of Winnipeg suggests that we need to *re-vision* a curriculum around student success by building on what students know and love rather than the opposite. Proverbs, storytelling, choral readings, spoken word poetry, biographies, and artistic collages can be catalysts for newcomer youth to express themselves. Students coming from cultures with rich oral traditions should be given more opportunities to share their knowledge. Kuly explains that "part of the dilemma with enacting teaching practices that support marginalized youth is the challenge of imagining alternatives to the status quo" (Kuly, this volume). How might a class be organized in a way that invites students to dream and envision a hopeful future for themselves? Marc Kuly's chapter reminds us that what you teach and how you teach can make a significant difference in the lives of individual learners. A transformative literacy curriculum could be built around the voices, stories, hopes, and challenges of learners in ways that would reduce social and psychological boundaries in the classroom and in the larger classroom of life. Multicultural and global texts can encourage inclusion, critical thinking, and a deeper appreciation of new or diverse perspectives. Kuly emphasizes that thoughtful and reflective teaching "requires a realization that the process of reproducing and naturalizing inequity is part of what happens in schools" (Kuly, this volume). Students too often leave school without experiencing belonging, mastery, and self-confidence. Kuly draws upon his own personal experiences as a teacher and a learner in providing a more positive vision for education.

In chapter 3, Michelle Honeyford describes the rich opportunities for multimodal literacy learning in an afterschool program for culturally diverse youth. Honeyford writes that we need literacies of compassion as well as critical literacies if we wish to break down systemic inequities that include racism, multiple forms of discrimination, and a fear of difference. Service learning opportunities, afterschool programs, and related alternative education contexts can help pre-service teachers disrupt misconceptions they may have about their students. Healthy educational contexts reduce stress and anxiety, and instead, increase students' motivation, engagement, and well-being. Transcultural literacies, as Honeyford observes, can help learners make sense of their experiences as they navigate new sociocultural locations. Honeyford emphasizes the importance of grounding teaching in that ability to understand the complexity of learning from the learner's point of view: "All of these 10- and 11-year-old students bring with them multiple subjectivities: their interests and affiliations, curiosities and fears, gifts and abilities; their cultural, linguistic, and gender identities; their beliefs, and perspectives, and worldviews." Developing "literacies of compassion" requires an emphasis on building relationships and engaging in shared activities—for example, as "teacher candidates sit shoulder to shoulder with students" as they create music, art, drama, hip-hop, and other texts (Honeyford, this volume). In these contexts, learning becomes a way of being.

In chapter 4, Lloyd Kornelsen examines the "cultural divide" that exists between two communities that produce and interpret knowledge differently: academic institutions of higher education (specifically, teacher education programs) and the practical knowledge of teachers working in the field of education. His chapter explores George Sefa Dei's imperative that communities that produce knowledge in different ways need to create a space for discussion. Drawing on his experiences facilitating a global citizenship practicum in Costa Rica, Kornelsen's chapter examines the politics of education within a discussion of transcultural literacies. Like the other authors in this book, Kornelsen emphasizes that the teacher-student dynamic is precious and potentially life changing. How can we prepare teacher candidates to be more sensitive and appreciative of cultural diversity? The work that teachers do in the field should inform and advance the knowledge of teaching in more subtle and more overt ways. Innovative curriculum design, the consideration of alternative places for learning, creative assessment, and the development of an educational system that embraces innovation would encourage literacy learning as a life-widening skill.

Karen Magro explores the connection between transcultural literacies processes and transformative learning in chapter 5. Her work with secondary English language arts teachers highlights the value of integrating emotional intelligence qualities and social justice themes such as planetary sustainability, human rights, oppression and inequity, the plight of refugees, and discrimination through literacy and non-fiction texts. Reading can be viewed as an act of empathy; it is through an awareness and understanding of different perspectives that transcultural literacies can develop. In studying the work of "transcultural writers," for example, readers are introduced to new cosmopolitan genres and ideas. Dagnino (2012) explains that

> it is not just a question of literary definitions and genres. It is instead a question of changing mindsets, different cultural approaches, heterogeneous identities, deterritorialising dynamics and, subsequently, of emerging new imaginaries that are being created in the process, through the active interaction between transcultural writers and transcultural readers. (p. 14)

A transcultural literacy curriculum that uses global and multicultural texts could benefit students in many ways, note McCaffrey and Corapi (2017). These benefits include: (1) A more engaging reading experience, where students become more interested in understanding how their experiences differ from those in other cultures. They may also be interested in learning new languages and in reading texts in other languages. Close attention to detail in reading and critical thinking skills can develop as students explore themes and issues that they may be unfamiliar with. (2) Students gain an expanded worldview as they broaden their perspectives and learn to think more deeply and critically about global issues such as poverty, oppression, ecological crises, and a lack of resources. Students can begin to understand how these challenges are manifested in countries around the world. (3) Increased self-confidence for English language learners. Reading books that reflect different immigrant experiences can enable English language learners to value their own experiences that might involve crossing numerous geographic, linguistic, social, and cultural borders. (4) An opportunity to help students make connections between the issues they are reading about and their own lives. Current issues can be integrated with international news stories in ways that inspire and enrich learning. In addition, using multicultural and global texts can help students improve their reading, speaking, and listening skills (McCaffrey and Corapi, 2017, p. 9).

In chapter 6, Burcu Yaman Ntelioglou and Tim Skuce explore Richard Wagamese's (1994) *Keeper'n Me* within the framework of transcultural literacies. Yaman Ntelioglou and Skuce remind us that reading is not a passive act; rather, it can be viewed as a transformative learning journey that invites a dialogue with existential issues. Reading can encourage empathy and insight into a character's experiences of injustice and alienation. Literacy texts should portray different forms of oppression and address structural inequality. Dialogue and discussion that can lead to repair, redistribution of resources, and reconciliation may then occur. Barriers to educational inclusivity include "contestations over knowledge, power, representation, identity, culture, resistance, and the possibilities of transgressive pedagogy."

In chapter 7, David Anderson challenges Eurocentric models of education that have negated and trivialized the concepts and ideas of Aboriginal peoples. The *Kenanow* ("All of Us") model of learning emphasizes that "who we are and how we come to know and understand the world are interconnected." A transcultural and transformative education would provide alternative spaces and places where new forms and celebration of Aboriginal ancestry, identity, and culture are fully embraced. Oral storytelling traditions, notes Ander-son, can help both educators and students become more fully engaged. Egan (2015) writes:

> Stories are instruments for orienting human emotions to their content. That is, stories do not just convey information about events and char-acters, nor do stories just convey information in a way that engages our emotions; stories orient, or shape our emotions to the events and char-acters in a particular way.... In an oral culture one knows mostly only what one remembers and the story is one of the most effective tools for encoding important social information.... Stories shape events into emotionally meaningful patterns. (p. 11)

This book comes at a timely moment. In a recent 2017 Statistics Canada Report, the data show that our country is more diverse than ever before. Com-pared to 4.7% of people surveyed in 1981, 22.3% of Canadians identify them-selves as a visible minority, and by 2036, 35.9% of the population in Canada will be composed of visible minority individuals (Statistics Canada, 2016). Canada's immigrant population continues to grow, and each year, schools are receiving students from China, the Philippines, India, Ethiopia, Eritrea, South Sudan, Syria, Iraq, Iran, Eastern Europe, and many other countries around the world. How do trajectories of immigration impact learning? Liv-ing in multiple places, acquiring several languages, and holding memories of places and spaces very different from the geographic and sociocultural ter-rain of Canada will influence the way learners interact within multi-layered communities and societal structures. Educators today have a responsibility to appreciate the richness newcomers bring to the teaching and learning context. Dagnino (2012) writes that in a globalizing world, "cultures, as well as soci-eties and identities, tend to be more fluid and intermingled, less irreducibly different and less 'territorially fixed' than in the past" (p. 13).

How can we build literacy programs around the strengths, linguistic di-versity, and experiences of all of our students? Reading, writing, listening, viewing, and representing are developed when teachers gain in-depth in-sights into learners' thought processes. The classroom can be seen as a cre-ative atelier where new investigations, discoveries, and forms of knowledge can emerge. Students today have a range of literacy expressions that include writing, digital communication, storytelling, art, drama, photography, and experiential learning. Learning is complex and nuanced and involves psychological, social, imaginative, intuitive, cognitive, analytical, creative, and kinesthetic dimensions.

To reach these dimensions, teachers today are challenged to conceptualize learning in more expansive ways. In *The Posthuman Child*, Murris (2016) notes that a deeper challenge of educational systems involves teachers preparing for the uncertainty and risk involved in "planning for lessons that democratically accommodate children's own questions and ideas" and that "draw on pedagogies with which they are unfamiliar" (p. 195). Yet, barriers stand in the way and, too often, students who are from marginalized backgrounds are left out; their skills and strengths lie dormant, and they may be vulnerable to feeling a sense of alienation and isolation. This book addresses some of the ways that all students can feel a part of the educational enterprise. Relationships between students, teachers, and administrators in educational systems can be viewed with new potential and possibility. Transcultural literacies emphasize evolving, flexible, and life-centred curricula that encourage human capacity building. In her book *Immigrant Children in Transcultural Spaces*, Orellana (2016) writes:

> Perhaps if schools relinquished just a little their tight hold on the distinction between truth and fiction, science and narrative, information and entertainment, data and story, we might imagine and build a more utopian and loving world. (p. 85)

Further, Orellana (2016) suggests that teachers play an important role as "socio-cultural mediators" who have "the power to shape the direction of [students'] growth" (p. 47). This book explores key questions such as: How do we create more effective learning contexts that value and validate learners' existing literacy practices while at the same time encourage a creative climate that continues to shape and expand literacy practices? How can educators break down psychological, situational, and institutional barriers that prevent literacy learning? How can we re-vision a dynamic curriculum that includes global literacies?

Effective teaching involves empathy and positive relationship building across and beyond borders—cultural, geographic, linguistic, socio-economic, and psychological. Teaching should energize, engage, and enlighten. Teachers in this context are co-investigators with their students; they are visionaries, challengers, advocates, artists, mentors, and facilitators of learning. It is our hope that new insights into learning and literacy within the context of cultural, psychological, and social transformation will emerge.

Tilleczek (2016) writes that authentic voices from learners do "not fracture or reduce lives into small places, but rather invite open-ended and imaginative ways" (p. 37) to understanding learning processes and the complex lives of youth who do not feel a sense of belonging in school. We need to create literacy and learning opportunities that help students succeed. The challenges and struggles of youth are contextualized by families, friends, schools, communities, the natural world, and society. She further explains that "most of the young people we work with and for are those who have been made marginal to society, their voices never heard or carelessly erased or ignored. Many struggle in school due to poverty and/or discrimination and/or mental health issues" (p. 36). Tilleczek (2016) suggests that more opportunities for students to be researchers, writers, ethnographers, and anthropologists who are observing, interviewing, photographing, and crafting stories would succeed in creating a dynamic climate of learning. Assessing literacy learners' needs began by connecting with the learner in a holistic way that encouraged learners to "tell their teachers what they cared about, what they hoped for, where they felt safe, who their most important people were, what they were really good at, and what cultural practices were important to them" (p. 78). Our hope is that this book will provide helpful insights into ways that literacy barriers can be removed and that the strengths of all learners can develop.

While the focus of this book is not on delineating social class and connecting it to the potential for literacy learning among children, youth, and adults, it is vital to recognize the way in which systemic barriers (e.g., food insecurity, mental health, unsafe housing, family fragmentation and hardship, exposure to violence) can hinder learning processes and human capacity building. Our overall well-being is influenced by our living conditions. It is important to note that conceptions of social class vary depending on the study, but in general, SES (social-economic class) "describes an individual's or a family's ranking on a hierarchy according to access to or control over some combination of valued commodities such as wealth, power, and social status" (Sirin, 2005, p. 418). Collective health and literacy would improve in a transformative way if social programs prioritized the needs of individuals, families, and communities and worked in a systematic way to remove psychological, situational, and institutional barriers. We must ask: How could public policy be shaped in ways that would benefit all?

Determinants of health are a broad range of psychological, cultural, social, economic, and environmental factors that determine individual and population health (Brownell et al., 2005; Fernandez, MacKinnon, & Silver, 2010). Socio-economic status and overall health have been linked to how well or poorly an individual performs in school and in the achievement of life goals. Studies have linked income and social status, parental occupation, employment history, working conditions, neighbourhoods, school size, and physical environment to both health and learning outcomes/academic achievement in childhood and adulthood (Brownell et al., 2005; Sirin, 2005). Brownell and her colleagues (2005) write that "it is also well known that there is a strong relationship between health status and socio-economic status. Those with higher incomes, higher levels of education, and higher status jobs live longer and healthier lives than those with lower incomes" (p. 1). These researchers further correlate low socio-economic status and parental occupation and income as "predictors" of academic achievement among children and youth. They conclude their analysis of social determinants of education and health by stating that universal education programs should "ensure that those children with the greatest needs receive whatever extra support is required to help them improve their outcomes, regardless of where they live" (p. 12).

It is important to recognize that sociological and educational studies linking SES with learning outcomes are limited in their scope. The voices of the children, youth, and adults who are central to these studies are often left out. The authority and authorship of learners to activate change in their lives is undermined, and the complex and rich tapestries of family, traditions, community networks, and individual differences that could inform a study about learning barriers can be left unexplored (Thiessen, 2007). Little emphasis is placed on creative potential and individual talent; for example, parental occupation alone does not determine a child's motivation to excel. Growing research (including examples in this book) suggests that transformative change can occur and new spaces for growth and talent development can emerge anywhere (Cain & Boydell, 2010; McCluskey, Treffinger, Baker, & Wiebe, 2016; Sirin, 2005). From an Indigenous perspective, Steinhauer and Lamouche (2018) assert that "western-based competencies" should be interpreted more from a community-based, Indigenous worldview. They write that "concepts such as family, security, child development, parenting, and health can be understood very differently" (p. 84). Steinhauer and Lamouche assert that students who have a strong grounding in their own cultural traditions and languages would be better prepared for the future. They highlight the need for a holistic education that integrates spiritual, emotional, social, and cognitive dimensions:

> Most mainstream [educational] programming does not include a spiritual component; often uses a problem-solving or deficit model; frequently ignores traditional kinship mapping and family organization; does not address the trans-generational impacts of history; and does not include the use of Indigenous languages, traditional teachings, or ceremony. With Indigenous program design, delivery, and evaluation, understanding is based in meaning as opposed to measurement, and in process as opposed to outcome—and it is in these differences that the expectation of different and better outcomes will result. (Steinhauer & Lamouche, 2018, p. 83)

Education policy makers must critically question how the marginalization, silencing, and social devaluing of some individuals based on race, culture, religion, class, gender, schooling, neighbourhood, and language occurs. Rummens and Dei (2010) explain that "marginalization is a process, not a label—a process of de-valuation that serves to justify disproportional access to scarce societal resources. As social actors, we do this to each other" (p. 50). These researchers present the example of minority and refugee youth coming from countries of war and conflict who may be coping with multiple stressors such as navigating an unfamiliar culture, language, and customs. Others may be overcoming loss and trauma. They may feel a sense of social isolation as well as the responsibility of assuming adult roles in the family. However, to undervalue or negate their strength, resilience, existing skills, and talent is to shortchange these youth as they navigate new pathways.

Researchers like Sirin (2005) assert that SES is also not a static phenomenon; people and communities can develop and transform in significant ways when resources and opportunities are available. The assumptions, predictions, and interpretation of outcomes can be misconstrued (e.g., a parent not completing secondary school does not "determine" a child's talent and skill in setting their sights to complete higher education; a parent without a high school education still has the potential to achieve and advance their learning or education). A fatalistic narrative of impending failure or inevitable problems can also create a climate of hopelessness, fear, and apathy. "We hear marginalized youth described as 'deviant, criminal, substance users, culturally impoverished, overtly different, bored and powerless'" (Caine & Boydell, 2010, p. 43).

These labels are harmful, misleading, and can be used to further alienate vulnerable youth who feel that their stories and experiences are not acknowledged or heard.

Caine and Boydell's (2010) qualitative research exploring the narratives of youth who are often considered marginalized in society points to individuals who are "imaginative, creative, and resourceful human beings with social, cultural, and political agency" (p. 43). A "sociological imagination" that listens to the aspirations, fears, and hopes of the life worlds of young people is needed. "By listening to marginalized youths, we ground our knowledge in their lives, accounting for the intersection of representation and identity as well as the multi-faceted mingling of the social, cultural, and psychological elements in their lives" (p. 43). Rummens and Dei (2010) advocate for significant policy changes to break existing patterns of social dislocation and marginalization to ensure the realization of education-, success-, and associated life-outcomes for students who have been historically marginalized. They write that "to do this we need to better understand, consider, and respond to the social location and life circumstances of our diverse students" (p. 58).

What is clear is that we need to move beyond labels and stereotypes and work to create communities and classrooms that restore, reclaim, and recognize the value and potential for all individuals to contribute. We need social and educational policy to interconnect in ways that improve access and opportunity for individuals who are most in need. The chapters in this book provide new pathways to consider as we strengthen educational opportunities for all learners.

It is the authors' intent to encourage and extend discussions and critical inquiry into the multi-faceted dimensions of transcultural literacies. The specific design features of this text invite you to participate in a critical and creative dialogue with the text chapters, with your colleagues, "with imagined possibilities" for literacy learning, and with the critics (Jarvis, 2006; Magro, 2015). The chapters encourage you to think of significant personal and professional learning experiences that have shaped your perspectives of learning and literacy. Reflective questions, visual organizers, and additional resources offered for further reading and classroom use will, we hope, contribute to enriching the dialogue as you read, and serve as a valuable reference for you in your ongoing professional journey. You are encouraged to approach the book iteratively, returning to the visual organizers and revisiting the reading notes and questions so they may be a catalyst for you to make connections between and across the chapters. Ultimately, we hope you will expand the dialogue that we have begun, critically and creatively engaging in this work of transcultural literacies—the work of all of us in all the transcultural dimensions, spaces, and contexts of our lives.

REFERENCES

Brownell, M., Roos, N., Fransoo, R., Guevremont, A., MacWilliam, L., Derksen, S., Dik, B., Bogdanovic, B., & Sirski, M. (2005). *Why do educational outcomes vary with socioeconomic status? Key findings from the Manitoba Child Health Atlas, 2004.* Winnipeg: Manitoba Centre for Health Policy.

Caine, V., & Boydell, K. (2010). Composing lives: Listening and responding to marginalized youth. *Canada Education, 50*(5), 42–45.

Dagnino, A. (2012). Transcultural writers and transcultural literature in the age of global modernity. *Transnational Literature, 4*(2), 1–14.

Epstein, S. E. (2009). "[T]o carve out new orders in experience": Imagination in a Social Action Literacy Project. *English Journal, 99*(2), 61–66.

Fernandez, L., MacKinnon, S., & Silver, J. (2010). The social determinants of health in Manitoba. Winnipeg: Canadian Centre for Policy Alternatives.

Freire, P. (1993). *Pedagogy of the oppressed.* New York: Seabury Press.

Jarvis, C. (2006). Using fiction for transformation. In E. Taylor (Ed.), *Teaching for change: Fostering transformative learning in the classroom. New Directions for Adult and Continuing Education, 109,* 69–78. San Francisco: Jossey-Bass.

Magro, K. (2015). Teaching for social justice and peace education: Promising pathways for transformative learning. *Peace Research: The Canadian Journal of Peace and Conflict Studies, 47*(1/2), 109–142.

McCaffrey, M., and Corapi, S. (2017). Creating multicultural and global text sets: A tool to complement the CCSS text exemplars. *Talking Points, 28*(2), 8–17.

McCluskey, K. W., Treffinger, D. J., Baker, P. A., & Wiebe, A. C. (2016). *Lost prizes: Identifying and developing the talents of marginalized populations.* Ulm, Germany: International Centre for Innovation in Education.

Murris, K. (2016). *The posthuman child.* London: Routledge.

Orellana, M. F. (2016). *Immigrant children in transcultural spaces.* New York: Routledge.

Pennycook, A. (2010). *Language as a local practice.* New York: Routledge.

Rummens, J. A., & Dei, G. S. (2010). Including the excluded: De-marginalizing immigrant/refugee and racialized students. *Canada Education, 50*(5), 48–53.

Sirin, S. R. (2005). Socioeconomic status and academic achievement: A meta-analytic review of research. *Review of Educational Research, 75*(3), 417–453.

Statistics Canada. (2016). 2017 Annual Report to Parliament on Immigration. http://www.cic.gc.ca/english/resources/publications/annual/report-2016/index/

Steinhauer, D., & Lamouche, J. (2018). Miyo-pimâtisiwin: "A good path": Indigenous knowledges, languages, and traditions in education and health. In M. Greenwood, S. de Leeuw, & N. M. Lindsay (Eds.), *Determinants of Indigenous Peoples' health: Beyond the social* (2nd ed.; pp. 80–92). Vancouver and Toronto: Canadian Scholars Press.

Thiessen, D. (2007). Researching student experiences in elementary and secondary schools: An evolving field of study. In D. Thiessen & A. Cook-Sather (Eds.), *International handbook of student experience in elementary and secondary school* (pp. 36–52). Dordrecht, the Netherlands: Springer.

Tilleczek, K. (2016). Voices from the margins: Educative research with, for, and by youth. *Canada Education, 56*(4), 34–38.

Wagamese, R. (2011). *One story, one song.* Toronto: Douglas & McIntyre.

Acknowledgements

The writing of this book was a collaborative endeavour. As writers and educators, our work is always inspired by, in dialogue with, and responsible to communities. The essence of transcultural literacies is relational, and so we wish to begin by acknowledging the importance of learning to live in relationship. In the words of Richard Wagamese (2016):

> I've been considering the phrase "all my relations" for some time now. It's hugely important. It's our saving grace in the end. It points to the truth that we are all related, that we are all connected, that we all belong to each other. The most important word is "all." Not just those who look like me, sing like me, dance like me, speak like me, pray like me or behave like me. ALL my relations. That means every person, just as it means every rock, mineral, blade of grass, creature. We live because everything else does. If we were to choose collectively to live that teaching, the energy of our change of consciousness would heal each of us—and heal the planet. (p. 36)

In this work, we are deeply grateful to Heather Hunter, the inspiration and catalyst for this book. Our thanks to Heather for inviting us to collaborate in the early days of planning the MERN (Manitoba Education Research Network) symposium that was the impetus for this book. Heather's passion for bringing educators together with the goal of providing greater access and opportunity for all learners is both relentless and inspiring. As we worked with Heather on our initial plans for this book, her kindness, creative spirit, and guidance provided motivation for our writing, and as the book took shape, Heather read and provided feedback for many of the chapter drafts. Heather's work as the director of MERN has been paramount in creating a dynamic space in Manitoba for collaborative educational research and inquiry and for the production of new knowledge and theory in K–12 and post-secondary contexts.

We are grateful to Ken McCluskey for his generous support and encouragement of innovative educational projects, including the writing of this book.

We would also like to acknowledge George Sefa Dei (Nana Adusei Sefa Tweneboah), who gave the opening address at the transcultural literacies symposium and whose anti-racist, anti-colonial, and Indigenous knowledge frameworks and global vision for transformative education are strong through-lines in this book. We are grateful to him for his critical insight and wisdom—for powerful truth-telling that our students need us to listen to and enact.

To our colleagues and collaborators, we thank you for taking up this invitation and for writing about the important ways this work matters—personally, professionally, and politically. Our inquiries are borne out of our experiences in classrooms, communities, and research contexts. We are grateful for the opportunity to learn with and from one another. We also acknowledge that the work we do is always in relationship, and thus we wish to thank the students, adult literacy learners, teacher candidates, teachers, and colleagues who shape our practice, provoke our questions, inspire our theories, and make possible our research.

We are also grateful to those who have joined us on the journey of co-editing this book. Our vision was that the book would be pedagogical in its orientation, inviting dialogue in classrooms and professional learning communities. We are grateful to Karla Costa for reading each chapter and creating the visual organizers for our book and contributing to the questions, readings, and resources. We treasure her diligence, patience, and imagination as we worked to visually "map" the theories and ideas in each chapter. We are grateful to Gary Evans, who provided editorial guidance and content expertise. Paulo Freire wrote that teaching is not just an act of courage but an act of love, and it is with this expression that we see this book as the start for further discussions and research possibilities.

We express our deep gratitude to Canadian Scholars Press for understanding and sharing our vision and for their exceptional guidance in realizing this book.

We also wish to acknowledge the readers of this book. We believe deeply in the strength of collaborative inquiry and dialogue, of creating communities of compassion and resistance that work together across boundaries and borders to imagine and effect real change. We acknowledge the lessons we need to learn about living with one another in humility, and with respect, courage, honesty, wisdom, truth, and love. To those who have walked before us, to those who walk this path with us, and to those who are still to come, we honour and thank you.

Decolonizing Education for Inclusivity: Implications for Literacy Education

We must move literacy education from knowing how to read and write to engaging learning as a process of sharing, reciprocity, respect, collaboration, healing, and creating sustainable relationships.

—*George J. Sefa Dei*

OPENING THE CONVERSATION: READING NOTES

How can we transform education systems in positive and inclusive ways if we do not critically identify, examine, and change the socio-political and cultural systems that continue to exclude so many? In this chapter, George J. Sefa Dei (Nana Adusei Sefa Tweneboah) explores the context for educational change. He illustrates how historical, political, ideological, economic, and social foundations must be taken into account in any discussion of education and learning. Dei examines the barriers that impact literacy and learning: ongoing global challenges such as racism, xenophobic attitudes, terrorism, conflict and war, the refugee crisis, and land claims. He reminds us of the larger contexts of our classrooms and schools, and argues there is a vital need for us as educators to critically examine our own views of culture, literacy, belonging, and identity.

With a focus on inclusion, Dei draws on post-colonial theory to critique Eurocentric models of knowledge production that focus on "selected capacities and potentialities" to the exclusion of other belief systems, identities, bodies of knowledge, and voices. From a colonial perspective, notes Dei, literacy education is seen as an "end in itself"—a prescribed curriculum privileging individualism and competition. Dei writes that "we must move literacy education from knowing how to read and write to engaging learning as a process of sharing, reciprocity, respect, collaboration, healing, and creating sustainable relationships."

Dei provides a decolonial framework for education rooted in anti-oppressive and holistic tenets. He proposes that literacy education can create opportunities for teachers, students, families, institutions, and the wider community to engage in ongoing dialogue that resists oppression and develops critical consciousness, informed by Indigenous knowledge and transgressive pedagogies. Educational experiences, as Dei observes, cannot be fragmented and disconnected from one's experiences in, responsibilities to, and relationships with the wider community. In efforts to work toward a transformative and visionary education, education processes should welcome "underrepresented narratives," embrace "social difference," and critically engage in "dealing with violence" and "unlearning privilege."

As you read this chapter, consider Dei's conceptualization of a future literacy educational agenda informed by change and inclusion in relationship to your context. In our specific locations, how can we work together to listen, co-produce, "rewrite" and "tell" stories that resist, respect, and heal our transcultural communities? What strategies can we take up to apply the intellectual agencies and voices of our students and communities for educational and relational transformation?

THINKING VISUALLY: CHAPTER ORGANIZER

Dreaming about ...
Imagining ...
New Futures for
(Canadian)
Educational Contexts

Framework/ Philosophical Paradigm/ Perspective	Colonial Educational Agenda/ Eurocentric	Decolonial Educational Agenda/ Indigenous	New Politics of Global Futurity Educational Agenda/Transcultural
Purpose	Global Western capital reach	Resistance to oppression	"Epistemic break"
	Neo-liberal thoughts and markets	Development of critical consciousness	Inclusivity
	Western knowledges	Social difference knowledges	"Wholeness"

Framework/ Philosophical Paradigm/ Perspective	Colonial Educational Agenda/ Eurocentric	Decolonial Educational Agenda/ Indigenous	New Politics of Global Futurity Educational Agenda/Transcultural
Learning and Pedagogical Orientation	Linear approach to learning how to read and write Specific or pre-determined skills Learning is more limited and narrow Traditional pedagogy	An encouragement to read and write the word and the world (Freire, 1993) Learning is not sequential, but rather holistic and integrated Critically engaged with social difference Learning how to share, respect, think critically, and create sustainable relationships Elders are guides in helping learners through life lessons Elders are mentors in the teaching/learning dynamic Learning is not separate from community building, family relationships, and relationship to the land Learning is more fluid, lifelong, and connected to personal, social, and community transformation Transgressive pedagogy	An encouragement to read and write the word and the world (Freire, 1993) Critical knowledge Individual & collective voices Learning is interconnected with local and global events Learning involves personal, social, and ethical development Learning is a journey and process of becoming Learning is creative, critical, and collaborative Learning is more fluid, lifelong, and connected to personal, social, and community transformation Transgressive/ disruptive/ subversive pedagogy
Authority and Intellectual Agency	Western canon Specialized disciplines and discourses Knowledge and authority are hierarchical Competitive and individualistic	Collaborative, holistic, and collective Interconnected systems of knowledge	Knowledge systems are ever-evolving A commitment to anti-racist and social justice advocacy Listening to and learning from diverse knowledge systems, cultures, and identities

Source: Figure by Karla Costa

The table highlights key concepts discussed in the chapter and suggests ways to think about how these ideas work in relationship to policies and practices at work in colonial and decolonial approaches. Think about the theories and practices embedded in a specific educational system or context you know: What approach is being taken? What evidence do you see of that approach? The third column represents Dei's educational agenda for a new politics of global futurity. Think about your context: What would such a future look like? What would need to change to enact such a vision?

CHAPTER 1

Decolonizing Education for Inclusivity: Implications for Literacy Education

George J. Sefa Dei (Nana Adusei Sefa Tweneboah)

What does it mean to educate for change and inclusion in today's schools? How do considerations of inclusivity, equity, culture, and identity factor into discussions of literacy education? This chapter explores some of the challenges of decolonial educational politics highlighting the implications for inclusivity as they relate specifically to questions of literacy education. This chapter considers a broad understanding of literacy education to advance the interplay of knowledge, identity, culture, and educational politics. I assert that discussions of literacy education must highlight systemic barriers to education inclusivity pointing to contestations over knowledge, power, representation, identity, culture, resistance, and the possibilities of transgressive pedagogy. The structural and systemic challenges that confront contemporary learners (e.g., racism, navigating culture, language, power, and the politics of social exclusion) call for developing and implementing practical strategies for achieving educational inclusion. We are also challenged to imagine and to revise new educational futures. We need to consider the growing impact of world events and global changes on learning, literacy, and social justice. For example, struggles over land and identity, a rise in racist exclusions, the impact of oppression in a xenophobic world, persistent terrorism of multiple forms, and the overall fragile state of the world all impact educational systems and individual learners' lives. Our work as educators is urgent, so how do we move forward to envision an education that helps solve some of the prevailing global challenges? What do we see as the role of education in mobilizing human agency and resilience for change?

A primary concern is the pursuit of educational resistance in the search for a new global futurity working with critical knowledge anchored in individual and collective intellectual agencies and voices. In my own work, I continually grapple with what it means for a politics of global futurity where scholarship counts and is relevant in the face of human lives. Clearly, we will need to co-produce critical knowledge, deploying our intellectual agencies and authentic voices for change. There are enduring systemic challenges with particular impacts on marginalized, racialized, and Indigenous students' success in schools (Castagno & Brayboy, 2008; Dei et al., 1997; Savage et al., 2011). The salience and silence of race and Indigeneity (e.g., the ongoing legacies of anti-Black racism, settler colonialism, Islamophobia) are among the challenges that readily come to mind.

A prevailing neo-liberal educational agenda continues to lay bare limitations of schooling and a restrictive education in the context of a global capitalist modernity. We are witnessing in our schools, colleges, and universities a disciplining of bodies and knowledges (through regulation, deregulation, competition) intended to ensure that what is deemed education and/or how such education is approached serves individualized, private, corporate market interests (Dei, 2008, 2017b; Ball, 2003; Bertelsen, 2008; Bragg, 2007; Campbell, Proctor, & Sherington, 2009; Davies, 2005; Gibbs, 2001).

We must uphold new critiques of the "global publics," i.e., a recognition of an emerging "transnationally-organized global public" very critical of the ways globalization has actually intensified global socio-economic inequalities (Mundy, 2008). On the global landscape, rising levels of poverty are linked with the logics and mechanics of globalization and global forces. Globalization, contrary to its much-touted benefits, has been accompanied by differential or asymmetrical benefits of "modernization" to the Global North and the Global South. For example, while in the Global South some may point to the benefits of education as a core avenue for "global redistributive justice" (Mundy, 2008) the links of "democracy," "good governance," and "human rights" in the context of the primacy of global markets and capitalism are disturbing. The "rights" of global capital continue to be met unchallenged. The global reach of Western capital is extensive. The regulatory potentialities of global capital to create and to dominate "space and spatial economies," to determine literally who lives and who dies, who is deemed worthy of education, and whose future is predetermined, is awesome. Clearly, there is everyday resistance to globalization; however, the fact remains that the power of global capital to define and to determine what is knowledge, what constitutes a worthwhile intellectual project, and the acquisition of a local cultural resource as property of the powerful nation/state/empire is indisputable. When matched with the seduction of the communication capacities of global capital, it reveals the extent, nature, and enormity of what confronts the task of education for transitioning into new futures. It is imperative that we be aware of the material conditions that would make transformative education possible.

In the discourse of global and transcultural literacies, many scholars are writing about some specific impacts of schooling and education (see also Magro, 2008, 2015; Magro & Ghorayshi, 2011, among many others). For example, in order to promote education for global diversity it is insisted that we critically engage social differences and what they mean for teaching, learning, and administration. I see this call as more than a knowledge of the cultural politics of schooling. It is about the pursuit of decolonial resistance in everyday schooling and education. It is about understanding how the different bodies in our school systems come to navigate culture and power in a new place, especially when bodies are caught within the "bifurcated regimes of citizenship" that include the divide of "citizens with rights" and "subjects to be governed" (Spencer, 2006). For many learners, their very existence, within and outside school spaces, is about struggling for inclusivity and resisting the dictates of "capitalist citizenship" (Hall, 2002; Spencer, 2006). For Indigenous peoples who have been dispossessed of their Lands, the legacies of cultural genocide, residential schooling, and colonial settlerhood are yet to be fully addressed. In such a context, what can we say about the integration of new migrants into these communities and schools as they deal with social alienation, devalued identities, and social and racialized exclusions? As noted elsewhere (Dei, 2008; Fiedler, Schuurman, & Hyndman, 2006; Dion, 2001; Biles, Burstein, & Frideres, 2008), among the crises of voluntary and involuntary migrants today are racialized and gendered poverty, homelessness, and displacement; post-traumatic stress as a result of coming from war zones; and increasing discrimination in the housing and social service sectors. All of these affect people's sense of belonging. Refugees are navigating unfamiliar legal, financial, educational, cultural, and social contexts, often with limited resources. When we speak of global extremism, it is not just terror by fringe groups. We must include state-sanctioned violence and how this violence has contributed to the fragile state of the world.

As many have noted, extremism—such as religious extremism, racial bigotry, and the perception of Islam as a threat—as a current global concern has links to terrorism of all forms. Transformative education can help counter forms of extremism. The possibilities of literacy education could prevent youth from joining extremist groups and enable youth to critically analyze extremism and its consequences (Davies, 2009) and to create learners who would transform their communities. We can only pursue this agenda if we confront the questions: What sort of literacy education is required in schools? And how can literacy education be meaningful for young learners?

THE FRAMING OF LITERACY EDUCATION

There are many works on literacy and multiliteracies education (e.g., Cope and Kalantzis, 2000; Norton, 2007; Luke, 1997). Traditional or "dominant" conceptions of literacy are about knowing how to read and write in colonial languages, predominantly English (see critiques by Norton, 2007; Luke 1997). Colonialism as a framework can be used to understand conceptions and articulations of literacy. Traditional notions of literacy are guided by a rationalization that presumes the acquisition of English reading and writing skills is the only mode to becoming literate. Colonial dimensions of literacy can be highlighted when we begin to understand the processes by which English becomes the standard of measure. Those who are literate enough are allowed to enter spaces of knowledge production, while those who are not become knowledge consumers. Those who produce wield power, while those who consume become the servants of the production process. Literacy is the conduit through which knowledge and power flow; those who are thus defined as illiterate are subjugated and meant to serve those who are literate.

Street (2001) has called for understanding "the uses and meanings of literacy practices to local people themselves" (as cited by Norton, 2007, p. 12). There have also emerged significant works that have argued for a "spatial analysis of literacy and transcultural literacy" as well as pedagogical work around developing multiliteracies. For example, Kostogriz & Tsolidis (2008) lament how dominant conceptions of literacy are filled with notions of "placeless or decontextualized knowledge acquisition, emphasizing the instrumental role of literacy in accessing the cultural knowledge needed for every citizen of the nation-state" (p. 127). Their work points to the importance of embracing local conceptions of literacy that subvert "the technologies of dominant knowledge production [and the] affective states of ambivalence, detachment and even of non-existence that emerge in [Indigenous] groups due to their rejection and exclusion from dominant cultural and linguistic norms" (pp. 126–127). The engagement of critical literacy education must focus on the workings of the social in meaning-making, challenging the location of literacy learning within the individual mind and contesting "the homogenizing ideology of decontextualized literacy" (Kostogriz & Tsolidis, 2008, p. 127; see also Street, 1993; Gee, 2000). Kostogriz & Tsolidis (2008) argue that "the spatial imagination of literacy has ... significant implications for how we envisage the future of literacy education in a multicultural, global society and, indeed, the future of multiculturalism. While boundary politics are important tools in understanding inequalities and technologies of power in literacy education, they can also [be] a means of portraying places and spaces as homogeneous and uniform" (pp. 130–131). These scholars push for a "conception of transcultural literacy [grounded in] new geographies of identity that are characterized by the multiple spatial and temporal scales of identification" (p. 132). Our understanding of literacy education must bring to the forefront questions of language, knowledge, power, resistance, and decolonization. The processes of racialization are encountered differently by different bodies in the sociocultural and political contexts of schooling and education. The understanding of literacy is, in fact, encoded in deep meanings that characterize rewards, discipline, and punishments in a Foucauldian sense. To subvert these meanings, we must begin to think differently.

We must move literacy education from knowing how to read and write to engaging learning as a process of sharing, reciprocity, respect, collaboration, healing, and creating sustainable relationships. In other words, we must perceive literacy not as an end in itself, but as a process and a movement of transitioning in life for different learners (Edwards, McMillon, & Turner, 2015). The conventional definition of literacy is completely the opposite of literacy in the Indigenous community. Indigenous conceptualizations of literacy promote Indigenous/cultural knowledges and philosophies of education as both political and intellectual acts (Semali & Kincheloe, 1999). These conceptualizations of literacy call for situating inclusivity and decolonization as key aspects of literacy education. Indigenous-community literacy is beyond knowing how to read and write. In fact, Indigenous peoples do not look at literacy from this Eurocentric lens, but rather, they look at learning as a process of sharing, respecting, collaborating, healing, and creating relationships. Literacy that is built on such a platform troubles and decolonizes colonized concepts of learning, which are competitive and individualistic. Literacy becomes a process of learning together where those who are "good" in one area can assist those who are struggling. Schooling is seen as a "community of learners" on a journey to learn together, not as individual learners competing with each other for high scores and attention. Storytelling, visual representation, and the strong interconnections among the spirit, animal, and human world are valued. Understanding "non-Western" ways of knowing is key to psychosocial and cultural development. Non-Western ways of knowing embrace intuition and the neglected art of storytelling. Books like Michael J. Caduto & Joseph Bruchac's (2001) *Keepers of the Night* include selected First Nations tales with experiential activities that encourage learners to explore astronomy, weather, vegetation, and the animal world in a way that engages the whole child with their emotions, thoughts, senses, and actions. Literacy education in the Indigenous community is all about transitioning, that is, transitioning from an infant to an adult, and in between these stages of life, there is relationship building. Literacy as a process and a movement of growth allows for the articulation of different literacies such that it is an evolvement and growth of different ways of learning, teaching, and coming to know. This way of reading literacy disrupts the centrality of one understanding of literacy as the totalizing tool.

In today's education system, inclusivity is an important aspect of literacy education. The critical literature looks at school inclusivity as acknowledging all axes of differences and relations of power (Gorski and Swalwell, 2015). These axes of differences are gender, race, sexuality, ethnicity, religion, ableism, culture, and language. In thinking through the questions of educational transformation, we need to centre the question of social difference and schooling. Rather than social difference becoming a site of oppressions, social difference must be a tool to make a change. Earlier on, Darling-Hammond (2002) argued that "a critical task in becoming an effective teacher of diverse students is coming to understand individual young people in non-stereotypical ways while acknowledging and comprehending the ways in which culture and context influence their lives and learning" (p. 209). It is therefore important for the educator to enter a literal space with openness while recognizing that spaces are informed by different cultural meanings and symbols. Educators must work with our cultural symbols to enhance multiple knowings. This is where social difference can be a point of empowerment and recognition in literacy. Educators must also understand how their own life experiences, schooling contexts, and the settings in which they currently teach, shape their teaching (Watson et al., 2006, p. 407). Teaching social difference as critical self-reflection is important. Social difference as a literacy component must recognize our myriad identities, roles, and responsibilities. I have written elsewhere (2010) that "identity is an important site of knowing. Identity has in effect become a lens of reading one's world. Young minority learners continually lament the absence of teacher representation in their school" (p. 119). Students coming from linguistically and culturally diverse backgrounds need to see this representation in their schools. In a study exploring young adults' educational experiences, Mila (in Dei, 2010) compares the experience with past schooling and laments the fact that not being able to make racial connections with her educators can be limiting:

> [In my high school] I found that it was different having teachers who were all Black because in my former public school there was only one Black teacher in the whole school. It was just because of the area and location of the school. I felt that I could relate to the teachers a bit more and that they could understand my background because most of the Black teachers were West Indian (Caribbean). You kind of felt like they were looking out for your best interests on a more personal level and you felt that you could talk to them about whatever. It's more personable. It was more of a family feeling. There was competitiveness but there was still a great group. (Dei, 2010, p.119)

Mila conveys the degree of connectedness and understanding that some learners may experience when they work with teachers who share similar cultural, racial, ethnic, gender, and sexual backgrounds. Students may feel a stronger sense of inclusion that can ultimately impact the motivation to learn and to persist in academic settings.

Cultures are diverse, and so to claim a dominant or hegemonic culture is to engage in oppression. All learners are situated in their cultures, whether home, school, or out-of-school cultures. There is indisputable evidence that all learners want to be centred in the schooling process in ways that acknowledge their diversity, differences, and equity. Learners would like to see their lived experiences being respected and reflected in and out of the classroom and educators responding to discrimination, oppression, and hierarchal relations (Lepp Friesen, 2016; Gorski & Swalwell, 2015).

The subject field of literacy education continues to expand into new areas. Quite recently, Flood, Heath, and Lapp (2015) have presented different views of literacy as encompassing not only reading, writing, speaking, and listening, but also the multiple ways through which learners gain access to knowledge and skills. Edwards, McMillon, and Turner's (2015) work addresses four major debates: the fight for access to literacy; supports and roadblocks to success;

theories and perspectives on teaching African American students; and the role of African American families in the literacy lives of their children.

The recognition that home, community, and parents have responsibilities to ensure effective literacy education for young learners is significant in pointing to literacy as more than ensuring academic competence. Cleovoulou et al. (2016), pursuing literacy education as visual education, contribute to an understanding of social inclusion through the use of self-produced family photograph books. The whole area of visual culture can be engaged as knowledge and representation. Self-expression and new cultural ways of knowing can be a catalyst to cross-disciplinary learning and overall enrichment. An asset model of literacy learning that involves not only children but their parents is critical. Taylor, Kumi-Yeboah, and Ringlaben's (2016) research on multicultural education and teaching of culturally and linguistically underrepresented diverse students shows the importance of transcultural literacies. Similarly, the connection between literacy education and disability studies is shown in Collins and Ferri (2016). Disability studies in education is an alternative way to reframe, to understand, and to teach students who are positioned as struggling in literacy classrooms. There is a growing area of literature for young adults that can help demystify conceptions of disability (Brenna, 2010). Transcultural literacies must also embrace science and technology in the classroom. Price-Dennis, Holmes, and Smith (2015) have assessed the impact of digital literacy practices toward an inclusive classroom, creating a community of learners, using digital tools to make curriculum more accessible, and linking the academic to the practical.

The International Science New Zealand's Literacy Education Program has been regarded as one of the world's most successful approaches to teaching literacy skills to young children, yet it has come under serious critique (Tunmer & Chapman, 2015). Are there some useful lessons and some cautions to be aware of when embracing literacy education in transcultural contexts? Chapman, Prochnow, and Arrow (2015) make a point to further challenge the myth in New Zealand education, that of the superiority of its approach to literacy instruction. Epstein & Gist's (2015) excellent discussion of "racial literacy" has emphasized the strategic instruction about race that teachers use in a New York City public school to ensure academic success. Particular curriculum approaches and/or teaching/learning strategies that these "successful" programs use include open and frank discussions about why race is important to schooling and education; asking learners to identify the self as significant entry points to their discussion; how their communities implicate these discussions; how race is significant in the analysis; and how racial identities impact schooling processes and learning outcomes.

In their work, Gorski and Swalwell (2015) highlight key aspects of equity literacy as critical in every subject area. An equity literacy approach is "integrative and interdisciplinary" and educators are challenged to pursue "teaching for equity literacy [as] a political act" (p. 37). Equity literacy is about teaching social justice, power, resistance, social responsibility, accountability, transparency, and ethics (see also Taylor, Kumi-Yeboah, & Ringlaben, 2016). The most effective equity literacy approach is holistic, linking "academics" to the "practical" (see also Flood, Heath, & Lapp, 2015; Price-Dennis, Holmes, & Smith, 2015). Given the saliency of race and Indigeneity in Euro-Canadian schooling and education, the whole area of racial equity literacy (strategic instruction about the saliency of Indigeneity, race, Blackness, and the intersection of social difference that includes gender, disability, class, and sexuality) is paramount for decolonization education and specifically for literacy education (see also Epstein & Gist, 2015; Collins & Ferri, 2016).

TOWARD DECOLONIAL LITERACY EDUCATION

Decolonizing is a word that is very much in vogue today. One needs to be clear what is meant when calling for decolonization. Decolonization is about changing power relations. It is about the politics of knowledge for subversion and to challenge colonial thinking. It is about a practice and a process to affirm the colonized mind in challenging imperial thought and practice. Decolonization and hegemonies cannot co-exist. Decolonizing literacy is not about mainstreaming literacy practice. In fact, as many have noted, a truly decolonial project cannot look for legitimation and validation from the dominant. Colonial relations have been about oppression, subjugation, domestication, and containment. A decolonial project is about resistance and assisting learners in developing a critical consciousness of oneself as a learner, having a sense of place, history, identity, culture, and memory. Decolonization is also about "abandoning all reflexes of subordination" (Diop, 1974, p. 123).

In earlier work (Dei, 2017a, 2017b), I assert that decolonial teaching and learning is anchored in the question of the Land and is place-based (concrete and metaphorical), while at the same time resisting "the slippage into a hegemonic thinking that only non-(authenticized) Indigenous bodies need to decolonize" (Dei, 2017a, p. 54). We cannot frame decolonization in ways that offer neither space nor possibility to address either "autodestruction" or the intersectionalities of struggles for peoples trying to shed the chains of colonialism (see also Doyle-Wood, 2016). To this end, decolonization involves the psyche, cultural memories, and resisting internalized colonial relations of thought and practice, including acknowledging diverse experiences of peoples who conceptualize Land and place differently for transnational anti-colonial praxis (Dei, 2017a, 2017b).

In the pursuit of critical literacy education, decolonization is about positionality, voice, and authority. It is about the recognition that knowledge production is a social, political, and cultural process. The implication of the self as a knower, the self in coming to know (hooks, 1994), and the self in producing knowledge means engaging our cultural and spiritual memories as consequential. Knowledge is open to contentions, contestations, contradictions, struggles, and challenges. Truth is constructed in the contest of power relations. What is perceived as "truth" lies not simply in the "facts" as presented, nor in their mere "interpretations, constructions and representation of events and meanings, but [also] in the dialogue between the reader, writer and events being described and analysed" (Chisholm, 2005, p. 83). Thus, we can have multiple meanings of truth or multiple truths, and these can be contesting and contested. We see ourselves in stories differently, and a version of a story can be narrated from one's personal experience, politics, and location, implying multiple accounts of the story. The significance of this for literacy education is to be aware of the body politics of knowledge. Formal education can create critical spaces of knowledge production for resistance and liberation. Educational sites have also been spaces for colonization, domination, and oppression. Allowing the privilege of Western science knowledges over Indigenous knowledges is a case in point. Historically, we have witnessed higher institutions of learning becoming "laboratories of modernity" (Chisholm, 2005, p. 81). They have been places where symbols of modernity abound.

I will highlight four key philosophical contentions for decolonizing literacy education and the relevance for new cultural framings of diversity, difference, and social inclusion. First is the *politics of identity and knowledge production*. Who we are and how we come to know and understand the world are inextricably linked. We make our knowledges and produce our own knowings. Yet, in the contestations over knowledges, this is either lost or dismissed for certain bodies. Schooling must accord legitimacy of voice to every learner. In colonial contexts where certain bodies and their knowledges are continually privileged, decolonization literacy education can only be purposeful if it helps challenge this coloniality and empower the disempowered voice. In other words, literacy education has to critically embrace the relative saliencies of our different identities in responding to the dictates of inclusion and equity education. Bodies and identities matter in schooling and education and there is no universal learner or voice. What is often seen as universal, for example, learner/experience/culture/history, is the particular reality of the dominant.

A second point is the power of cultivating *diverse communities*. We create communities through the acknowledgement of differences, the creation of new systems, knowledges, and power sharings. Our communities must be sites and places of learning and healing, respectful of diverse knowledges and experiences and promoting sharings, reciprocity, and "giving back." Similarly, communities are about differences and sameness; shared experiences are never singular. As communities come into a global public sphere, we are confronted with broader questions and challenges of inclusion (e.g., migration, family reunification, and community development). As a consequence, communities are always tension-filled (e.g., individual/group; group/nation; cooperation/competition). Communities work if we acknowledge our differences and relative strengths. Communities do not take away our individualities. Communities acknowledge how we connect to each other in terms of shared and contingent histories, identities, and cultures. Literacy education is meaningful if the learner is strengthened to understand our shared responsibilities to each other, as well as our collective destinies and aspirations. Our successes and failures are shared successes and failures.

A third consideration for decolonizing literacy education involves the notion of *difference*. Difference is political and there are dangers in depoliticizing that difference. Difference calls for both affirmation and response. Thus, there is the importance of moving beyond a mere acknowledgement of difference to concretely respond to difference. The interstices of social difference (e.g., ethnicity, gender, class, sexuality, disability) complicate human subjectivities and identities and help subvert naturalized/totalizing discourses. Difference pushes us to learn from that which is not familiar. Difference is not the flip side of sameness. Difference is an acknowledgement of voice, positionality, place, context, and history. Given the tendency to sweep differences under the carpet, the accentuation of difference has implications for literacy education. For example, the power of sub-altern and sub-intern differences and voice must be seen as a process of authentication that allows the marginalized, subjugated, and downplayed differences to surface. Difference also has implications for how we speak about inclusion in literacy education. Decolonized literacy education must promote a discourse of radical inclusion that defines inclusion as more about beginning anew, not simply adding to what already exists. This definition of inclusion centres power and power relations. Inclusion is only meaningful if everyone is in a centred space. Radical inclusion also works with multiple models of social justice (e.g., treating everybody the same, targeting differentiated responses to groups, recognizing that there is no universalized subject).

The fourth quality is *Indigenous literacy as transgressive pedagogy*. For the dominant culture, a decolonial literacy education is teaching students to understand their Euro-ancestry privilege. For all learners, this means learning to challenge or to subvert hegemonies (whether ontological, epistemological, or axiological). I have argued elsewhere (Dei, 2016) that there is a particular place for Indigenous epistemologies to help us re-imagine alternatives to colonial thinking and practice. The complex problems and challenges facing the world today defy universalist solutions. They require that we promote Indigenous literacies as part of multiliteracies. Indigenous knowledges have their own internal and historical processes of knowledge production that must be acknowledged, validated, and legitimized in their own right. Beyond claims of multiple epistemes and ways of knowing as shaped by the long-term experiences of local environments, cultures, histories, and the Land, we also need to understand the context, politics, and desires that we each bring to knowledge.

MOVING FORWARD: SUGGESTIONS WITH PRACTICAL IMPLICATIONS

In this final section I offer suggestions on what schools and educators can do at the institutional level to promote the philosophical ideals of decolonized literacy education in Canadian contexts. Schools and school boards, including provincial ministries of education, can develop effective institutional policies to achieve inclusivity, diversification of educational curricula with clear guidelines, well-defined equity standards, timelines, expectations, and measures of accountability. Establishing guidelines, timelines, and accountability is significant. Most institutions claim to have equity policies; however, it is one thing to have the policy on the books and it is another to actually implement and hold people accountable for the policy.

It is also important that any critical approaches to educational inclusivity through institutional, school, and school board policies be framed within anti-racist, anti-Black racism, Indigenous, anti-Islamophobic, and anti-xenophobic perspectives. There has to be a clear communication of institutional equity policy and its implications for all within the school community. To be effective, educational policies should be aligned with the cultural climate of the school. In other words, policies must be developed from bottom up in order to get "buy-in." There must be an identification and a sense of collective ownership of knowledge from the very people who will implement and oversee the policies. Where there is a disconnect between the cultural climate and the policies, we cannot expect the policies to bring any gains and benefits or promote change.

There can be no way of looking at education today which is anything but anti-racist, anti-homophobic, anti-sexist, and anti-Islamophobic. How grounded are future teachers in these bodies of knowledge? How is this type of education central in the preparation of school teachers in faculties of education? Courses about such topics as race, gender, class, and equity speak about our world today. If we understand equity as inclusion, making everyone feel part of our diverse communities, and as connecting our distinct but shared histories, the promotion of these courses constitutes educational practices for a common good. The pursuit of knowledge cannot just be for knowledge's own sake. Knowledge must mean something. Knowledge must propel action and bring about positive personal and social change. Therefore, what we teach in our faculties of education, how we prepare our student teachers, and how education is allowed to confront possibilities and challenges of our growing diversities matter very much. Knowledge, social relevance, and responsibility must go hand in hand. We must start to do things differently. Hence, there is a place for mandates and expressed expectations in our schooling and the educational system. We must have mandates for faculties of education so that faculty and students alike take courses in Black/African/Indigenous education, as well as anti-racist and equity studies before certification. The selection of teacher candidates for training should proportionally reflect student population demographics. Greater representation from diverse cultural groups and closer attention to the emotional and social skills of pre-service teachers are needed. Students need to see reflection of the wider society in their classrooms. Educators must understand the communities from which their students come. Looking for the "best" or "excellent" teacher with criteria so abstractly defined and yet removed from the realities of the communities and the question of practical relevance of the knowledge we have acquired must end. Academic freedom must boldly embrace academic integrity in all that it entails. When we make this connection we can easily see the need for schools to put in place specific equity initiatives that ask educators and schools to embark upon academic programming initiatives with social conscience. Such initiatives cannot strictly be subjected to economic arguments and rationalizations of "demand/supply" (Goldberg, 1993).

As educators, we have our work cut out for us. There are no easy and quick solutions. There can be no illusions either. Let us look at the future that currently stares us in the face. There are new forms of racism, such as anti-Blackness, anti-Black racism, settler colonialism, anti-Indigeneity, anti-Semitism, xenophobia, anti-different racism, profiling of particular bodies/populations, the "hypervigilance of perceived Black physical formidability" (Wilson, Hugenberg, & Rule, 2017), and Islamophobia. In fact, while not drawing any hierarchies, the misconception of Islam is a major global worry. It is important for literacy education to help learners understand why and how the construction of Islamophobia is a threat, and the impact it has on Muslims worldwide. Learners must be able to ask and to respond to the question: Who benefits from the "Othering" of Muslims? There is an issue of the power to define the problem as the "Other." A decolonial literacy education must help examine state and institutional policies aimed at targeting Muslims. Specifically, decolonial literacy education should be developing an anti-Islamophobic policy framework for educating young learners (Zine, 2002a, 2002b, 2004). People's bodies are visibly racialized. While not taking away from the saliency of Blackness, it is important to note how particular religions such as Islam and dress attire (e.g., the hijab, niqab, burka) are racialized regardless of the body's skin marker in those instances. Decolonial literacy education is necessary to resist and to counter Islamophobia, especially when in the dominant's imaginings, the notion of being Muslim is solely connected to the "inferior" and racialized geography. Fortunately, today we see such intersections and convergence of political struggles in multiple forms of resistance, such as rallies, demonstrations, and marches.

The recognition of intersectionality and how it impacts people's lives and everyday individual and collective experiences should also be part of decolonial literacy education. We must not deny the existence and intersectionality of Black Muslims among other intersectionalities/identity markers such as gender, dis/ability, and dress attire. We must see how the social construction of what constitutes a person who is Black, who is Muslim, is embedded in the dominant's imaginings; how these imaginings affect how one is perceived and whether one is included/excluded as, for example, Black, Muslim, Black Muslim; and the materialized impact/consequences they endure. The recognitions of the intersections provide us with a demand to work in solidarity and to counter the colonial tactic of pitting our oppressed peoples against each other. Classroom teachers might apply these important insights into teaching practice through the resources they might use, such as texts from different vantage points, including those with intersectional identities, and undertaking discursive approaches that show how the individual subject is of multiple selves wearing the multiple hats of race, gender, class, and religious identities. Innovative teaching strategies must allow learners to connect their different histories and cultures, to see themselves in each other's culture and history, and to speak about these intersections of histories and identities in ways that create learning communities and collectives rather than pitting one group of learners against another.

A troubling feature of schooling and education is that some educators conveniently work with curriculum that hardly references the scholarship and writings of minority and Indigenous scholars. Yet these educators claim to teach critically and to be presenting inclusive knowledge. Decolonial literacy education must aim to integrate Indigenous literatures and minority scholarship into school curricula. We can hope that individual teachers will make a greater effort to radically transform their curricula and classroom practices. At the institutional level it may require an official insistence on annual/periodic curriculum reviews informed by the thought that academic freedom has matching responsibilities to learners.

The existing literature on institutional change has emphasized the importance of having policies that seek the development and implementation of proactive strategies for diverse administrative staff and faculty recruitment, retention, and promotion into top-level administrative positions. Schools and educational institutions that have either direct or indirect impact on youth learning could change hiring practices so that prior to people being hired, it is ensured that candidates have a foundational awareness of these issues and how to counter them, are conscious, and are willing to continue growing through the process of (un)learning. We must scrutinize hiring practices themselves; for example, we clearly need equitable union practices where seniority would not override equity and avenues toward liberation. There are educators who may be "saved" by the union even though they continue to create violent, hostile, unsafe, and unhealthy spaces for the youth, their peers, and the general public. We cannot allow these educators to be educating our youth.

Approaches to African-centred and Indigenous schooling work with Indigenous philosophical ideals of community, social responsibility, reciprocity, sharing, connectedness, relationality, local language, and culture (Asante, 1991; Dei & Kempf, 2013; Agyepong, 2010; Radebe, 2017). Decolonized literacy education can apply these cultural values and ideals in everyday school and classroom settings. Decolonial literacy education must aim at promoting healthy, dynamic, and spiritually centred learning spaces. Alternative places and spaces for learning must be envisioned. The development of community centres working from within schools; community and youth workers running programs inside schools; increasing the presence of Elders and families in schools through community programming and events; and having each school assigned to a community centre in order to build relationships, could develop literacy learning practices that are life-widening. Such decolonial educational approaches would seek to replace the increased police presence in schools with caring adults/Elders (e.g., to facilitate teaching [not enforcing] discipline and to nurture and mentor rather than criminalize learners). The school site must be a place for learning and cultivating healthy relations that make academic and social excellence possible. We need educational support initiatives that help learners transition from middle school to academic streams in secondary school and post-secondary institutions. Stronger connections between academic contexts and career and professional trajectories can then be made.

CONCLUDING THOUGHTS

Can we offer a reading of literacy education that is about the possibilities of working with healing, hope, and productive futures amidst global violence and oppression? There is always the danger of reading counter and oppositional discourses as necessarily hegemonic. Presenting oppositional readings is about a search for new futures, working with the knowledge that "something else/different is possible." A decolonized literacy education is possible if we are serious about re-imagining education differently than we currently have. There is the urgency of nurturing a political-epistemic community working for new educational futures. In this search for new futures, Indigenous cultural knowing has a place. These knowledges help us to respond to the desire for wholeness. Wholeness is only possible when we start to think in terms of relations, connections, reciprocity, sharing, and a connection of body, mind, soul, and spirit. Wholeness challenges compartmentalization, individualization, and atomization of selves. Wholeness demands that we see literacies in terms of a completeness of the learner in body, mind, soul, and spirit. Education is about the physical and metaphysical realms of existence, and the integration of teaching, learning, and the administration of education to ensure learners' and educators' myriad identities are connected to questions of history, culture, knowledge, and politics.

The world today is about a continuation of the past, the present, and the future. Our communities have long shared histories with significant continuities and discontinuities across time and space. There are Indigenous and diasporic continuities and discontinuities that cannot be discounted. They present us with possibilities to create new ontologies and epistemologies to account for the diversity of human experience. Just as our diversity is a strength, the noted continuities and discontinuities also allow for rewriting the human story in ways that promote inclusion rather than exclusion. Colonial education has been oppressive and violent. We need more subversive pedagogies with the potential to liberate minds, ideas, and practices. Subversion is a violent act. It is about fighting to bring a new educational and social order. So the question is not whether there is a place for violence in creating new futures. Violence has been part of the human existence. Franz Fanon (1963) wrote that, by its nature, colonization was a violent phenomenon that would require an equally violent response. This form of violence has been the normal of subservient education. Our work as educators must be to provoke new critical consciousness to re-imagine new worlds and futures.

We must continually look for and promote "epistemologies of the South" to advance the cause of social and educational disruption and subversion. Any education that fails to address the needs of what is currently going on "out there" in our communities is no education. As educators, we must see learners for who they are and for what their potential might be. The saying that "when the teacher is ready the learner always appears" must mean something. Teaching to subvert and to transform cannot be an idealist thought. So how can we do even more disrupting of the status quo in classrooms, school spaces, or other social settings? This is disrupting the normal, which has been exclusive, hegemonic, and works with epistemic certainty. We can continually use counter and oppositional narratives as a way of disruption. The stories we tell must disrupt the meta-narrative. These stories must bring new meanings of the human experience. These stories must be consequential and affirming of ourselves and our communities. We fail in education if our pedagogies of disruption do not lead to new futures. If our pedagogies merely reproduce and sustain hegemonic thoughts and practices, transformation can only be a wishful idea. As educators, we betray our promise to young learners if education fails to transform ourselves and our communities.

We must have a vision of the educational future we want in order for us to strive for it. This future can be contested. The whole idea of educational futurity is to be able to dream new ways of schooling and education. As Sium (2014) opines, dreaming must be a "metaphor for resistance" anchored in the anti-colonial realm of spiritual resurgence. Dreaming has been a core site of knowing within Indigenous philosophies. Dreams are always part of the future and the imagination of a new world (Lattas, 1993). Sium (2014) further argues that "dreams must be taken seriously as a subversive realm for one's anti-colonial dialogue with the spiritual and political self and collective" (p. 77). Dreams evoke both the physical and metaphysical realms of life and human existence, and educators must be able to "think outside the confines of dominant thought [and engage] deeper theoretical and spiritual mediations of the [new educational] future" (Sium, 2014, p. 74). I believe a decolonial literacy education working with multiple knowledges and promoting critical views of what inclusion, equity, difference, and community mean holds great possibilities for us all.

For teachers who wish to apply this decolonial and transformative approach to their teaching, the journey begins by engaging the self as a learner, seeking new knowledge as part of understanding decolonization as a violent process that calls for unlearning what we have learned. It also calls for seeing decolonization as about the many things we do to bring about productive and meaningful change in the classroom, in the school setting, and in the lives of our learners, including appreciating the Land and Earth-wide teachings of respect, humility, sharing reciprocity, relationality, ethics, and accountability. This journey calls for questioning our relative power and privileges and asking how history has brought us to where we are and what it means to make a difference in the lives of the learners we teach. Making this difference is not possible unless we are prepared to divest ourselves from our colonial investments and colonial inheritance.

QUESTIONS FOR REFLECTION AND DISCUSSION

1. What is decolonizing education and what does this mean for literacy education?

2. How do we educate for change and inclusion in today's schools? Identify three to five practical steps that teachers and learners can take to activate meaningful change.

3. How do considerations of inclusivity, equity, culture, and identity implicate literacy education?

4. What is the impact of world events on learning, literacy, and social justice (e.g., impact of forced migration, persistent terrorism, climate change)? Research one global dynamic from the lens of learning and education.

5. Moving forward, how do we envision schooling and education in addressing some of these challenges?

6. What speculative imaginaries are called for as we collectively envision a new, different future? What is your vision for education in such a future?

7. How do we openly address race/racism and not simply engage with the language that talks around race and difference?

DEEPEN YOUR INQUIRY: RELATED READINGS AND RESOURCES

Brewer, C. A. (2016). *Immigrant and refugee students in Canada.* Toronto: Brush Education.

Cabral, A. (2016). *Resistance and decolonization.* London: Rowman & Littlefield.

Coulthard, G. (2014). *Red skins, white masks: Rejecting the colonial politics of recognition.* Minneapolis: University of Minnesota Press.

Cope, B., & Kalantzis, M. (2000). *Multiliteracies: Literacy learning and the design of social futures.* New York: Psychology Press.

Darling-Hammond, L., French, J., & Garcia-Lopez, S. P. (Eds.). (2002). *Learning to teach for social justice.* New York: Teachers College Press.

Darling-Hammond, L., Ramos, B., Padnos-Altamirano, R., & Hyler, M. (Eds.). (2016). *Be the change: Reinventing school for student success.* New York: Teachers College Press.

Dei, G. J. S. (1996). *Anti-racism education: Theory and practice.* Halifax: Fernwood Publishing.

Fleras, A. (2016). *Racisms in multicultural Canada: Paradoxes, politics, and resistance.* Waterloo, ON: Wilfrid Laurier Press.

Grande, S. (2015). *Red pedagogy: Native American social and political thought* (10th anniversary ed.). New York: Rowman & Littlefield.

Johnson, L. L., Jackson, J., Stovall, D. O., & Taliaferro, D. (2017). "Loving blackness to death": (Re)imagining ELA classrooms in a time of racial chaos. *English Journal, 106*(4), 60–66.

Lysicott, J. (2017). Racial identity and liberation literacies in the classroom. *English Journal, 106*(4), 47–53.

Mackey, Eva. (2016). Unsettled expectations: Uncertainty, land and settler decolonization. Halifax: Fernwood Publishing.

Magro, K. (2015). Teaching for social justice and peace education: Promising pathways for transformative learning. *Peace Research: The Canadian Journal of Peace and Conflict Studies, 47*(1/2): 109–142.

Michael, A. (2016). *Raising race questions: Whiteness and inquiry in education*. New York: Teachers College Press.

Palmater, P. (2016). *Indigenous nationhood: Empowering grassroots citizens.* Winnipeg & Halifax: Fernwood Press.

Price-Dennis, D., Holmes, K. A., & Smith, E. (2015). Exploring digital literacy practices in an inclusive classroom. *The Reading Teacher, 69*(2), 195–205.

Samuels, D. (2016). *The culturally inclusive educator: Preparing teachers for a multicultural world.* New York: Teachers College Press.

Tuck, E., & Yang, K. W. (2012). Decolonization is not a metaphor. *Decolonization: Indigeneity, Education, & Society, 1*(1), 1–40.

Willinsky, J. (1998). *Learning to divide the world: Education at empire's end.* Minneapolis: University of Minnesota Press.

Zaidi, R. (2017). *Anti-Islamophobic curriculums.* New York: Peter Lang.

Zygmunt, E., & Clark, P. (2016). *Transforming teacher education for social justice.* New York: Teachers College Press.

AUTHOR'S NOTE

I would like to thank Dr. Rose Ann Torres, Dionisio Nyaga, Yumiko Kawano, Andrea Vasquez, and Cristina Jaimungal, all of the Department of Social Justice Education at the Ontario Institute for Studies in Education, University of Toronto, for literature work for this paper. I also acknowledge the work of Professor Karen Magro of the Faculty of Education, University of Winnipeg, Manitoba, for reading through and commenting on the early draft of the paper. Portions of this text were initially presented as keynote addresses in two places: (a) at the Manitoba Education Research Network Symposium, "Transcultural Literacies for Inclusion and Change in Education," Manitoba Teachers' Society, Winnipeg, Manitoba, September 30, 2016; and (b) at the Centre for Creativity, Sustainability and Educational Futures, Graduate School of Education, University of Exeter, Exeter, England, on

Decolonizing Teacher Education: An Expert Seminar, C, March 10, 2017. I thank the audiences for their comments.

REFERENCES

Agyepong, R. (2010). *Black-focused schools in Toronto: What do African Canadian parents say?* Unpublished PhD dissertation. University of Toronto. Toronto, Canada.

Asante, M. (1991). The Afrocentric idea in education. *Journal of Negro Education, 60*(2), 170–180.

Ball, S. J. (2003). *Class strategies and the education market: The middle classes and social advantage.* London: Routledge Falmer.

Bertelsen, E. (2008). The real transformation: The marketisation of higher education. *Social Dynamics, 24*(2), 130–158.

Biles, J., Burstein, M., & Frideres, J. (Eds.). (2008). *Immigration and integration in Canada in the twenty-first century.* Montreal & Kingston: McGill-Queen's University Press.

Bragg, S. (2007). Student voice and governmentality: The production of enterprising subject. *Discourse: Studies in the Cultural Politics of Education, 28*(3), 343–355.

Brenna, B. (2010). Assisting young readers in the interpretation of a character with disabilities in Iain Lawrence's juvenile novel Gemini Summer. *English Quarterly, 41*(1/2), 54–61.

Caduto, M. J., & Bruchac, J. (2001). *Keepers of the night: Native stories and nocturnal activities for children.* Calgary: Fitzhenry & Whiteside.

Campbell, C., Proctor, H., & Sherington, G. (2009). *School choice: How parents negotiate the new school market in Australia.* Sydney: Allen & Unwin.

Castagno, A. E., & Brayboy, B. M. J. (2008). Culturally responsive schooling for Indigenous youth: A review of the literature. *Review of Educational Research, 78,* 941–993.

Chapman, J. W., Prochnow, J. E., & Arrow, A. W. (2015). Eleven myths about literacy education in New Zealand. In W. E. Tunman & J. W. Chapman (Eds.), *Excellence and Equity in Literacy Education* (pp. 214–235). London: Palgrave Macmillan.

Chisholm, L. (2005). The politics of curriculum review and revision in South Africa in regional context. *Compare. A Journal of Comparative and International Education, 35(1),* 79–100.

Cleovoulou, Y., et al. (2016). Using photographic picture books to better understand young children's ideas of belonging: A study of early literacy strategies and social inclusion. *Journal of Childhood Studies, 38*(1), 11–20.

Collins, K., & Ferri, B. (2016). Literacy education and disability studies: Re-envisioning struggling students. *Journal of Adolescent & Adult Literacy, 60*(1), 7–12.

Cope, B., & Kalantzis, M. (2000). *Multiliteracies: Literacy learning and the design of social futures*. New York: Psychology Press.

Darling-Hammond, L. (2002). Educating a profession for equitable practice. In L. Darling-Hammond, J. French, & S. P. Garcia-Lopez (Eds.), *Learning to teach for social justice* (pp. 201–212). New York: Teachers College Press.

Davies, B. (2005). The (im)possibility of intellectual work in neoliberal regimes. *Discourse: Studies in the Cultural Politics of Education, 26*(1), 1–14.

Davies, L. (2009). Educating against extremism: Toward a critical politicization of young people. *International Review of Education, 55*, 183–203.

Dei, G. J. S. (2008). *Racists beware: Uncovering racial politics in contemporary society*. Rotterdam, the Netherlands: Sense Publishers.

Dei, G. J. S. (2010). The possibilities of new/counter and alternative visions of schooling. *English Quarterly, 41*(3/4), 115–134.

Dei, G. J. S. (2016). Indigenous philosophies, counter epistemologies and anti-colonial education. In W. Lehman (Ed.), *Education and Society* (pp. 190–206). London: Oxford University Press.

Dei, G. J. S. (2017a). *[Re]theorising blackness, anti-blackness and black solidarities through anti-colonial and decolonial prisms*. New York: Springer.

Dei, G. J. S. (2017b). Reframing education through Indigenous, anti-colonial and decolonial prisms. In P. McLaren & S. Soohoo (Eds.), *The Radical Imagine-Nation* (Vol. 2). New York: Peter Lang Publishing.

Dei, G. J. S., & Kempf, A. (Eds). (2013). *New perspectives on African-centred education in Canada*. Toronto: Canadian Scholars Press.

Dei, G. J. S., Mazzuca, J., & McIsaac, E. (1997). *Reconstructing dropout: An ethnography of Black students' disengagement in school*. Toronto: University of Toronto Press.

Dion, K. L. (2001). Immigrants' perceptions of housing discrimination in Toronto: The Housing New Canadians Project. *Journal of Social Issues, 57*(3), 523–539.

Diop, C. A. (1974). *The African origin of civilization*. Chicago: Lawrence Hill.

Doyle-Wood, Stan. (2016). Personal communication. Equity Studies, New College, University of Toronto.

Edwards, P. A., McMillon, G. T., & Turner, J. D. (2015). *Change is gonna come: Transforming literacy education for African American students*. New York: Teachers College Press.

Epstein, T., & Gist, C. (2015). Teaching racial literacy in secondary humanities classrooms: Challenging adolescents' of color concepts of race and racism. *Race Ethnicity and Education, 18*(1), 40–60.

Fanon, F. (1963). *The wretched of the earth*. New York: Grove Press.

Fiedler, R., Schuurman, N., & Hyndman, J. (2006). Hidden homelessness: An indicator-based approach for examining the geographies of recent immigrants at-risk of homelessness in greater Vancouver. *Cities, 23*(3), 205–216.

Flood, J., Heath, S. B., & Lapp, D. (2015). *Handbook of research on teaching literacy through the communicative and visual arts, volume II: A project of the international reading association*. New York: Routledge.

Freire, P. (1993). *Pedagogy of the oppressed*. New York: Seabury Press.

Gee, J. P. (2000). New people in new worlds: Networks, the new capitalism and schools. In B. Cope & M. Kalantzis (Eds.), *Multiliteracies: Literacy learning and the design of social futures* (pp. 43–68). London: Routledge.

Gibbs, P. (2001). Higher education as a market: A problem or solution. *Studies in Higher Education, 26*(1), 85–94.

Goldberg, D. (1993). *Racist culture: Philosophy and the politics of meaning*. Malden, MA: Blackwell Publishers Ltd.

Gorski, P. C., & Swalwell, K. (2015). Equity literacy for all. *Educational Leadership, 72*(6), 34–40. Available at http://www.edchange.org/publications/Equity-Literacy-for-All.pdf

Hall, B. L. (2002). The right to a new utopia: Adult learning and the changing world of work in an era of global capitalism. In E. V. O'Sullivan, A. Morrell, and M. A. O'Connor (Eds.), *Expanding the boundaries of transformative learning* (pp. 35–46). London, UK: Palgrave.

hooks, b. (1994). *Teaching to transgress: Education as the practice of freedom*. New York: Routledge.

Kostogriz, A, & Tsolidis, G. (2008). Transcultural literacy: Between the global and the local. *Pedagogy, Culture & Society, 16*(2): 125–136.

Lattas, A. (1993). Essentialism, memory and resistance: Aboriginality and the politics of authenticity. *Oceania, 63*(3), 240–267.

Lepp Friesen, H. I. (2016). Student engagement with difference at a Canadian university. *Canadian Journal for New Scholars in Education, 7*(1), 74–83.

Luke, A. (1997). Critical approaches to literacy. In *Encyclopedia of language and education* (pp. 143–151). Dordrecht, the Netherlands: Springer.

Magro, K. (2008). Exploring the experiences and challenges of adults from war-affected backgrounds: New directions for literacy educators. *Adult Basic Education and Literacy Journal, 2*(1), 24–33.

Magro, K. (2015). Teaching for social justice and peace education: Promising pathways for transformative learning. *Peace Research: The Canadian Journal of Peace and Conflict Studies, 47* (1/2): 109–142.

Magro, K., & Ghorayshi, P. (2011). *Adult refugees and newcomers in the inner city of Winnipeg: Promising pathways for transformative learning.* Winnipeg: Canadian Centre for Policy Alternatives.

Mundy, K. (2008). Global Education in Canadian elementary schools: An exploratory study. *Canadian Journal of Education, 31*(4), 941–974.

Norton, B. (2007). Critical literacy and international development. *Critical Literacy: Theories and Practices, 1*(1), 6–15.

Price-Dennis, D., Holmes, K. A., & Smith, E. (2015). Exploring digital literacy practices in an inclusive classroom. *The Reading Teacher, 69*(2), 195–205.

Radebe, P. (2017). *Afrocentric education: What does it mean to Toronto's black parents?* Unpublished PhD dissertation. Vancouver: University of British Columbia.

Savage, C., Hindle, R., Meyer, L. H., Hynds, A., Penetito, W., & Sleeter, C. E. (2011). Culturally responsive pedagogies in the classroom: Indigenous student experiences across the curriculum. *Asia-Pacific Journal of Teacher Education, 39*(3), 183–198.

Semali, L. M., & Kincheloe, J. L. (Eds.). (1999). *What is Indigenous knowledge? Voices from the academy.* New York: Falmer Press.

Sium, A. (2014). Dreaming beyond the state: Centering Indigenous governance as a framework for African development. In G. J. S. Dei & P. Adjei (Eds.), *Emerging perspectives on "African development": Speaking differently* (pp. 63–82). New York: Peter Lang.

Spencer, B. (2006). *The purposes of adult education: A short introduction* (pp.75–78). Toronto: Thompson Publishing.

Street, B. V. (1993). *Cross-cultural approaches to literacy.* Cambridge, UK: Cambridge University Press.

Street, B. V. (2001). Contexts for literacy work: The "new orders" and the "new literacy studies." In J. Crowther, M. Hamilton, & L. Tett (Eds.), *Powerful literacies* (pp. 13–22). Leicester: NIACE.

Taylor, R., Kumi-Yeboah, A., & Ringlaben, R. P. (2016). Pre-service teachers' perceptions towards multicultural education and teaching of culturally and linguistically diverse learners. *International Journal for Innovation Education and Research, 3*(9), 42–48.

Tunmer, W., & Chapman, J. (Eds.). (2015). *Excellence and equity in literacy education: The case of New Zealand.* New York: Palgrave Macmillan.

Watson, D., Charner-Laird, M., Kirkpatrick, C. L., Szczesiul, S. A., & Gordon, P. J. (2006). Effective teaching/effective urban teaching: Grappling with definitions, grappling with difference. *Journal of Teacher Education, 57*(4), 395–409.

Wilson, J. P., Hugenberg, K., & Rule, N. O. (2017). Racial bias in judgments of physical size and formidability: From size to threat. *Journal of Personality and Social Psychology, 113*(1), 59–80.

Zine, J. (2002a). "A framework for anti-Islamophobia education." Paper presented at the Canadian Sociology and Anthropology Association, Congress of the Social Sciences and Humanities. Toronto: University of Toronto.

Zine, J. (2002b). Inclusive schooling in a plural society: Removing the margins. *Education Canada, 42*(3), 36–39.

Zine, J. (2004). Anti-Islamophobia education as transformative pedagogy: Reflections from the educational frontlines. *American Journal of Islamic Social Sciences, 21*(3), 110–119.

Rethinking Remedial English in the Light of Dei: The Relevance of Transcultural Theory to Practice

Part of the dilemma with enacting teaching practices that acknowledge and support marginalized youth is the challenge of imagining alternatives to the status quo.

—*Marc Kuly*

OPENING THE CONVERSATION: READING NOTES

Why is there widespread suspicion of theory in education? What happens when we fail to think about why we do what we do? This chapter provides a context for thinking with the powerful ideas introduced by George J. Sefa Dei in chapter 1. Marc Kuly begins this chapter by raising questions about the "divide between theory and practice" and the tensions that such a division creates in education. He provides a specific example in his own experience as a novice teacher assigned to teach "Upgrading English," a class for students whose scores on school assessments were judged as indicating that they were in "need [of] remedial work on their literacy skills." While acknowledging that the school may have had good intentions, in the "light of Dei," Kuly troubles the assumptions of "Upgrading English" and its implications. He reflects on how being unaware of the theoretical assumptions informing his decisions as a teacher contributed to reinforcing oppressive pedagogical practices.

At the heart of this chapter is an unexpected encounter with Alice, a refugee from Rwanda and new student in Upgrading English. It is Alice who prompts Kuly to begin questioning the assumptions that informed the design and teaching of Upgrading English. Kuly's story reminds us that educational policy and day-to-day practice are always grounded in theory; however, when they remain unexamined, theories can often exert great "influence with no scrutiny."

To illustrate, Kuly draws on the anti-racist, anti-colonial, and Indigenous theoretical frameworks of Dei to explicate the vital connection between theory and practice in the case of Upgrading English. In the process, Kuly demonstrates how theories can help us understand complexity in educational practice and "bring about change and transformation" (Dei & Asgharzadeh, 2001, p. 298) by re-visioning teaching and learning.

For Kuly, a transcultural theoretical framework needs to position students' cultural and racial identities in respectful relationship at the centre of the classroom in order to build understanding and appreciation for students' diverse voices and knowledge. As you read this chapter, consider Kuly's story in the light of your own experiences: What evidence do you see of a theory/practice divide? What are the implications in your context of literacy-related assumptions about students, teaching, and learning that have great "influence with no scrutiny"? How can anti-racist, anti-colonial, and Indigenous theoretical frameworks become more central to choices, decisions, and actions in literacy policy and practice?

THINKING VISUALLY: CHAPTER ORGANIZER

This graphic explores visually how the different theoretical frameworks and experiences of Marc Kuly and his student Alice come together in their exchange about the "good life." Each of them comes to the educational setting with a set of assumptions that inform their actions and ways of thinking. In their encounter, these differences are embodied as ways of thinking, communicating, and acting. When Kuly reflects on the encounter—years later—with a transcultural theoretical framework, a much more complex "reading" of the encounter emerges. In the light of theories that illuminate the racist and colonial patterns of educational practice, Kuly calls for educators to engage in praxis, to become critically aware of the oppressive discourses that circulate in school spaces and to resist their power with theories and practices that honour the transcultural lives of our students and communities—attentive to issues of history, culture, identity, representation, community, knowledge, and power. What kinds of spaces do we wish to create in our schools? Who (or what) is at the centre of educational theory and action? What assumptions are at work? How do they need to change?

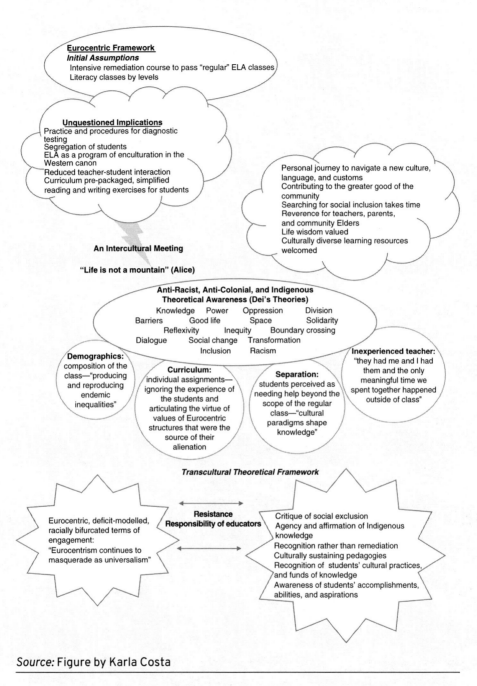

Eurocentric Framework
Initial Assumptions
  Intensive remediation course to pass "regular" ELA classes
  Literacy classes by levels

Unquestioned Implications
Practice and procedures for diagnostic testing
Segregation of students
ELA as a program of enculturation in the Western canon
Reduced teacher-student interaction
Curriculum pre-packaged, simplified reading and writing exercises for students

Personal journey to navigate a new culture, language, and customs
Contributing to the greater good of the community
Searching for social inclusion takes time
Reverence for teachers, parents, and community Elders
Life wisdom valued
Culturally diverse learning resources welcomed

An Intercultural Meeting

"Life is not a mountain" (Alice)

Anti-Racist, Anti-Colonial, and Indigenous Theoretical Awareness (Dei's Theories)
  Knowledge   Power   Oppression   Division
Barriers   Good life   Space   Solidarity
    Reflexivity   Inequity   Boundary crossing
  Dialogue   Social change   Transformation
        Inclusion   Racism

Demographics: composition of the class—"producing and reproducing endemic inequalities"

Curriculum: individual assignments—ignoring the experience of the students and articulating the virtue of values of Eurocentric structures that were the source of their alienation

Separation: students perceived as needing help beyond the scope of the regular class—"cultural paradigms shape knowledge"

Inexperienced teacher: "they had me and I had them and the only meaningful time we spent together happened outside of class"

Transcultural Theoretical Framework

Eurocentric, deficit-modelled, racially bifurcated terms of engagement: "Eurocentrism continues to masquerade as universalism"

Resistance Responsibility of educators

Critique of social exclusion
Agency and affirmation of Indigenous knowledge
Recognition rather than remediation
Culturally sustaining pedagogies
Recognition of students' cultural practices, and funds of knowledge
Awareness of students' accomplishments, abilities, and aspirations

Source: Figure by Karla Costa

CHAPTER 2

Rethinking Remedial English in the Light of Dei: The Relevance of Transcultural Theory to Practice

Marc Kuly

I recently emigrated from the land of public school classroom teaching to the land of teacher education in the university. I use the immigration metaphor purposefully. The school and the university are much like two separate countries who share borders, geography, and customs but are divided by distinct cultural practices and assumptions. However, the divisions are not readily apparent until one has lived in both lands. Becoming a citizen of the university has prompted me to reckon with one of the key areas of difference, the relative value given to the study of theory in schools as opposed to universities. This difference in values was evident in the reaction my public school teaching colleagues had when, years ago, I told them that I was starting graduate studies in education. Apart from being envious that my university night class on Tuesdays meant I was allowed to leave monthly staff meetings 15 minutes early, they were largely puzzled by my motivation. Comments such as "I guess you'll get a pay bump when you are done," "My university profs didn't even know how to teach!" or "When did writing a paper ever help you become a better teacher?" revealed an ambivalence bordering on enmity between the culture of classroom teaching and the culture of university-based teacher education. While these colleagues were thoughtful and creative teachers, they did not express any faith in the value of the knowledge or approaches that I was going to study at the university.

This is a tension that has troubled me. The divide between theory and practice in teacher development is not new. Much writing has been done about getting teaching preparation right through balancing practical and theoretical concerns (Bezzina, 2006; Kettle & Sellars, 1996; Kyriacou & Stephens, 1999; McIntyre, 2005) as well as about the unique content of thought and action that make up teacher knowledge (Connelly, Clandinin, & He, 1997; Elbaz, 1991; Sutherland, Howard, & Markauskaite, 2010). In working through this tension I have reflected on my own K–12 teaching experience and wondered how theory did and did not influence my practice. Although I know now that much of my early teaching decision making was influenced heavily by my time as a student and the sociocultural connotations of the profession (Britzman, 1986; Weber & Mitchell, 1995), at the time, I did not recognize that my decisions were influenced or mediated by anything other than my own supposedly "natural" thought processes.

Eventually, I became aware that my reasoning was not, in fact, distinct from my sociocultural and intellectual milieu, and slowly I problematized that in my practice. This is not to say that my teaching ended up as an elegant synthesis between theories of learning or culture and the organization of classroom experience. What I am saying is that my gradual opening up to theoretical frameworks for thinking about teaching led to a broader range of possibilities for thinking about teaching, my school, and the students who attended it. Recognizing this, I have come to believe that it is important to break down the opposition between theory and practice that is so common within schools. To explain why, I will recall a moment in my early teaching practice and then explore that moment in the light of the theories of educational sociologist George Sefa Dei in order to better understand the significance of that moment. In doing this I hope to show that even when I thought I was simply engaged in the practical business of teaching, I was unknowingly being influenced by theories of knowledge and culture. From there I will argue that the study of theory creates the potential for creating new and better practical approaches in the school and the classroom. My hope is to show that the space between the things we do (practice) and the reasons why we do those things (theory) is always interwoven and that becoming aware of how the threads between them connect allows us to create a better fabric to support the lives of children in school.

UPGRADING ENGLISH AND ALICE'S ARRIVAL

Early in my teaching career in an inner city high school, I was tasked with teaching a course called Upgrading English. The course was specific to the school and was developed by teachers and administrators to support a specific group of students. All students enrolled in English Language Arts at the school were given a diagnostic literacy test designed by teachers in the school, and those deemed to need remedial work on their literacy skills were assigned to Upgrading English. The students in my class were all Indigenous boys between the ages of 15 and 18. Some were from the local neighbourhood and others were from northern First Nations who had moved to the city to complete high school. The class was small, composed of about 15 students. There were two assumptions at play in the creation of this course. The first was that by identifying students in need of intensive remediation we would be able to help them attain the skills required to pass "regular" English language arts classes. The second assumption was that it would be helpful to all involved if students in classes had literacy skills that were somewhat homogenous. By putting this group of students together, the other classes were presumed to have students with a more uniform set of higher level skills, which was supposed to reduce the need for differentiation in all of our classes. Neither of these assumptions were questioned or discussed in department or planning meetings. The procedure for testing students and the curricular materials for both the Upgrading English and regular English language arts classes were well established parts of the routine of the school. I inherited them from the teacher who I was hired to replace in much the same way that I inherited the classroom he had taught in.

Looking back on my practice at the time, I can see that I entered my teaching career with a relatively unscrutinized academic rationalist stance (Eisner & Vallance, 1974; Vallance, 1986). As such, I believed that the logical and natural goal of English language arts education was enculturation of students by revealing the brilliance of the Western canon. Prepared to teach the classics, I was not prepared for students who struggled with grammar, composition, and vocabulary. I did, however, believe that remediation was necessary and took up the task, accepting the logic behind it. Lacking training with helping struggling readers and writers, I leaned heavily on the pre-packaged materials that I had inherited for the course, which were composed of reading and writing exercises that were simplified versions of what was being taught in the more advanced classes. For instance, rather than studying a whole play by Shakespeare and composing an essay about it, the students would read a sonnet and do assignments that asked them to decode the language within it. Most of the work was focused on building reading comprehension and writing fluency, and nearly all of the work was done through booklets of materials that students could work through at their own pace. As a result, there was limited interaction between us.

Despite the lack of interaction in class, I did come to know the students who attended the class outside of it. Our meaningful interactions happened over noon hours when I would play football, basketball, and floor hockey with students in pick-up games outside or in the gym. Our class was always right after lunch, so we would play until the buzzer signalled the end of lunch and make our way together back to the classroom. I enjoyed the routine and I think the boys did as well. Over time, a sense of informal camaraderie developed within the classroom. Lacking any common experience beyond our gym time and the resulting sweatiness in class, we seized on that and made the best of our time together.

Midway through the semester the flow of life that had evolved in Upgrading English was interrupted by a new arrival. Alice entered the class shortly after her family arrived in Canada. They had come from Rwanda as refugees. As the oldest child in her family, Alice was the only one who had a living memory of the brutal realities of the genocide that had unsettled them and forced their migration. I learned this about Alice long after I met her. What I learned about Alice immediately upon meeting her was that she dressed very well. On her first day in my class she was wearing clothes that others might wear if they were going to church or a job interview. Day after day, this trend continued. Alice stood out in the school because of her dress and in my class, where the boys and I regularly were wearing the same clothes we had just sweated through a floor hockey match in, the contrast was particularly pronounced. Over time I expected that Alice would gradually conform to the norms around attire common within the rest of the school, but I was wrong. I was taken with and perhaps even a little bothered by this. Alice was a hardworking, extremely polite student and she was making great progress through her booklets. However, her dress felt incongruous. I wanted her to fit in. One day I called her aside after class to fill her in on the norms around the place.

"Alice," I said, "I noticed you dress really nicely."

"Oh, thank you, Mr. Kuly," she replied.

"No, Alice, I mean, you don't understand. It's just school. Take a look around, we don't dress up for school here. Why do you feel the need to dress so well?"

Alice pursed her lips thoughtfully and smiled. "Oh, Mr. Kuly, it's because life is not a mountain."

I had no idea what she meant. I toyed with the idea of nodding and moving on but my curiosity made me ask, "What do you mean, life is not a mountain?"

Alice smiled again and said, "Mountains last forever."

UNPACKING ALICE'S ARRIVAL

You are walking well-trod ground if you say that teaching develops through cycles of reflection on experience (Dewey, 1933; Van Manen, 1995). However, claims that you know exactly how to prompt teachers to engage in reflective processes emerge from far less certain terrain (Eraut, 1985, 2002). One suggestion for prompting teachers to reflect is to have them focus on the "bumpy moments" of their practice (Romano, 2005, 2006). I can attest to the potential in such an approach, as Alice's words were a bump; they forced me to reckon with myself. Her words put a crack in the everyday for me, and, echoing Cohen (1992), that crack let in a transformative kind of light. In its glow, I had to rethink and re-see what was going on in my classroom. I later learned that Alice's expression was an English translation of a proverb she had learned as a child. Even in translation, the words were illuminating. The inner city remedial classroom was changed, revealing a space that approached the sacred. Through Alice's words, I saw that my room was the next waypoint on a journey from a place so beautiful that people in central Africa refer to it as the place where God goes to sleep at night (Dallaire, 2009). Alice's journey was precipitated by one of the most brutal examples of inhumanity that history has managed to give us. She fled her home without hope of ever returning, without time to mourn the loss of classmates, neighbours, or family. She moved from hovel to hovel in the international shuffle of the landless, finally ending up on the snow-swept prairies registered for Upgrading English in my classroom. She wasn't just going to school every day. Alice was reclaiming the chance at a good life we should all enjoy simply by virtue of being born human. My classroom was her next step toward that future. Moreover, Alice's words didn't just reveal the significance of her presence in my class to me, they also made me realize my responsibility. This space she had worked so hard to arrive within was the one for which I was responsible. Things began to shift after that day, beginning with me bringing a shirt to change into after floor hockey.

George Sefa Dei is an accomplished theorist, active in academic knowledge generation and in community action to promote the academic and social success of marginalized youth. His work is particularly germane here because it theorizes schooling for marginalized students like those I taught in Upgrading English, but also because it directly addresses the connection between how we think and what we do. Dei lays out his stance on the vital connection between theory and practice as follows:

> The relevance of a theory should be seen in how it allows us to understand complexity of human society and to offer a social and political corrective—that is, the power of theories and ideas to bring about change and transformation in social life. (Dei & Asgharzadeh, 2001, p. 298)

Taking him at his word, what follows is a brief survey of Dei's work with anti-racist, anti-colonial, and Indigenous theories in order to re-examine the Upgrading English class to find out what sort of "social and political corrective" might be discovered.

Dei's work spans a time of resurgent interest in the persistent and pervasive inequities facing racialized and other minority students in schools. During the same time span, the academy has grappled with questions about whose voices and knowledge count within its own traditions. Dei's attention is focused on the implications of both of these movements. Through surveying his development of the concept of "integrative anti-racism" (1995), his expansion of those ideas into an "anti-colonial discursive framework" (Dei & Asgharzadeh, 2001), and most recently, into the exploration of Indigenous philosophies (2011a, 2011b), some common theoretical elements in Dei's approach emerge.

One of the fundamental questions in Dei's writing is about whose knowledge and experience is considered valuable within social interaction and decision making. Answering this reveals the link between knowledge and power as well as the asymmetry that characterizes the relationship between the two. The old adage that "knowledge is power" is indeed true but should be followed by the proviso that not everyone's knowledge gets equal access. By tracing power relations, Dei identifies race as a key category that gives some in society power while denying others. However, from his first writing on anti-racist theory through to his more recent works on Indigeneity, Dei has pointed to the need to recognize that "race is mediated with other aspects of oppression" (1995, p. 14) and that since the task of the theorist and educator is "to critique and deal with human injustice, all the different forms of oppression, defined along racial, ethnic, class, and sexualities, must be problematized" (1995, p. 16). Dei recognizes intersectional oppression, but he does not equate all discrimination, and cautions, "We risk trivializing social oppression by claiming that we are all oppressors and oppressed" (1995, p. 17). Such a caution emanates from Dei's insistence on theory that is ethically bound to the lived experience of embodied subjects, particularly those embodied within oppressive contexts. He is constantly mindful that "philosophy as a discursive category neither is apolitical nor does it occupy an ahistorical space" (Dei, 2011a, p. 2). As a result, his theories advocate direct and mindful action on the part of teachers and administrators to address the biggest barriers faced by marginalized children in their pursuit of a good life.

Dei urges a broad approach to considering the construction of oppression within the arena of knowledge production. He takes issue with the potential for theoretical models to take part in the very processes they critique. Western hegemony is a totalizing narrative, and taking issue with its attempts to encompass and categorize all human experience is as important as critiquing its effects. Therefore, Dei points to the tendency within the fields of Marxism and feminism to create critiques of hegemonic treatments of class and gender that are so all encompassing that they subsume the experience of marginalized groups within them. An example of this comes from his choice of *anti-colonial* terminology as opposed to *post-colonial* in order to underline the fact that colonial relations are only "post" for a relatively small and relatively lucky slice of the world's population. At the other end of the spectrum, Dei cautions against the potential erosion of any claim to shared experience (and thus common action) that some post-structuralist and postmodern theories create. Dei and Asgharzadeh carve out a theoretical space wherein critiques based in race, gender, class, power, Indigenous philosophy, and post-colonial analysis embrace a "common zone to resist oppression" through solidarity with each other (2001, p. 318). Such a space is characterized by analysis that resists two opposing polarities, on the one side the pull to efface the texture of individual experiences in the service of assembling a unified critique, and on the other, the pull to focus myopically on the individual in ignorance of the shared experience and common sources of inequity. Dei develops a method for working within this space. His method is characterized by a discursive reflexivity wherein he preserves the salient critiques of power from many fields and combines them in a flexible framework that evolves in relationship to social change within the arenas where the reproduction of power relations are at play.

Schooling plays a fundamental role in building society and as such, it is a key arena for the imposition of and resistance to power. Dei sees the imposition of power in schools as being based in the assumptions that guide the decisions made within them. Schools commonly use "White, Euro-American culture(s) as the norm from which to evaluate other cultures and treat people differently"

(1995, p. 12). To move beyond the assumptions that have guided schooling for so long, Dei states that "educators and students must cross boundaries into different territories and create spaces to engage in conversations and dialogue with each other for genuine social change and transformation" (1995, p. 15). But where are the boundaries that need to be crossed? For Dei, to find them we must "interrogate the processes by which certain groups are singled out for unequal and differential treatment on the basis of real or imagined cultural, racial, gender, and class differences" (1995, p. 20). Examining how students, subjects, teachers, space, and resources are grouped or distributed within schools will reveal that things that may seem innocuous to some, such as setting up a remedial English class like the one I recalled earlier, might also divide and exclude.

Dei recognizes that examining schools in this way will create resistance. Because "Eurocentrism continues to masquerade as universalism, and old school sentinels fiercely discredit any political academic projects that seek to break the silence that surrounds marginalized knowledges" (Dei, 2000, p. 53), schools will often defend their practices before considering changing them. This is part of a pattern of action to resist change that has a long history. Taking a historical view of how Eurocentric ideas have been defended reveals

> how the dominant has used biological, physical, and cultural characteristics to inferioritize and subsequently dominate that which is different, which is "the other," now resorting to religious dogma, now to skin colour, imaginary biogenetic differences or illusory scientific explanations, and now to sophisticated forms of cultural and linguistic racisms. (Dei & Asgharzadeh, 2001, p. 308)

Looking at how people are included, excluded, and treated differently reveals the operation of power within school structures, and that awareness can assist educators to gain greater agency in their approach to teaching thoughtfully.

Thoughtful teaching requires a realization that the process of reproducing and naturalizing inequity is part of what happens in schools. From that perspective, teachers are equipped to examine their context with questions about change. These questions begin with a teacher examining their practice and school for evidence of what is wrong, and these questions motivate decisions about adding, deleting, and re-imagining. The goal of such revision is to establish the hopes, skills, experiences, and presents and futures of all young people as the centre of educational action. For Dei, that means careful attention to issues of history, culture, identity, representation, community, knowledge, and power (1995, pp. 21–23; see also this volume). Significant to schools in general, but perhaps more particularly poignant here on the prairies where the historical and contemporary processes of Canadian colonial action has had such a ruinous effect (Aboriginal Justice Implementation Commission, 1999; Daschuk, 2013), Indigenous reality must be a constant focus. As Dei indicates clearly, perhaps more than any other group, "Indigenous bodies know too well that structures and institutions script individual lives differently" (2011b, p. 22). With these suggestions in mind, it is time to return to Alice and Upgrading English.

RETURNING TO THE CLASSROOM

My conversation with Alice revealed the difference between how she saw our shared experience at school and how I saw it. The place and time we shared were critical to her journey toward fulfillment. That was an important realization and I like to think that my practice after that day was more attentive to my responsibility to help all my students toward that end. However, in the light of Dei's work, I see that interaction, the students in the classroom, and the factors that brought us all together were influenced by much more than my own inattention to the perspectives of my students. The influence of racist and colonial assumptions in establishing the terms of our meeting were also very present.

Four aspects made Upgrading English unique. First, the class was, until Alice's arrival, demographically homogenous. Even after Alice's arrival into the exclusively Indigenous group of students, there were significant connections between the students' ethnocultural histories and identities. While the particulars were different, the racial geographic realities of all of the students in the class were marked by the legacy of colonialism. Second, the curricular materials in the class were simplified versions of the same Western canonical texts and grammar lessons used in the more advanced English classes. Instruction was focused on offering support as students worked at their own pace through their booklets of pre-packaged materials, unlike the other classes where students benefited from discussion, debate, group work, and choice. Third, the decision to create this class was motivated by the perceived need to have a place where remediation would presumably be easier because students would have uniform reading comprehension and composition skills, but this decision simultaneously created a classroom of students separated from their peers because of their supposed deficits. Fourth, the class was assigned to me, a settler-colonial novice teacher with no training or experience in remedial English instruction. Each one of the decisions that created this situation was seen as a natural, logical, and well-intentioned response to student needs. It is in analyzing decisions like these which are justified by recourse to "common sense" that Dei's critique is most effective at exposing the assumptions that underpin the status quo.

Consider the composition of the class. The class was established after all students took a diagnostic test that consisted of reading a passage, responding to questions about the content, and defining a list of words. Sadly, I no longer have a copy of this test, nor do I remember what the passage or vocabulary words were. However, given that the diagnostic test identified only Indigenous learners, I have to wonder about the cultural context from which it came. Is it a reasonable assumption that in a school that served a broad range of students from a variety of ethno-cultural groups and socio-economic backgrounds the only students requiring remediation would be Indigenous? Looking back, the notion is absurd, and yet the results of the test were never questioned by my department, my students, or by me. The veneer of objectivity offered by the test was enough for us to decide to remove a whole group of Indigenous students from the regular English class that would earn them credits toward graduation and place them into a remedial class. Finding evidence of "the role of societal/institutional structures in producing and reproducing endemic inequalities" is not difficult once you know how to look for it (Dei & Asgharzadeh, 2001, p. 300).

The materials and practices within Upgrading English offer another glimpse into the ways in which some students' experiences are received differently from others. The material in the booklets the students worked through was designed by English teachers at the school and excerpted from the texts, readings, and language study traditionally used in the regular English class. The difference was in the amount that had to be read and written. The logic behind this decision, as it was explained to me, was that students in Upgrading English would learn these materials and, much like an inoculation with a small amount of a virus, the students would then take the regular course, prepared for the more rigorous material. In the regular class, students read novels together and did group projects and presentations as well as individual reading and writing assignments. In Upgrading English, all work was individual, as students progressed through the reading, writing, and grammar assignments contained in the booklets. This decision was made because in previous classes of Upgrading English, students often had trouble with regular attendance, and so it was decided that, given how hard it is to conduct communal activities without the predictable presence of a consistent group of students, individual work would better serve these students. In re-examining these decisions from the perspectives of anti-colonial and anti-racist theory it becomes clear why there had been attendance problems in Upgrading English. Success in the class meant demonstrating proficiency with content drawn from the Western literary canon, which ignored the experience of the students and articulated the virtue of values of Eurocentric structures that were the source of their alienation from the rest of the school. Success also meant working on your own without interacting with peers and the reward for success was, absurdly, redoing more of the same material the next semester.

The premise of the class was that these students needed help beyond the scope that they would receive in the regular English class. This premise was by no means secret. The students in the class knew it and their schoolmates knew it. It was also not lost on anybody that the students in the class were also Indigenous. The cumulative effect was a powerful message about the relative worth of knowledge within the school. Indigenous students were constructed as knowing less and needing help. Dei states that "cultural paradigms shape knowledge" (2011a, p. 4) and the cultural paradigm in place within the school recognized one form of knowledge as desirable. Ironically, or perhaps purposefully, the course had me as its teacher—the most inexperienced teacher available within the school. If the claim that the students needed special help was actually well-intentioned, perhaps the school might have assigned a teacher to the class who knew even a little about how to teach the technical aspects of composition and reading comprehension to struggling students. Instead, they had me and I had them and the only meaningful time we spent together happened outside of class. Informed by Dei, I understand now that significant learning about or with each other, or even about the intended curricular material, was nearly completely foreclosed upon by the Eurocentric, deficit-modelled, racially bifurcated terms of engagement that underpinned our gathering.

When I look back on it, I realize that very little about Upgrading English was set up with a sensitivity to the experiences or needs of the students assigned to it. However, I also know that the course was not set up as part of a consciously planned and overtly racist conspiracy on the part of scheming, mean-spirited teachers in the English department at my school. Rather, as mentioned earlier, "Eurocentrism continues to masquerade as universalism" (Dei, 2000, p. 53) and it is experienced as such by those socialized within its ideological assumptions. The decision to create that course was as natural as taking attendance or starting and ending class with the sounding of a buzzer. However, it was not inevitable. Dei asserts that resistance is possible, desirable, and the responsibility of educators. Following the dismal dissection of the oppressive assumptions that created Upgrading English, it is both useful and hopeful to turn to a consideration of what resistance might have looked like had the anti-racist, anti-colonial, and Indigenous critiques considered earlier been at play within the school.

Part of the dilemma with enacting teaching practices that acknowledge and support marginalized youth is the challenge of imagining alternatives to the status quo. Yet, by looking through the frameworks developed in theoretical imaginations, new realities that might otherwise not be apparent become possible. Returning to Upgrading English, the question can be asked, what might have been? To start, we can consider how the segregation of certain students into the class itself could have been prevented. Following that, we can see how, even within the severely limited space created by the class, there may have been a place for transformative action.

The class was based on two self-reinforcing assumptions. First, that there is only one form of knowledge that counts, and second, that the goal of school is to educate students into the logic and practices of that knowledge. Had a different set of assumptions been present, different actions would have resulted. For instance, had the school operated under the premise that society values an exclusionary set of norms and its job was to help students who are mistreated by those norms develop a self-sustaining critique of it, the diagnostic tool used to assess students' skills would have been very different. Recognizing that students gain strength from their home cultures, the tool may have asked students to tell their teachers what they cared about, what they hoped for, where they felt safe, who their most important people were, what they were really good at, and what cultural practices were important to them. After all, "an understanding of local experiences provides the requisite building blocks for the development of strategies that will be both relevant and insurgent" (Dei, 2000, p. 51). With this information, the school could have organized curriculum and instruction around nurturing student success by building on what students knew, did, and loved, rather than the opposite. Furthermore, the school could have recognized that in their Indigenous population, and likely amongst newcomers like Alice, there were funds of knowledge ready to be welcomed. Dei argues that "Indigeneity and Indigenous knowings provide intellectual agency to marginalized, colonized peoples" and that the reclaiming and affirmation of that within schools "provides a space for colonized and oppressed people to interpret their own experiences on their own terms and understandings, rather than being forced through Eurocentric paradigms" (2011a, p. 4). Rather than remediation, the students placed in Upgrading English could have been seen as needing recognition. If so, the segregation would never have happened because there would have been no need to see one group of students as being at a deficit in relation to another. And while it is true that no amount of theorizing would alleviate the troubles that the students in Upgrading English had with English comprehension and composition, is it not a far more certain proposition that their skills would have developed more in an environment that affirmed rather than effaced the values encoded in their cultural and racial identities?

It is fair to object to a re-visioning of school practice like the one above on the practical grounds that it is rare to find a school that is willing to organize itself with an overt, coherent, anti-racist, anti-colonial, pro-Indigenous model. However, resistance can occur within the classroom as well. Even though the Upgrading English class was created to exclude, there was still space within it for me to have acted differently. It was neither inevitable nor legislated that I had to use the booklets I inherited when I was assigned to teach the class. Teachers in my province still retain significant autonomy over what they teach and how they teach it. The shock that Alice's proverb provided me prompted me to wear different clothes. After realizing how she saw the school, I wanted my deportment to show that I respected her reality. However, had I been able to view that moment or the lack of interaction that happened in the classroom through the lenses critical theories of race in education might have provided, more substantive changes would have been possible. Dei suggests that "the incorporation of marginalized knowledges into mainstream educational sites would not only contribute to general educational improvement, it would foster collective reliance, mutual interdependence and strengthening of individual/group identity" (2000, p. 48). What would have happened if the day after I spoke with Alice I asked the students to put away their booklets and then I shared the proverb she had shared with me? Given the low level of student interest within the class before that point, it is likely any change would have been welcomed. Likewise, the presence of this well-dressed newcomer amongst us hadn't gone unnoticed by my students and hearing the traditional knowledge she had brought with her from the other side of the world would have likely helped answer some of the questions they had about her. Possibly, as was my experience later in my career (Kuly, 2015), such a moment might have prompted more and deeper sharing. Perhaps one of the students in the class would have chosen to share a piece of the wisdom from his own tradition that he relied on in making it through school. Sharing cultural sayings in class may not seem like a revolutionary move in the struggle against hegemony, but

> folkloric production (as in proverbs, story forms, folk music, dance, art, etc.) is about the totality of a people's experience, a way of life that speaks to the cultural, political, economic, social, and spiritual interconnections of human life and/or psycho-existential existence. (Dei, 2011a, p. 8)

Nothing that the students were reading and writing about spoke to anything remotely as affirming of their experience. Inviting Alice's wisdom may well have provided the necessary crack in the everyday to my students that it did for me. Perhaps through that crack we might have imagined a different future together within Upgrading English in which their gaps in composition and reading would have been sublimated by the centring of their accomplishments, abilities, and aspirations. Perhaps that re-centring would have provided a foundation for tackling the dilemmas they had with reading and writing. Perhaps not, but the time definitely would have been better spent.

CONCLUSION

At the outset I recalled the ambivalence I experienced from my classroom teaching colleagues about the worth of the theoretical work involved in graduate studies in education and then set about reconciling a teaching moment with the theoretical framework established by George Sefa Dei. The process has left me wishing for another conversation with those colleagues. Had I been aware of the theoretical assumptions I held and those that underpinned the school's practices before being assigned to teach Upgrading English, things may have been better. As Peter McLaren (2015) pointed out, a central realization of critical educational theory is that the things we do unconsciously are not natural but learned as we are made by our environment. The implication of the fact that we are constructions of our experiences and environments is emancipatory because, as McLaren states, "the point to remember is that if we have been made, then we can be 'unmade' and 'made over'" (2015, p. 153). If I had been aware of how I was made, I may well have been open to being remade in light of critiques like those found in Dei's work. If I was, I am confident that students entrusted to me would have learned more about each other and the world they were living in.

Later in my teaching career, after entering graduate school and studying the theories profiled here, I discovered that "relevant and insurgent" space could in fact open up within my classroom (Dei, 2000, p. 51). Alice was not the only student in the school who had valuable cultural experiences to share. With increased awareness, I began to make changes in my teaching strategies and in the curriculum content. I included more relevant learning resources and I listened to the interests and motivations of my students. These changes came together to create a storytelling project that exemplified the value of intercultural literacy.

Personal stories are a rich means of creating both collective and individual meaning (Egan, 1986). Key aspects of stories for Egan are: they resist easy reduction into morals (but do touch on the moral dimension); they proceed through a pattern of compelling conflicts and imaginative resolutions; they grapple with both the affective and cognitive dimensions of learning; and, rather than being prescribed or preplanned, their effect emerges in a gradual way. Sanchez (2009) studied the use of family stories from ethnically diverse student experiences as one way to develop an authentic curriculum that is relevant and meaningful to students who have historically been marginalized. The use of storytelling and personal narratives can help students discover their own voices and the biased nature of the voices represented in mainstream curricula (Sarris, 1990). Storytelling as a learning process can enhance social bonding and community building and nurture emotional well-being, developing self-confidence, self-expression, and personal empowerment. Senehi (2002) views storytelling as a peace-building process that provides tellers and listeners with a narrative form that negotiates meaning and "serves as a rationale for action" (p. 43). She asserts that storytelling events create movements suspended from the regular part of the day. The ability that story has to suspend a moment and enrich it with memories of other moments allows people the pause required to examine and record their actions. Storytelling can open up spaces and possibilities for people to reconsider their connection to each other in more nuanced and richer ways. For many Indigenous students, oral storytelling traditions centre relational learning, belonging, and better understanding of one's purpose in life. Oral storytelling can also be a catalyst for creative writing, artistic creations, drama productions, and poetry. Wagamese (2012) writes:

> We all have stories within us. Sometimes we hold them gingerly, sometimes desperately, sometimes as gently as an infant. It is by sharing our stories, by being strong enough to take a risk—both in the telling and in the asking—that we make it possible to know, recognize, and understand each other. (p. 85)

The storytelling project (Kuly, 2015) occurred, in part, as a response to a rapid increase in cultural diversity within the school community that resulted in cultural stratification between ethno-cultural student groups. I hoped to encourage self-expression and community spirit among the students with storytelling as the vehicle. The students involved in the project volunteered to participate after completing a unit based on reading *A Long Way Gone: Memoirs of a Boy Soldier*, Ishmael Beah's (2007) book about his experiences as a child soldier in Sierra Leone. The book was extremely popular with students and it emboldened students who had been refugees to begin speaking more openly about their experiences, at the same time piquing the interest of their Canadian-born classmates in those experiences. The storytelling project began as a simple way to respond to the students' interests by engaging them in storytelling circles. The group of students involved was composed of between 20 and 30 students depending on the day. Approximately half of the students were from urban and rural, white and Indigenous, poor and middle-class Canadian backgrounds. The other half of the students came from largely rural backgrounds in Sierra Leone, Sudan, Ethiopia, Eritrea, Liberia, Ghana, Afghanistan, and Burma. As they shared stories the project took on a life of its own, moving from a teacher-directed initiative to one animated by the students' growing sense of shared understanding and common cause.

In the beginning, storytelling sessions would start with students standing in a circle, bowing to each other and then sitting in a circle. The storytelling structure was framed around key themes that included the meaning of their names, memorable experiences, fears, life goals, and dreams that they hoped to realize. The storytelling prompts that the students were given began simply. For instance, students would tell each other the story of their names, the oldest person they knew, their favourite childhood game, or something similar. These stories served to establish rapport and the understanding that there was much they shared despite their apparent differences. After establishing rapport with each other, the students began to tell stories that touched on the differences in their backgrounds. Much of the interest for this class emerged from their shared reading of Ishmael Beah's memoir; as a result, many of the stories told in the earlier classes focused on the harrowing experiences of the refugee and immigrant students in the group. However, in fairly short order, the students developed an interest that extended beyond the trauma of refugee experience. Everyone had a story that needed to be heard, valued, and validated.

As the storytelling project moved from considering Ishmael Beah's experiences into a consideration of their own experiences, the cultural practices, values, and beliefs of the students became a central part of its curriculum. The effect of this was multi-faceted. The first was to acknowledge and address misperceptions and a lack of understanding that existed between the cultural groups in the project. These gaps in understanding were evident in the fact that students had to explain what it meant to be Muslim, what the Koran was, and what it meant to be Indigenous. While the potential for mutual discovery exists with any multicultural group, the centrality of story to this group allowed the ignorance and accompanying explanations to happen in an educative and non-judgmental way. Story requires a lack of knowledge on the part of the listener so that the gaps in cultural understanding become an essential part of the storytelling project (Senehi, 2009). This stands in contrast to normal school practices wherein differences between people are often ignored in order to cover more content, or glossed over for fear of divisiveness (Noddings, 2008).

After both the Canadian-born and newcomer students had heard all of each other's stories and discovered a common experience of struggle and joy across their culturally constructed differences, they wanted to take action. The action they chose was to perform their stories with each other to highlight their dissatisfaction with the inequity of treatment and circumstances that they had learned about from listening to one another. The students performed for a school staff meeting, for a student assembly, and at a storytelling festival. Each performance was tailored for the audience in question through the students deciding which stories would be told. The students determined which stories would be told and how they would be told based on how to best express the mutual understanding and common desires that existed between them, despite their differences.

From a position of understanding, students could share their sense of longing for stability, a desire to realize their dreams, and a need to counter and overcome discrimination, hardship, and tragedy.

Hopefully, by juxtaposing this story of teaching with the one I told about Upgrading English, the benefits of embracing transcultural literacies is clear. Additionally, I hope it is clear that for those benefits to be recognized, an engagement with the theories that guide school structure and teacher practice is required. The opposition between theory and practice is based on a flawed assumption about the basis for the decisions commonly made in schools. The truth is that theory is deeply relevant and influential in everyday school practice. However, for the most part it exerts its influence with no scrutiny. It is not accurate to say that I began teaching Upgrading English without theoretical assumptions about teaching, learning, students, or schools and that the process of graduate studies equipped me with a theoretical framework. It is accurate to say that I began teaching Upgrading English unaware of the theoretical assumptions I did hold and further study helped me become aware of them. Sadly, those Eurocentric, colonial, racist assumptions about what knowledge mattered and what the aims of schooling should be impeded the progress of real people. The theories held by my colleagues were equally unscrutinized and that is the topic of the conversation I wish I could have now. Dei contends that "the worth of a social theory should be judged both on its philosophical groundings/merits, as well as the ability of the theory to offer a social and political corrective" (2011a, p. 9). By that criteria, the lack of worth of the theories that prompted my colleagues and me to feel good about labelling, segregating, and poorly educating a group of already marginalized students in the name of helping them is painfully evident.

QUESTIONS FOR REFLECTION AND DISCUSSION

1. As a student or as a teacher, consider times when you experienced school as preventing some students from being successful. (It might help to think of times when familiar practices or events in school were considered strange to some students, or vice versa.) How have these issues been brought up for consideration (or if they have not, why do you think that is the case)? What have the results been?

2. Consider how students are grouped, resources are distributed, space is allocated, and teachers are assigned to students and subjects in your school: How do factors of race, gender, social class, sexuality, or ability intersect with these processes? What do these groupings, distributions, and assignments say about the values of the school?

3. When you think about what ideas and experiences are most prominent in the teaching you do, what can you conclude about the theories that guide your practice? Have your theories about education changed over time? If so, how and why?

4. Based on your reading of Kuly's chapter, identify three to five tenets of anti-oppressive teaching. Now think of a course, class, program, or school with which you are familiar. What would need to change if those theories/tenets were enacted? What might be the goals or principles of such a course, class, program, or school? What texts, activities, resources, people, strategies, and spaces can you envision including?

5. Gabo Ntseane (2007) explains that African education traditions value practical knowledge, the preservation of cultural heritage, a participatory education for the common good, storytelling, and the interpretation of dreams, visions, and proverbs. How might you include some of these features in designing your curriculum and in your assessment of student learning?

6. Are there particular books, films, and/or other texts that have informed or challenged your understandings and/or assumptions about different cultures? How should we address cultural representations, stereotypes, and counter-stereotypes in the texts and resources we read, view, and/or bring into the classroom?

7. "Each of us is put here in this time and in this place to personally decide the future of humankind. Do you think you were put here for something less?" (Chief Arvol Looking Horse, in Ellis, 2013). Imagine that Chief Arvol was invited to be a guest speaker in Kuly's class—what might he say about "Upgrading English"?

DEEPEN YOUR INQUIRY: RELATED READINGS AND RESOURCES

Booklist: The refugee experience for teens. Available at http://www.yalsa.ala.org/thehub/tag/deborah-ellis/ (a list of Young Adult books focusing on newcomer and refugee youth experiences)

Brewer, C., & McCabe, M. (2014). *Immigrant and refugee students in Canada.* Edmonton: Brush Education.

Canadian Museum of Human Rights Teaching Resources. Available at https://humanrights.ca/human-rights-education-activities-grades-10-12

Capacity building K–12: Supporting students from refugee backgrounds. (2016). Toronto: Government of Ontario. (a resource book for teachers and counsellors. PDF format available at http://www.edu.gov.on.ca/eng/literacynumeracy/inspire/research/cbs_refugees.pdf)

Ellis, D. (2009). *Children of war.* Toronto: Groundwood Books. (narratives of children who have survived war and conflict)

Farrell, E., & Seipp, K. (2008). *A road to peace curriculum: A teaching guide on local and global transitional justice.* Minneapolis: The Human Rights Advocates. Available at http://peacefulschoolsinternational.org/wp-content/uploads/road_to_peace_curriculum.pdf

Sarasvati Productions. www.sarasvatiproductions.com. (*Home 2.0* is a theatre production based on narratives of newcomer and refugee youth. The Sarasvati website provides ideas for popular and transformative theatre productions.)

Short, D., & Boyson, B. A. (2012). *Helping newcomer students succeed in secondary schools and beyond. Report to the Carnegie Corporation.* New York & Washington, DC: Centre for Applied Linguistics. Available at https://www.carnegie.org/media/filer_public/ff/fd/fffda48e-4211-44c5-b4ef-86e8b50929d6/ccny_report_2012_helping.pdf

Stewart, J. (2011). *Supporting refugee children: Strategies for educators.* Toronto: University of Toronto Press.

Students from refugee and displaced backgrounds: A handbook for schools. (2007 updated). Fairfield, Queensland, Australia: Queensland Program of Assistance to Survivors of Torture and Trauma. Available at https://qpastt.org.au/wordpress/wp-content/uploads/2014/05/handbook-2007-updated-2014.pdf

UNESCO Associated Schools Teaching Resources. Available at https://en.unesco.org/events/unesco-associated-schools-aspnet-innovative-and-collaborative-teaching-and-learning-context

Venn, D. (2017). Supporting newcomer students through storytelling and mentorship. Victoria, BC: Community Foundations of Canada. Available at https://communityfoundations.ca/supporting-newcomers-storytelling-mentorship/

AUTHOR'S NOTE

For a personal and professional perspective on how certain student experiences are privileged over others, see: https://www.ted.com/talks/victor_rios_help_for_kids_the_education_system_ignores. For an example of an alternative approach to cultural and language differences in classrooms, see: www.bullfrogfilms.com/catalog/story.html. For an example of the interplay of theory and practice, see: *To Teach: The Journey in Comics* (Ayers & Alexander-Tanner, 2010). For an example of how school decisions create unequal opportunities, see *Unfinished Business: Closing the Racial Achievement Gap in Our Schools* (Noguera & Wing, 2008) and "Humiliating Ironies and Dangerous Dignities: A Dialectic of School Pushout" (Tuck, 2011).

REFERENCES

Aboriginal Justice Implementation Commission. (1999). Report of the aboriginal justice inquiry of Manitoba. Winnipeg: Government of Manitoba.

Ayers, W., & Alexander-Tanner, R. (2010). *To teach: The journey in comics.* New York: Teachers College Press.

Beah, I. (2007). *A long way gone: Memoirs of a boy soldier.* New York: Farrar, Straus, and Giroux.

Bezzina, C. (2006). Views from the trenches: Beginning teachers' perceptions about their professional development. *Journal of In-Service Education, 32*(4), 411–430.

Britzman, D. (1986). Cultural myths in the making of a teacher: Biography and social structure in teacher education. *Harvard Educational Review, 56*(4), 442–457.

Cohen, L. (1992). Anthem. On *The future.* New York: Columbia.

Connelly, F. M., Clandinin, D. J., & He, M. F. (1997). Teachers' personal practical knowledge on the professional knowledge landscape. *Teaching and teacher education, 13*(7), 665–674.

Dallaire, R. (2009). *Shake hands with the devil: The failure of humanity in Rwanda.* Toronto: Vintage Canada.

Daschuk, J. W. (2013). *Clearing the plains: Disease, politics of starvation, and the loss of Aboriginal life* (Vol. 65). Regina: University of Regina Press.

Dei, G. J. S. (1995). Integrative anti-racism: Intersection of race, class, and gender. *Race, Gender & Class, 2*(3), 11–30.

Dei, G. J. S. (2000). *Removing the margins: The challenges and possibilities of inclusive schooling.* Toronto: Canadian Scholars' Press.

Dei, G. J. S. (2011a). Introduction. In G. J. S. Dei (Ed.), *Indigenous philosophies and critical education. A reader* (pp. 1–13). New York: Peter Lang.

Dei, G. J. S. (2011b). Revisiting the question of the Indigenous. In G. J. S. Dei (Ed.), *Indigenous philosophies and critical education: A reader* (pp. 21–33). New York: Peter Lang.

Dei, G. J. S., & Asgharzadeh, A. (2001). The power of social theory: The anti-colonial discursive framework. *Journal of Educational Thought, 35*(3), 297–323.

Dewey, J. (1933). *How we think*. Chicago: Henry Regnery.

Egan, K. (1986). *Teaching as storytelling*. London, ON: University of Western Ontario.

Eisner, E. W., & Vallance, E. M. (Eds.). (1974). *Conflicting conceptions of curriculum*. New York: McCutchan Publishing.

Elbaz, F. (1991). Research on teacher's knowledge: The evolution of a discourse. *Journal of Curriculum Studies, 23*(1), 1–19.

Ellis, D. (2013). *Looks like daylight: Voices of Indigenous kids*. Toronto and Berkeley: Groundwood Books.

Eraut, M. (1985). Knowledge creation and knowledge use in professional contexts. *Studies in Higher Education, 10*(2), 117–133.

Eraut, M. (2002). Menus for choosy diners. *Teachers and Teaching: Theory and Practice, 8*(3), 371–379.

Kettle, B., & Sellars, N. (1996). The development of student teachers' practical theory of teaching. *Teaching and Teacher Education, 12*(1), 1–24.

Kuly, M. (2015). Crossing the divide: Storytelling as a bridge to student-teacher connection. In D. Sisk (Ed.), *Accelerating and extending literacy for diverse students* (pp. 195–204). New York: Rowman & Littlefield.

Kyriacou, C., & Stephens, P. (1999). Student teachers' concerns during teaching practice. *Evaluation & Research in Education, 13*(1), 18–31.

McIntyre, D. (2005). Bridging the gap between research and practice. *Cambridge Journal of Education, 35*(3), 357–382.

McLaren, P. (2015). *Life in schools: An introduction to critical pedagogy in the foundations of education* (6th ed.). New York: Paradigm.

Noddings, N. (2008). Spirituality and religion in public schooling. In J. R. Wiens & D. L. Coulter (Eds.), *Why do we educate? Renewing the conversation* (pp. 185–195). Chicago: National Society for the Study of Education.

Noguera, P., & Wing, J. (Eds.). (2008). *Unfinished business: Closing the racial achievement gap in our schools*. San Francisco: Jossey-Bass.

Ntseane, G. (2007). African Indigenous knowledge: The case of Botswana. In S. B. Merriam and Associates (Eds.). *Non-Western perspectives on learning and knowing* (pp. 113–136). Malabar, FL: Krieger.

Romano, M. E. (2005). Preservice teachers' reflections on observed "bumpy moments" in teaching: Implications for teacher education. *The Teacher Educator, 40*(4), 257–277.

Romano, M. E. (2006). "Bumpy moments" in teaching: Reflections from practicing teachers. *Teaching and Teacher Education, 22*(8), 973–985.

Sanchez, C. (2009). Learning about students' cultures and language through family stories elicited by dichos. *Early Childhood Education Journal, 1*(37), 161–169.

Sarris, G. (1990). Storytelling in the classroom: Crossing vexed chasms. *College English, 52*(2), 169–185.

Senehi, J. (2002). Constructive storytelling: A peace process. *Peace and Conflict Studies, 9*(2), 41–63.

Sutherland, L., Howard, S., & Markauskaite, L. (2010). Professional identity creation: Examining the development of beginning preservice teachers' understanding of their work as teachers. *Teaching and Teacher Education, 26*(3), 455–465.

Tuck, E. (2011). Humiliating ironies and dangerous dignities: A dialectic of school pushout. *International Journal of Qualitative Studies in Education, 24*(7), 817–827.

Vallance, E. (1986). A second look at conflicting conceptions of curriculum. *Theory into Practice, 25*(1), 24–30.

Van Manen, M. (1995). On the epistemology of reflective practice. *Teachers and Teaching: Theory and Practice, 1*(1), 33–50.

Wagamese, R. (2012). *One story, one song*. Toronto: Douglas & McIntyre.

Weber, S., & Mitchell, C. (1995). *That's funny, you don't look like a teacher!: Interrogating images and identity in popular culture* (No. 3). New York: Psychology Press.

"It's Resonating": Transcultural Literacies in Unexpected Moments

Like tide pools, transcultural literacies create dynamic spaces characterized by particular local ecologies, all the while affected by the waves of global flows that are in constant flux.

—*Michelle A. Honeyford*

OPENING THE CONVERSATION: READING NOTES

How do we respond to the unexpected moments in our lives as learners, educators, administrators, and researchers? What do our responses show about what we value in our relationships with students? What do these moments reveal about what we believe is most important in education? What might they tell us about who we are as educators?

Like Kuly and his exchange with Alice, the teacher candidates in this afterschool program reflect on unexpected and potentially transformative moments of their time with the Grade 5–6 students during the evening's activities. These are moments that the teacher candidates identify as "resonating" for them: moments of uncertainty, surprise, and joy that they begin to unpack in terms of their significance or implications. In this chapter, Michelle Honeyford highlights how the actions of the teacher candidates "in the moment" and their reflective dialogue afterwards reveal what happens when learning spaces are organized primarily around building relationships with students and co-constructing learning communities that value play, joy, and students' interests in collective creative experiences.

Grounded in her analysis, Honeyford contributes dynamic ways to think about transcultural literacies as enacted through *hacceity*, being present and open to what may emerge; as *embodied knowledge*, visceral, physical understandings shared or revealed experientially; and as *epistemic knowledge*, specialized knowledge learners bring as part of their backgrounds and experiences that often remains invisible and untapped due to the cultural, racial, economic, religious, gender, geographical, and historical biases of curriculum, assessment, and educational programs and practice.

As you read this chapter, consider what is unexpected for you: What surprises you and why? Think about the design of Afterschool U in relationship to other educational spaces you know: To what extent would you agree that a relational focus has the potential to change teaching and learning in powerful ways? What are the barriers educators might experience in orienting education to more meaningfully connect with students' passions and interests, and to be more intentionally organized around shared activity? How could those barriers be mitigated? What kinds of "becoming" can you imagine for students, schools, and communities?

THINKING VISUALLY: CHAPTER ORGANIZER

In this graphic organizer, the elements of Afterschool U are explored in relationship to the kinds of spaces they create. After you read the chapter, you might return to this diagram and annotate it, adding ideas for how:

- classrooms can become translocal spaces;
- curriculum can honour the transcultural flows of our students' knowledges and experiences;
- situated meaning-making with others invites new ways to theorize and approach transcultural literacies in other contexts;
- relationships and shared activity can contribute to more intentional and reflexive transcultural pedagogies;
- inquiring into "unexpected moments" with colleagues can create opportunities for professional learning and growth;
- the interests and passions of students, teachers, and communities might inspire deeper and more meaningful and interdisciplinary curricular inquiries.

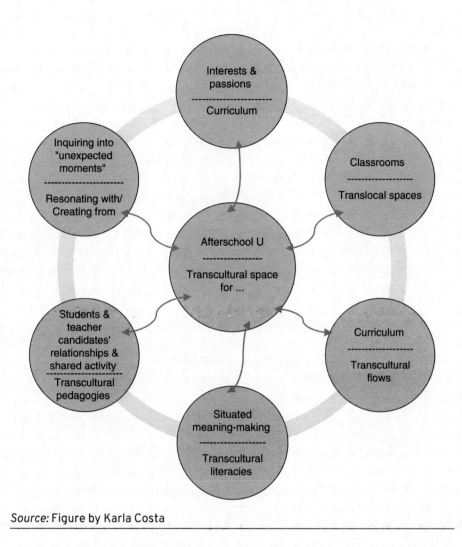

Source: Figure by Karla Costa

CHAPTER 3

"It's Resonating": Transcultural Literacies in Unexpected Moments

Michelle A. Honeyford

There is always the danger in education to dismiss new theories and ideas as "just another fad" or to quickly conclude that an idea is not new at all, simply rebranded, and we "already know/do that." It can be easy to critique what we hear or read about as irrelevant, not pertaining to us/our students, as too removed, complex, "research-y" or theoretical to be of value in the classroom—in the day-to-day demands of our work or the real "nitty-gritty" of teaching. Far too often, we fail to see the connections between theory and practice (see Kuly, this volume), to identify the taken-for-granted assumptions that inform the many consequential decisions we make in the constantly moving and ever-changing moments of teaching. We neglect to see our roles as theory makers, perhaps because we are not often given the time and space amidst the multiple demands of our jobs to slow down, talk to one another, and think critically together about how our work relates to the challenges in our world, to the specific and situated lives of our students and communities, and to our own beliefs, concerns, and vulnerabilities as teachers. We are often too daunted by the challenges in front of us to consider what got us here or what alternatives we might make possible if we worked together to change the inequitable systems and politics of education.

"Re-imagining education differently" (Dei, this volume) is a critical concern in teacher education. Anti-oppressive theories and practice need to come together in complex sociocultural spaces where pre-service teachers have the same kinds of opportunities to build relationships, promote cooperation, and encourage self-reflection (Ellerbrock, 2014) that they will need to create in their own diverse classrooms. My research in Afterschool U focuses on what happens when these are the goals of an informal learning space. In this context, teacher candidates work in teams to collaboratively design, plan, lead, and then reflexively inquire into their experiences with a group of Grade 5–6 students. Through the dialogue of these pre-service teachers, it is possible to see how, in the unexpected moments of Afterschool U, new possibilities for thinking about transcultural relationships, knowledges, and literacies are produced. Theory and practice come together; moreover, they are entangled in more inclusive, reciprocal, responsive, and ethical understandings of teaching, learning, and being with one another.

TRANSCULTURAL SPACES: AFTERSCHOOL U

"Afterschool U" (pseudonym) is a large university-community partnership that began as a pilot project six years ago for 15 students in Grades 5–6. Since then, enrollment in the program has grown to 500 students and the program has expanded to include innovative options for students in Grades 7–9, as well as 10–12. However, students in Grades 5–6 continue to be a strong focus in the program's efforts to inspire hope and confidence, build relationships, and offer high-quality afterschool programming in collaboration with university departments, faculties, and programs.

One of the original partners in the pilot program was the Faculty of Education. Over the years, the faculty's participation in Afterschool U has evolved and grown quite dramatically. Initially, two teacher candidates offered tutoring that then developed (in response to students' interests) into a comic-themed writing workshop. In the year this study took place, over 30 teacher candidates participated, working in teams to design and lead seven different interest-driven "academy" programs for about 80 students.

The partnership creates an opportunity for teacher candidates to work with a highly diverse group of middle years students from schools across the downtown "core" and greater urban areas. Although the faculty has adopted a new diversity admissions policy aimed to create a more diverse teaching force in the province, a significant gap still remains between the ethno-cultural, linguistic, and racial backgrounds of teacher candidates and the students they will teach. Research has shown that partnerships in teacher education programs that serve to expand teacher candidates' social and cultural understandings of learners and learning can contribute to disrupting their assumptions regarding difference and diversity and to gaining new perspectives from the experience (McHatton, Thomas, & Lehman, 2006; Boyle-Baise &

Sleeter, 2000; Boyle-Baise, 1998). Providing more "real world" opportunities to teach also increases teacher candidates' self-efficacy (Cone, 2009), particularly in more constructivist methods and approaches they may not have seen demonstrated or experienced themselves. For teacher candidates, working in partnership spaces helps them: (i) more deeply understand the complexities of teaching and learning by observing and interacting with learners, developing strategies like questioning, reflecting, and responding (Baker, 2008; Cox-Peterson, Spencer, & Crawford, 2005); (ii) feel more confident and competent in those practices with real students in the classroom (Cartwright, 2012; Cox-Peterson, Spencer, & Crawford, 2005); and (iii) develop a greater sense of connection between theory and practice (Boyle-Baise, 2005; Carrington, 2011; Cartwright, 2012). Transformative experiences for teacher candidates also embed opportunities to engage in reflexive practices (Conner, 2010), including opportunities for journaling and collective discussions (Ryan, Carrington, Selva, & Healy, 2009; Cone, 2009).

As a partnership, Afterschool U offers flexibility to create for teacher candidates a unique experience. In the academy program, they are invited to work in teams to design their own six-week afterschool program for Grade 5–6 students with their interests and passions as the focus. Teacher candidates learn about Afterschool U when they attend orientation, as well as through the university's social media channels. Participation by teacher candidates in the academy program is voluntary and open to all. They submit a proposal to the program as a team, develop a budget, and create a video to show the Grade 5–6 students (who then choose which academy they wish to attend). Throughout their participation in Afterschool U, the teacher candidates are supported with space and time to engage in collective and reflexive inquiry into teaching and learning.

TRANSCULTURAL THEORIES AND PEDAGOGIES

Transcultural Spaces

Afterschool U is an example of what Orellana (2016) describes as a transcultural space, characterized by movement across geographic, cultural, linguistic, and academic/disciplinary borders (p. 3). More specifically, the academy program is characterized by movement within the liminal and temporary spaces that the teacher candidates have created. Every academy space is shaped by pluralisms and differences (e.g., age, gender, socio-economic status, as well as cultural, ethnic, racial, linguistic, and religious backgrounds) not just among the students who attend, but also among the program's many volunteers: high school students (peer leaders), university undergraduates (group leaders), and the teacher candidates (academy leaders).

The academies are held in the education building, at the same time as evening diploma and graduate courses. As participating teacher candidates finish their afternoon classes, they begin their work of transforming designated classrooms into performance spaces, crime labs, studios, and maker spaces in preparation for the arrival of the Afterschool U students. The program also represents a liminal space for them, both familiar and yet new. It is not a required component of the teacher education program, nor an evaluative space. It is a volunteer, co-curricular activity,[1] yet it is affiliated with the university and coordinated by an education professor. It is situated in the education building during the teacher candidates' course block,[2] but creates a concurrent opportunity to teach students. The teacher candidates remain on their academic "home turf," maintain their subjectivities as university students, and play host to the visiting Grade 5–6 students. There is also a subtle but dramatic shift in interacting with Grade 5–6 students outside of their home schools, and where instead they are potential future university students increasingly comfortable navigating the hallways and classrooms of the education building and campus. Here, teacher candidates are not limited in their experience by some of the specifications and expectations of their practicum courses: They can work with students outside their grade level focus (e.g., early or senior years) and teachable areas. They are invited to go beyond the provincial documents to create curriculum out of their passions, and to do so collaboratively. In this space, first-year students work with second-year students who boast a wide variety of majors, minors, and teaching experiences, and here, they teach together as a team.

Thus, as Orellana (2016) elaborates, using "trans" as a prefix signals the design of the academy program in Afterschool U as a space to invite new ways to experience, think about, and understand teaching and learning, for

> "trans" is not just a substitute for "multi" or "inter." It is not just about fluidity or movement, or even "just" transgression. "Trans" suggests a movement *beyond* borders, a transcendence or transformation of things that were being held apart, or artificially constructed as separate and distinct. This is not the same as hybridity, which presumes an even and presumably equitable blend of different forms. Nor is it the erasure of difference. Rather, it is about questioning the ontologies that

hold things apart. It involves the resolution of dialectic tensions and the emergence of something new—something that we perhaps cannot even imagine. (p. 91)

As will be discussed later, asking teacher candidates to think about the "unexpected moments" produced in the transcultural spaces of their academies prompted "the emergence of something new" and unimagined—of new questions, wonderings, and ideas, but also the consideration of new pedagogical possibilities and identities for students and themselves.

Translocality and Transcultural Flows

The Grade 5–6 students who attend Afterschool U are nominated by their teachers in partnering schools. The program provides bussing, snacks, supper, and (as a result of extensive fundraising, grants, and partnerships) all the materials and equipment the students need. The students have an opportunity in the fall program to choose the academy in which they wish to participate in January, and so they start anew with one another, re-grouped by their choices. Once they arrive at the education building and their group is complete, they walk to various locations on campus to eat, and then return to the education building for the academy program. By that time (5 p.m.), they have moved across multiple spaces, from their homes and neighbourhoods to their different community schools to the university campus. For some, even their journey to Canada is still quite recent. As the immigrant populations in the schools in this area continue to grow, with students from the Philippines, India, China, Somalia, Iraq, the Democratic Republic of the Congo, Eritrea, Ethiopia, and Syria, that diversity is reflected in Afterschool U. For some, their journeys here have been prolonged, arduous, and traumatic. Even some Indigenous students, whose connections to this land go back for many generations, are new to the city, having moved from their home communities in rural and northern areas. Many of these students are also experiencing the impacts of being disconnected from the land and their communities, displaced by decisions to move for economic or academic opportunities. All of these 10- and 11-year-old students bring with them multiple subjectivities: their interests and affiliations, curiosities and fears, gifts and abilities; their cultural, linguistic, and gender identities; their beliefs, perspectives, and worldviews.

When the teacher candidates submit their proposals for their academies, they are reminded that their plans should be tentative, open to being shaped and informed by the students who join. In their first evening with the students in particular, and in their debriefing and planning afterwards, they begin to see how their intended curriculum becomes *lived*—constructed through "dynamic [trans]cultural flows" that are "discursively produced in the local context" of their academy, but also embedded in students' "trajectories and movements across spaces, places, time, and people" (Medina, 2010, p. 40). This begins with the games they play to get to know each other. Each week, the teacher candidates are expected to begin the evening with games to build a sense of community and develop relationships with the students. In their reflexive discussions at the end of the evening, teacher candidates often note how much they learn from the students through playing games. This includes discovering more about students' interests and experiences, but also observations about what makes particular students laugh, how much risk students are willing to take, how creative they are, and how they respond to different social situations and challenges.

As the academies focus on shared passions and interests, and because the adult-to-student ratio is quite high, there is a lot of time and opportunity for teacher candidates to focus on developing relationships with the students. From a transcultural literacies perspective, Medina (2010) argues that "as opposed to [educators] asking what students' cultural backgrounds are and how those cultural backgrounds are made visible" in the classroom, "it is more significant to ask how the students are dynamically making sense of the multiple social locations they navigate (across time, places, and people) and what is being made visible, relevant, and accepted" in the students' participation "so that classrooms become a translocal space for cultural production" (p. 40). Those spaces are created as teacher candidates sit shoulder to shoulder with students, for example, in the art studio, as teacher candidates and students paint side by side, engaged in conversation together about their aunties, analyzing Beyoncé's latest video, or teaching each other words in their mother tongues.

Transcultural Literacies

Transcultural literacies are practices of navigating and moving through spaces (real and imagined), negotiating multiple social and cultural locations, and producing new ways of knowing, being, and doing in the process. The notion of transcultural literacies emphasizes the flow of people, materials, and practices across space and time and how they change from one context to another (Medina, 2010) or what is gained and lost in crossing one border or another (Orellana, 2016). Like tide pools, transcultural literacies create dynamic spaces characterized by particular local ecologies, all the while affected by the waves of global flows that are in constant flux. The space of an afterschool program is a rich habitat for transcultural literacies. The movement of adults, children, semiotic sign systems, materials, and practices creates an infinite number of possibilities in their intra-actions, the "mutual constitution of entangled agencies" out of which emerges, as with the cycle of each low tide, something new (Barad, 2007, p. 33).

As a theoretical and pedagogical concept, transcultural literacies focus attention on the ways literacy practices are embodied; how knowledge communicated through story, dance, or slam poetry, for example, can be viscerally experienced through its performance. Critical awareness and celebration of the body in literacy studies and literacy education has grown in dialogue with cultural studies, gender studies, critical race studies, disability studies, and anti-oppressive and anti-colonial education. These areas of research and critical pedagogy expand literacy practices beyond what happens in the mind. They highlight how literacy practices are experienced physically and physiologically, exploring affect, memory, touch, and perception, for example. They have contributed to expanding understandings of linguistic and communicative practices as conveyed through gesture, clothing, hair, jewellery, and body art. They have explored the ways knowledge is produced and understood through play, simulation, spiritual practices, and exercise. And they have examined the role of power and capital in relationship to how race, gender, age, ability, and dress influence how communicative practices are interpreted, valued, marginalized, or ignored in society. As Dei remarked, "Our anti-colonial intellectuality must consider the body of the knowledge producer, place, desires, politics and contexts in which knowledge is produced" (2016, slide 8).

Transcultural literacies call for expanding the literacy practices recognized and taught in classrooms: to note students' interests and dialogue with them to better understand the literacy practices they engage in (or desire to learn). Transcultural literacies are a celebration of identity and a movement of resistance[3] that draw attention to equity and social justice. As such, transcultural literacies are evident in the material and the symbolic—in rainbows, hashtags, raised black fists, orange shirts, and red dresses, as well as in speeches, chants, songs, and the movement of bodies in rallies, protests, and peace marches. Transcultural literacies are increasingly necessary to being able to read the material and artefactual that are present everywhere around us, as well as to critically engage in the multiple and contested histories of peoples and places from other times and places.

Transcultural literacies allow for simultaneity of experience: to be from multiple places, to identify with multiple groups, to be "both/and" (Honeyford, 2013). They enable multiple positions from which to enter into teaching and learning and multiple perspectives through which to relate to students, curriculum, and instruction. Such practices are dynamic and constantly on the move, adjusted and recalibrated in response to "reading the linguistic and cultural landscape" of a learning space (Orellana, 2016). They are thus difficult to measure or calculate (Medina, 2010). But when inquiry and relationship are the focus of learning and becoming, teaching involves wading into the tide pools, getting wet, and looking closely, learning to "see what kids ... [are] doing, ... the *complexity* of the tasks kids [are] engaged in ... [and then] deciding how [to] respond" (Orellana, 2016, p. 120). The next section describes what that looked like in Afterschool U.

REFLEXIVITY AND TRANSCULTURAL LITERACIES IN TEACHING

Every week, after they have said their goodbyes to the students and transformed their academy spaces back into university classrooms, the teacher candidates gather together for a debriefing. Once they have helped themselves to refreshments, they sit at a table with their team to engage in a reflexive discussion about the evening. The discussion is guided by a three-part inquiry framework designed for this purpose (see figure 3.1). After I lead the process

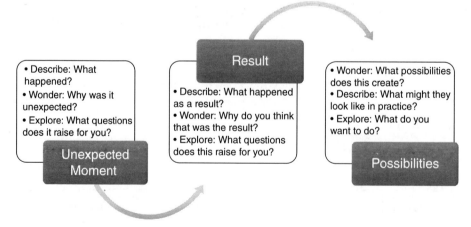

Figure 3.1: Inquiry Framework: Academy Team Debriefings

on the first night, the teacher candidates facilitate their own discussions in consecutive weeks. The discussion begins with teacher candidates taking turns identifying an unexpected moment, which opens up a conversation about why that moment was unexpected, what questions it raised for them, what happened as a result, and what possibilities it could create.

Inviting teams to begin their conversation with the "unexpected" is deliberately constructed as neither positive nor negative; the questions on the guide open up a space for teacher candidates to describe, wonder, and explore how they wish to respond. The process "involves supporting participants in identifying and taking up the issues that are of significance to them" (Campano, Honeyford, Sánchez, & Vander Zanden, 2010, p. 280). Notably, those moments and their ensuing inquiries focus on the students. In reflection, "relationships [are] at the heart of the process" (Campano et al., 2010, p. 280).

The debriefing creates another time and space for the teacher candidates to learn with and from the students and one another. As they discuss their unexpected moments, the teacher candidates "play back" the evening, pausing to describe what happened. In the process of revisiting the moments that were unexpected for each of them, the teacher candidates share with one another their perceptions, interpretations, and perspectives, weaving together their individual experiences into a "collective biography [of] pedagogical practice" (Davies & Gannon, 2009).

Inquiring into "unexpected moments" also invites teacher candidates to engage in critique, unsettling the already "sedimented roles and practices" they have learned "as teachers, researchers, students, community members ... [to] engage in new kinds of intellectual and creative labor" (Campano et al., 2010, p. 279). Asking themselves why such moments were unexpected and what such moments produced creates a "constructive disruption" (Cochran-Smith & Lytle, 2009) of teacher candidates' assumptions. Such disruptions often create additional "ruptures," opening up opportunities for the team to pose other questions, offer alternative perspectives, suggest opposing viewpoints, or voice tentative possibilities. Through this dialogue, teacher candidates learn to value multiplicity and complexity, to appreciate how such collaborative and reflexive inquiry affords "the creation of new subjectivities along the way" (Sitrin, 2006, p. vii). They are developing transcultural literacies in the practice of teaching, pushing the boundaries of their theoretical and pedagogical borders to see what possibilities might emerge.

"IT'S RESONATING"

It was during the debriefing of the musical theatre team, halfway through the six-week program, that Mia (all names are pseudonyms) and her group began by talking about how impressed they were that the students were remembering the dance steps and lyrics they had learned a full week before, that many students were practising on their own, and that they were anticipating their next session, coming with special requests for drama games and music. Mia turned the group's unexpected moment into a question: "I'm wondering—so clearly for some of them—it's resonating with them. My thoughts are why? Is it the material that we're using, the games that we're playing, is it us as teachers and our energy? What—what is it?" (Musical Theatre, Week 3, l. 48–51).

Mia's questions complement those educators often ask when things *do not* seem to be working: when we wonder why our efforts have not succeeded in making a meaningful connection with our students. In this case, Mia and her peers had evidence that what they were doing *was* working. To their credit, these future teachers did not simply pat themselves on the back and move on. Mia created a pause, a space and time for the group to think and inquire together. For teacher candidates who had just realized examples of students' deep engagement in programming they had designed, these questions were relevant not only to their present conversation, but also for the future. If they could figure out what it was that the students were responding to, they might be able to create more moments like these. Mia offered several possibilities for the team to consider: Was it the material (i.e., curriculum) they were using (i.e., the specific songs and music they had chosen)? Was it that the students were having fun because of the games they were playing? Could it be that the students were responding positively to the enthusiasm and energy of the teacher candidates and the positive environment they had created? What was it?

Over the six years I have been involved in coordinating this program, I have asked myself questions like these many times, and they have inspired the responsive research and design of the program. But as a teacher educator, I also find myself compelled to redirect Mia's questions to consider the participation of the teacher candidates. I know that the experience resonates for them, too. I know that it strikes a chord in the moment, as I observe them interacting with the students in their academies. I also know that they continue to think about their academies during the week, communicating and planning with one another. And, I know from conversations, emails, and letters that

I have received over the years that, for many, there are moments in their experience that continue to resonate, to "produce a loud, clear, deep sound for a long time; to have particular meaning or importance for someone: to affect or appeal to someone in a personal or emotional way" ("Resonate," 2019).

The debriefings of the teacher candidates are part of a broader multimodal ethnographic inquiry (Grenfell, Bloome, Hardy, Pahl, Rowsell, & Street, 2013) I have been engaged in over the years. Transcultural literacies offer a generative set of ideas to "plug in" (Jackson & Mazzei, 2012) to my thinking and analysis of the documentation generated by this work: my observations and reflective notes; the teacher candidates' notes and documentation, including artifacts, photos, and videos; the audio recordings of the debriefing discussions; and informal conversations with teacher candidates throughout the program. Mia's questions sparked my own: What would I find if I looked for moments of resonance for the teacher candidates in the unexpected moments they identified? In the next section, I "zoom in" to three such moments, and like Mia, I ask some more pointed questions: First, what is it that resonated for the teacher candidate(s)? How was that resonance produced? Second, what becomes salient in that moment (Dei, 2016; Medina, 2010)? Third, what possibilities are created in that moment for new pedagogies of transcultural literacies to emerge?

INQUIRING INTO THE UNEXPECTED: THREE MOMENTS

Moment 1: "Content to Sit There in Each Other's Presence"

The first moment was one I remembered Kris describing to her team as I circulated around the room during the teams' discussions. It was Week 3, and Kris and her peers in the art academy had spent the evening doing dot art with the students.

Kris: Maryam [a student] and I sat there a lot and, and just did the dot art. And we were just content to sit there in each other's presence just doing the dot art. And we would comment on each other's every once in a while. Well, she'd ask me to pass her a colour. But otherwise, like she was super into it, that we did not need to, you know, to have—like a flat conversation about the weather or something. Right? We were just comfortable being with each other and doing something together. (l. 169–175)

Kris's unexpected moment was a connection she felt to Maryam as they were both engaged in their art. The art academy was designed to foster a studio approach in which the teacher candidates would introduce a different painter, method, or movement each week. They would present key ideas, share multiple mentor texts (examples of art in that style), and lead a demonstration of the technique. More examples and all the resources and supplies students needed were available on the tables, and the teacher candidates then worked with students, helping them get started, answering questions, and then settling in side by side at the tables to begin a new piece alongside them.

What becomes salient in that moment for Kris is what Deleuze and Guattari call *hacceity*: the "just-thisness" of particular moments, when spaces take on a not-yet determined quality and the boundaries between self and other may dissolve (Davies & Gannon, 2009). As Orellana (2016) suggests, this is a "movement beyond borders, a transcendence or transformation of things that were being held apart, or artificially constructed as separate or distinct" (p. 91). In being "content to sit there in each other's presence just doing the dot art," Kris feels a transcendence from the traditional roles of teacher and student, and "the emergence of something new" (Orellana, 2016, p. 91): teaching and learning as co-activity. There is a transformation of physical proximity: Rather than standing and moving from student to student, Kris is seated at the table beside the student. There is a transcendence of the necessity for small talk, and instead, a realization of a new connection that can be enjoyed through easy, compatible silence. And there is a transformation of the learning space: Their parallel participation in co-activity creates contentment and comfortableness.

The sense of being in the "this-here-now" is described by Kris later in the same debriefing, first in association with time.

Kris: It really flew by, but yeah, when I looked [at the time], I was like: "Oh, I feel like I didn't talk to—like I did not talk to anyone."
Leah: Like sometimes it is just being with a group of people with the same intent and having that camaraderie.
Kris: But again, I could not even tell you what I did [someone giggles]. Like I, 'cause, I didn't do anything. (l. 163–168)

Tess: Like no one needed your attention. No one needed you to do something; they were all focused.
Zahira: They were all great!

Kris: They were all enjoying what they were doing. And it was like being in an art class—music is playing, everyone is doing something nice, like a really nice nirvana [there are murmurs of agreement from others].

Zahira: I agree.

Tess: Yeah, it really was. (l. 331–338)

Kris describes a transcendence of time, noting her surprise at how fast the time went. She notes that she did not have time to talk to the students, an activity the teacher candidates value in building relationships with students in the space of the art studio. As Burton (2000) notes, open-ended dialogue is an effective pedagogical tool in art education. Yet, in this instance, Leah suggests that talk wasn't necessary, that relationships were developed and experienced by "just being with a group of people with the same intent and having that camaraderie." She suggests that the ease they felt with one another (already in the third week) was due to their shared intent as artists to create. However, Kris struggles with the tension between *being* and *doing*. She makes a confession, with a sense of guilt, that in getting caught up in the painting she "didn't *do* anything" (i.e., as a teacher). Tess counters that the students were "all so focused" that they didn't need the teacher candidates "to do something" (e.g., demonstrate, problem-solve, replenish supplies, refocus students). Kris concedes that the students "were all enjoying what they were doing" and compares the afterschool space to an advanced art studio class, where the students have already taken on the processes and practices of being artists, are deeply engaged in their work, and where a sense of "nice nirvana" pervades.

What Kris has described is a sense of *flow*, "a state of deep absorption in an activity that is intrinsically enjoyable" (Shernoff, Csikszentmihalyi, Schneider, & Steele Shernoff, 2003, p. 160). In moments of flow, individuals like artists or athletes "perceive their performance to be pleasurable and successful, and the activity is perceived as worth doing for its own sake, even if no further goal is reached" (Shernoff et al., 2003, p. 160). The flow Kris has described is not realized individually, but collectively, shared by the other teacher candidates and the students. There is a dialectic tension between doing (as teachers) and knowing (as artists) that the teacher candidates resolve, a *hacceity* of "just being" that Battiste (2013) describes as "being present with the forces and energies—human, physical, natural, and spiritual—thus overcoming the forces of doubt and inertia. Action and sharing, rather than reflection, definitions, or categories best illustrate this concept" (p. 114).

"Being present" animates a pedagogy of transcultural literacies, where human, physical, natural, and spiritual forces and energies collide to create something new. Art-making became a material and relational experience lived "through the body ... [as] powerful ideas, feelings and moods, seeking wordless forms of expression" (Burton, 2000, p. 334). This is a pedagogy of action and sharing that is stronger than the individual, becoming powerful enough to overcome the anxiety and fear of doing teaching *right*, and instead, *being present* in that artistic process together.

Moment 2: "Feel It in Your Body"

The second example, also from the third week of the program, is a moment discussed by the teacher candidates leading the musical theatre academy. When it was Nadia's turn to share an unexpected moment, she addressed Sari and said:

Nadia: I love the moment where you and Raya [a student]—where she was struggling, and you like, grabbed her and suddenly she was able to do it. That was such a sweet moment! So nice! Yeah.

Sari: Well I think just having someone right there to like, do it with you, and if you're—if you're connected, you can kind of feel it in your body. (l. 167–171)

What resonated in this moment for Nadia was also an example of movement beyond borders, in this case, of the boundaries between mind and body that Orellana (2016) describes as "artificially constructed as separate and distinct" (p. 91). Rather than telling Raya what to do, or how to do it, Sari caught Raya's hands in hers to lead her in the dance steps, helping her feel how to move. Sari privileges embodied knowledge, the "ability to interact with a thought or an experience holistically ... with the total person" (Leonard, Hall, & Herro, 2016, p. 343). Merleau-Ponty (1945/1962), referring to the phenomenon of touch typing, described embodied knowledge as "knowledge in the hands" which comes "only when bodily effort is made, and cannot be formulated in detachment from that effort" (p. 166). In this case, the phenomenon is dance. Sari has an embodied knowledge of the dance, and when she notices that Raya is struggling to learn the choreography, she takes her arms and leads—allowing Raya to learn through shared physical connection.

Again, in this case, language is not needed. What becomes salient in the pedagogy of dance is to "feel it in your body." Sari articulates (probably from her own experience in dance) the understanding that "having someone right there ... to do it with you," and more so, someone to whom "you're [physically] connected," allows for movement to be felt and thus learned. Nadia (who does not have a background in dance) observed Sari come alongside Raya and lead her through the steps, and saw that "suddenly [Raya] was able to do it." For Nadia, watching Raya emerge from that moment as a dancer opened up new possibilities. Pedagogies of dance, drama, and music performance converged together, transcending boundaries in what was a playful and spontaneous moment. For Sari, this was instinctual, but for Nadia, this was unexpected, creating new possibilities for transcultural literacies in pedagogy.

Moment 3: "Knew More than We Thought"

The third example of an unexpected moment that resonated for teacher candidates was discussed by the team leading the secret agent academy in the second week of the session.

Tricia: I feel like we were in the same situation last week, where they knew more than we thought. Which I think is great.

Ali: And sometimes the terminology that they use? Like, when Darcy [student] said, "Maybe she took the Mona Lisa to sell on the *black market*." Like, that one [group laughs], I was like, "Whoa!"

Jas: And then they were doing that cryptic message—she made the connection that when you write too hard it pops through on the other sheet of paper.

Ali: Yeah, that was good.

Tricia: Or also, too, when they kept making connections, between last week's case?

Jas: They caught on right away. When you were doing the little history of the Mona Lisa? When you showed the image of the Louvre? They were like, "Oh! That was what was on the picture from the crime scene last week!" (l. 42–46, 48–52, 65–67)

What was unexpected for Tricia in this second week was something she and her peers had discussed already in their debriefing after their first session: that the students "knew more than we thought." Ali and Jas respond by providing examples: They are impressed by students' working vocabularies (e.g., Darcy's reference to the "black market"); by their ability to observe and learn from their experience (e.g., the effect of writing too hard on the paper); and by their capacity to remember and build connections from one week to the next, transferring knowledge from one context to another (e.g., recognizing the Louvre).

Students' knowledge and thinking can often remain invisible to teachers. When space and time is not made for experiential, dialogic learning, students' background knowledge and keen insights can go unnoticed and unheard. When students are evaluated primarily (and narrowly) to determine what they do not know, then the diversity and richness of everything they do know and understand is never acknowledged nor included in the curriculum. What teacher candidates often admit in Afterschool U is that they made assumptions that led them to underestimate what students knew or were capable of doing.

Tricia and her peers are realizing their secret agent academy is a translocal space where students are "dynamically making sense of the multiple social locations they navigate (across time, places, and people)" (Medina, 2010, p. 40). In this debriefing, they are collectively making students' knowledges "visible, relevant, and accepted" (Medina, 2010, p. 40). In fact, the conversation leads them to consider how they can open up opportunities for greater flows of knowledge production, recognizing they are not the only "knowers" in the room: They acknowledge that the students know a great deal and that they are bringing that knowledge with them or producing it in the space of the academy, in creative activity with one another.

Following the inquiry framework on the discussion guide, Ali poses the last big question to her team:

Ali: So ... what possibilities does this create? What might it look like in practice?

Tricia: Well one thing I thought was maybe we can tap into that knowledge a little more? And open it up to them to—'cause like, when we were talking about Paris and stuff. They might know some of that stuff already—

Jas: Yeah, instead of like, asking them, "Who do you think made the Mona Lisa?"

Sam: Or, "Where is it located?"

Jas: They can kind of—

Ali: Educate their peers

Jas: Like—"Where is Europe?"

Ali: They can like—teach that stuff

Sam: They may know that stuff
Tricia: Yeah like instead of us yappin'
Jas: I feel like they know—they know quite a bit!
Sam: Yeah!
Ali: Unexpected things. (l. 69–83)

The teacher candidates acknowledge that the secret agent academy space will be a more dynamic site for knowledge production if they stop "yappin'" and let the kids educate one another and "teach that stuff." What emerges through this discussion is a shift in pedagogy that is far more open to transcultural literacies. Specifically, they identify new "moves" they will take in their approach: tapping into students' knowledge by inviting them to share what they know already, asking open-ended questions, and creating new invitations for students to share their knowledge with one another. It is only then, Ali notes, that the "unexpected" can happen—that learning can become a new and exciting territory.

TRANSCULTURAL LITERACIES AND PEDAGOGICAL POSSIBILITIES

The inquiry framework that the teacher candidates responded to in their debriefing discussions invited them to describe, wonder, and explore. In this concluding section, my intent is to look across these moments and describe factors that contributed to their resonance, wonder what possibilities they afford for pedagogies of transcultural literacies, and explore their implications for education more broadly.

Produced in Relationship

These three moments reveal the ways the teacher candidates were listening to, observing, and responding to the students. From the moment they learn about the program, teacher candidates are told that the focus is on building relationships and having fun together through their interests and passions. Teacher candidates take that to heart: Most of the content of the debriefing discussions was focused on students' participation and what the teacher candidates were learning about the students. They "compared notes" about what students enjoyed and responded well to, and what they were learning about students' interests and ways of learning, and they worked together to troubleshoot how to address tensions they observed or felt. Teacher candidates considered in their planning not just what they wanted to do with the students and what they hoped the students would learn, but how to be more "present" with them in the limited time they had together.

Transcultural pedagogical practices emerged from a commitment to relationships. This is not to say that relationships were easily, evenly, or effectively established with all children, despite the high adult-child ratio. But these three moments (and many more like them) show that what resonated for teacher candidates were moments of socio-emotional, embodied, and intellectual connections, where learning was realized in more holistic and relational ways. The teacher candidates wanted to see the students "animated," to see signs of "a stirring or movement of the spirit from within" (Orellana, 2016, p. 55). This leads me to wonder: How might our schools and classrooms be different if we refocused our energy on learning what makes our students "light up" and fully animates the learning spirit within (Orellana, 2016; Battiste, 2013)? What would education look like if we intentionally focused on creating learning spaces where our priority was being present for and with our students?

Cultivated through Shared Activity

In addition to their focus on developing relationships with students, the moments highlighted in this chapter suggest the expanded literacies of learning through shared activity. While the teacher candidates had to submit a proposal with a tentative outline of the activities (and their "arc") for the six weeks of the program, they spent time in their debriefing discussions fine-tuning, revising, or completely changing their plans so that they would be more responsive to students' interests, background experiences, and goals. The diverse experiences of the teacher candidates (e.g., what they had learned through their practicum placements in early, middle, or senior years classrooms; their volunteer or work experiences with children; their own practices and experiences related to the focus of their academies) became a real asset in their collective planning, and the teams tended to take a very open-ended approach, considering everyone's suggestions and ideas. Without the pressure of evaluation teacher candidates may feel in other spaces of the teacher education program, they were inspired to take risks. Their collective attention was focused on students' enjoyment and participation; they were concerned most often about engaging students who seemed reticent to participate or who participated in ways that they had not anticipated. Thus, they paid close attention to participatory structures and routines that would allow them to connect with and engage every student more fully and positively. Moreover, the emphasis on experiential learning and shoulder-to-shoulder pedagogy pushed many outside the traditional role of teaching as "detached spectatorship" (as cited in Gustavson, 2013). They learned to balance predictable routines with ideas to "change it up" in order to keep things fresh and fun—both for themselves and for the students. They considered students' needs to move and talk, to have agency in making choices and decisions, and to look forward to activities with a range of visual, tactile, and sensory experiences.

The teacher candidates' ongoing efforts to plan engaging activities expanded the literacy practices valued in the academies and contributed to creating a sense of shared identity. For instance, in the musical theatre team's debriefing one evening, a teacher candidate recounted that after successfully singing in rounds, a student declared, "We sound like a choir!" Their shared focus and purpose contributed to a sense of community. For the teacher candidates, this also had the effect of providing a balance of structure and flexibility. When teacher candidates "riffed" from the plan to respond to students "in the moment," their peers applauded their efforts (as Nadia did for Sari in musical theatre) and often shared what they learned from watching their colleagues "in action." This leads me to wonder about the role of collaborative planning, peer observation, and practitioner inquiry in expanding transcultural literacies in our pedagogies. What would happen if we took up more participatory roles in our classrooms, engaged in meaningful activity with our students, and allocated time in professional learning communities for reflexive dialogue about what we were learning? What if we were more attentive to what our students were teaching us?

Where Interests and Passions Are the Curriculum

These moments also highlight what happens when students' interests and identities become the focus of teaching and learning. In the academies, teacher candidates are told to expect a wide variety of interests, abilities, and experiences. But because there are no expectations that students will all reach the same level of proficiency at the end of six weeks, the diversity of students' experiences is welcomed. That diversity contributes to a rich learning space where students and teacher candidates alike learn from one another. Activities are designed to give students the time, resources, opportunities, and mentors to try out and develop their interests. Within that story world (e.g., of being painters, secret agents, actors, superheroes, musicians, or scientists), the outcomes are open to students' needs, desires, and imaginations. One of the most surprising (and rewarding) outcomes for teacher candidates has been to hear from students that they have taken what they have learned and have initiated their own "academies" in their schools: For instance, two students excitedly told their academy leaders at the family festival (held a few weeks after the conclusion of Afterschool U) that they had initiated a lunchtime drama club at their middle school that regularly attracts 50 students. They thanked their leaders for everything they had learned, as they had gained the experience and confidence to provide such an opportunity for their peers.

These moments resonate for me. They suggest that in classrooms where we invite *becoming*—of ourselves and our students—in multiple ways, we provide opportunities for new identities, new ways of being, and new ways of knowing to emerge and develop. They point to how pedagogies of transcultural literacies can animate that process, drawing our attention to the unexpected and inviting us to describe, wonder, and explore. There are many things that are not working in our classrooms, schools, and educational systems. But there are also many things that are. They can point us to the change we need to be and the kind of world we wish to become.

QUESTIONS FOR REFLECTION AND DISCUSSION

1. Honeyford writes that "pedagogical practices emerged from a commitment to relationships. That is not to say that relationships were easily, evenly, or effectively established with all children, despite the high adult-child ratio." What are the challenges or difficulties you have faced in your efforts to build relationships with learners? What have you learned from some of your experiences? What can schools do to create more relational spaces and communities?

2. Honeyford explains that Afterschool U was shaped by "pluralisms and differences," not just among the students who participated, but among the volunteers, which included high school students, teacher candidates, and other community members. In what ways do you see (or not see) "pluralisms and differences" in the people, policies, and practices in your educational context? To what extent have the "ways of doing school" in your context been shaped (or not) by transcultural flows? What more could be done?

3. The research that informed this chapter took place in the context of an afterschool program where teacher candidates were given a lot of autonomy to design the curriculum, activities, and resources; to modify the physical space somewhat; and to collaboratively plan, co-teach, and collectively reflect on what they learned from the experience. What implications can such a study have for in-school spaces?

4. In *An Imaginative Approach to Teaching*, Kieran Egan (2005) explains that as learners mature, they develop a sense of abstract reality, a sense of agency, and a grasp of complex ideas and theories. They begin to develop a meta-narrative understanding of the world (pp. 155–157). How might the following dimensions enhance and/or hinder critical and creative thinking?
   · teaching style, prior experience, and teacher personality qualities
   · student/learner personality traits and preferred style of learning
   · community involvement
   · family background (e.g., culture, socio-economic factors, etc.)
   · linguistic knowledge
   · the physical setup of the classroom
   · other learners
   · classroom and school resources available
   · institutional norms and rules
   · approaches to assessing learning

   Based on your reading of this chapter, are there additional factors in the teaching-learning dynamic that would contribute to creative thinking and literacy learning?

5. What "unexpected moments" do you recall from your learning and/or teaching experience? What reflections emerge with them? Choose a couple of moments. Use the inquiry framework provided in the chapter to help you think of them and to consider the possibilities they produce. Share your insights with a peer or colleague.

6. What resonated for you in this chapter? List two or three ideas, moments, insights, or visualizations, and then set a timer for five minutes. Freewrite about these ideas and see where they take you in terms of thinking about your own teaching experiences, theories, tensions, and opportunities for change. When the timer stops, read what you wrote, underlining words or phrases that seem particularly interesting, revealing, problematic, or powerful. Write a found poem with those words.

7. Revisit the visual organizer in the preview for the chapter. In what ways are these ideas connected and complementary? Is there anything you would add? To what extent can such spaces be created in institutions, yet still remain open to change? What examples can you think of where curriculum, theory, and practice evolved as "lived" and "dynamic" experiences that embraced different ways of knowing and becoming? Why is it so important that we pay attention to the unexpected and that we make time to describe our experiences, to wonder about them, and explore their possibilities?

DEEPEN YOUR INQUIRY: RELATED READINGS AND RESOURCES

Boler, M. (1999). *Feeling power: Emotions and education*. New York: Routledge.

Duboc, A. P. M. (2013). Teaching with an attitude: Finding ways to the conundrum of a postmodern curriculum. *Creative Education, 4*(12), 58.

Egan, K., & Judson, G. (2015). *Imagination and the engaged learner*. San Francisco: Jossey-Bass.

Gee, J. (2003). *What video games have to teach us about learning and literacy*. New York: Palgrave.

Goulet, L., & Goulet, K. (2015). Teaching each other: Nehinuw concepts and Indigenous pedagogies. Vancouver, BC: UBC Press.

Goswami, D., Lewis, C., Rutherford, M., & Waff, D. (2009). *Teacher inquiry: Approaches to language and literacy research*. New York: Teachers College Press and National Conference on Research in Language and Literacy (NCRLL).

Greene, M. (1995). *Releasing the imagination: Essays on education, the arts, and social change*. San Francisco: Jossey-Bass.

Honeyford, M. (2015). Thresholds of possibility—mindful walking, traditional oral storytelling, and the birch bark canoe: Theorizing material intra-activity in an afterschool arts space. *Literacy Research: Theory, Method, and Practice, 64*, 210–226.

Honeyford, M., & Boyd, K. (2015). Learning through play: Portraits, photoshop, and visual literacy practices. *Journal of Adolescent & Adult Literacy, 59*(1), 63–73.

Hull, G., & Zacher, J. (2004). What is after-school worth? Developing literacies and identities out-of-school. *Voices in Urban Education, 3*(Winter/Spring), 36–44.

Leander, K., & Boldt, G. (2012). Rereading "a pedagogy of multiliteracies": Bodies, texts, and emergence. *Journal of Literacy Research, 45*(1), 22–46.

Orellana, M. (2017). Solidarity, transculturality, educational anthropology, and (the modest goal of) transforming the world. *Anthropology & Education Quarterly, 48*(3), 210–220.

Pahl, K., & Rowsell, J. (2005). *Literacy and education: Understanding the new literacy studies in the classroom*. Thousand Oaks, CA: Sage.

Roth, W. M. (2014). *Curriculum*-in-the-making: A post-constructivist perspective*. New York: Peter Lang.

Sanders, J., & Albers, P. (2010). Multimodal literacies: An introduction. In P. Albers & J. Sanders (Eds.), *Literacies, the arts, and multimodality* (pp. 1–25). Urbana, IL: National Council of Teachers of English.

Taguchi, H. L. (2011). Investigating learning, participation and becoming in early childhood practices with a relational materialist approach. *Global Studies of Childhood, 1*(1), 36–50.

Toward a brighter future: Teaching refugees with limited formal schooling. Available at http://teachingrefugees.com/. Calgary Board of Education; Government of Alberta, Education.

Wheatley, M. J. (2002). *Turning to one another: Simple conversations to restore hope to the future*. San Francisco: Berrett-Koshler Publications.

NOTES

1. Students may apply to have their participation in Afterschool U listed on their transcript as an institutionally recognized co-curricular activity.

2. The academic calendar for teacher candidates includes two nine-week course blocks and two six-week practicum blocks. The education program is a two-year after-degree program.

3. My thanks to Linda Christensen and her keynote address at the 2017 Adolescent Literacy Summit (Winnipeg, Manitoba, April 12, 2017) where she spoke about critical literacy as learning to read and write texts in the ways they celebrate students' racial, gender, cultural, linguistic, and religious identities and practices, and thereby name and negate the power of oppressive assumptions, stereotypes, and discourses.

REFERENCES

Baker, P. (2008). The ACCESS enrichment model for an undergraduate education program. *Gifted and Talented International, 23*(1), 17–22.

Barad, K. (2007). *Meeting the universe halfway: Quantum physics and the entanglement of matter and meaning*. Durham, NC: Duke University Press.

Battiste, M. (2013). *Decolonizing education: Nourishing the learning spirit*. Saskatoon: Purich.

Boyle-Baise, M. (1998). Community service learning for multicultural education: An exploratory study with preservice teachers. *Equity & Excellence in Education, 31*(2), 52–60.

Boyle-Baise, M. (2005). Preparing community-oriented teachers: Reflections from a multicultural service-learning project. *Journal of Teacher Education, 56*(5), 446–458.

Boyle-Baise, M., & Sleeter, C. E. (2000). Community-based service learning for multicultural teacher education. *Educational Foundations, 14*(2), 33–50.

Burton, J. M. (2000). The configuration of meaning: Learner-centered art education revisited. *Studies in Art Education, 41*(4), 330–345.

Campano, G., Honeyford, M., Sánchez, L., & Vander Zanden, S. (2010). Ends in themselves: Theorizing the practice of university-school partnering through horizontalidad. *Language Arts, 87*(4), 277–286.

Carrington, S. (2011). Service learning within higher education: Rhizomatic interconnections between university and the real world. *Australian Journal of Teacher Education, 36*(6), 1–14.

Cartwright, T. J. (2012). Science talk: Preservice teachers facilitating science learning in diverse afterschool environments. *School Science and Mathematics, 112*(6), 384–391.

Cochran-Smith, M., & Lytle, S. (2009). *Inquiry as stance: Practitioner research for the next generation*. New York: Teachers College Press.

Cone, N. (2009). A bridge to developing efficacious science teachers of *all* students: Community based service-learning supplemented with explicit discussions and activities about diversity. *Journal of Science Teacher Education, 20*, 365–383.

Conner, J. (2010). Learning how to unlearn: How a service learning project can help teacher candidates to reframe urban students. *Teaching and Teacher Education: An International Journal of Research and Studies, 26*(5), 1170–1177.

Cox-Petersen, A. M., Spencer, B. H., & Crawford, T. J. (2005). Developing a community of teachers through integrated science and literacy service-learning experiences. *Issues in Teacher Education, 14*(1), 23–37.

Davies, B., & Gannon, S. (2009). *Pedagogical encounters*. New York: Peter Lang.

Dei, G. S. (2016). Decolonizing education for inclusivity: Implications for literacy education. Manitoba Education Research Network (Opening Address, Sept. 30). Winnipeg, Manitoba. Manitoba Educational Research Network.

Deleuze, G., & Guattari, F. (1980/1987). (B. Massumi, Trans.). *A thousand plateaus: Capitalism and schizophrenia*. Minneapolis: University of Minnesota Press.

Egan, K. (2005). *An imaginative approach to teaching.* San Francisco: Jossey-Bass.

Ellerbrock, C. R. (2014). Cultivating a positive learning environment in college classrooms. In B. C. Cruz, C. R. Ellerbrock, E. V. Howes, & A. Vasquez (Eds.), *Talking diversity with teachers and teacher educators: Exercises and critical conversations across the curriculum* (pp. 28–52). New York: Teachers College Press.

Grenfell, M., Bloome, D., Hardy, C., Pahl, K., Rowsell, J., & Street, B. (2013). *Language, ethnography, and education: Bridging new literacy studies and Bourdieu.* New York: Routledge.

Gustavson, L. (2013). Influencing pedagogy through the creative practices of youth. In C. Lankshear & M. Knobel (Eds.), *A new literacies reader: Educational perspectives* (pp. 101–122). New York: Peter Lang.

Honeyford, M. (2013). The simultaneity of experience: Cultural identity, magical realism and the artefactual in digital storytelling. *Literacy, 47*(1), 17–25.

Jackson, A. Y., & Mazzei, L. A. (2012). *Thinking with theory in qualitative research: Viewing data across multiple perspectives.* New York: Routledge.

Leonard, A., Hall, A., & Herro, D. (2016). Dancing literacy: Expanding children's and teachers' literacy repertoires through embodied knowing. *Journal of Early Childhood Literacy, 16*(3), 338–360.

McHatton, P. A., Thomas, D., & Lehman, K. (2006). Lessons learned in service-learning: Personnel preparation through community action. *Mentoring & Tutoring: Partnership in Learning, 14*(1), 67–79.

Medina, C. (2010). "Reading across communities" in biliteracy practices: Examining translocal discourses and cultural flows in literature discussions. *Reading Research Quarterly, 45*(1), 40–60.

Merleau-Ponty, M. (1945/1962). *Phenomenlogy of perception.* London: Routledge.

Orellana, M. (2016). *Immigrant children in transcultural spaces: Language, learning, and love.* London: Routledge.

Resonate. (2019). *Merriam-Webster.* Retrieved from https://www.merriam-webster.com/dictionary/resonate

Ryan, M., Carrington, S., Selva, G., & Healy, A. (2009). Taking a "reality" check: Expanding pre-service teachers' views on pedagogy and diversity. *Asia-Pacific Journal of Teacher Education, 37*(2), 155–173.

Shernoff, D., Csikszentmihalyi, M., Schneider, B., & Steele Shernoff, E. (2003). Student engagement in high school classrooms from the perspective of flow theory. *School Psychology Quarterly, 18*(2), 158–176.

Sitrin, M. (2006). *Horizontalism: Voices of popular power in Argentina.* Oakland, CA: AK Press.

Transcultural Literacies: Bridging Field and Academy, a Personal Account

Many of the most transformational changes students undergo, I learned, happen not from the history/social studies being "taught" or because of any particular teaching strategy being employed, but from students seeing and understanding one another for the first time—overcoming stereotypes, chauvinisms, misunderstandings, and fears of others—often in classrooms brimming with difference and diversity.

—*Lloyd Kornelsen*

OPENING THE CONVERSATION: READING NOTES

In the preceding chapters, the authors have explored the significance of relationality in transcultural teaching and learning. In many cultures, parents are considered to be their children's first teachers. Learning occurs in relationship, through listening and observing; through story, song, and shared activity; through practice, feedback, and increasing independence. The relationships between Elders and children are imbued from the beginning with educational responsibility. In other contexts, relationships must first be created to build the trust and respect through which learning can occur: Teachers must get to know their students, and schools must build relationships with parents and communities. Relationships are critical to understanding and appreciating difference, to building trust in place of uncertainty, fear, or prejudice. As our local and global communities become more transcultural, building relationships of respect and reciprocity becomes all the more critical in education. How are such relationships made? In what contexts and through what experiences do students best learn (and unlearn) what it means to be a global citizen? What is the role of teachers and their professional experiences and knowledge in the production of global citizenship educa-tion theory, practice, and research?

In this chapter, Lloyd Kornelsen engages in a narrative inquiry about the nature of professional knowledge, educational theory, and their relationship. Like Kuly (this vol-ume) and the teacher candidates in Afterschool U (Honeyford, this volume), Kornelsen reflects on a moment of initial discomfort and vulnerability in his teaching experience. He tells the story as it unfolded in a schoolhouse one evening in Pedrogosso, Costa Rica: a spontaneous embrace that crossed linguistic and cultural barriers. In this first meeting between Canadian high school students and their host families, the surprise of the gesture sparked laughter, releasing the anxiety of everyone in the room. Despite their many differences, the encounter highlighted what they held in common—the dis-comfort of the unknown—and created a shared experience to begin getting to know one another.

Years later, in a study of the long-term impacts of the trip for the (then) Grade 11 and 12 high school students, Kornelsen finds that in large part, the goals of the global citizenship course were met through the home-stay experience—through the relation-ships the students developed with their host families in the activities of day-to-day living and their participation in the work life of the community. The study raises in-teresting questions about teaching in transcultural contexts, and Kornelsen pursues these through a multi-layered analysis of pedagogical knowledge, theoretical knowl-edge (Freire, 2007; Dewey, 1897; Buber, 2006), and their interweaving.

With this case as an example, Kornelsen argues for more meaningful dialogue about "knowledge production, teaching knowledge, and teacher education" so that field and academy might "inform, enrich, and affirm each other." In the context of transcultural literacies, Kornelsen echoes Dei's (2016) imperative for communities that produce knowledge differently to engage in conversation with one another and to "become literate of one another."

As you read this chapter, you might consider examples from your own experi-ences in unfamiliar contexts: What did you learn? How? What do we have to gain from expanding our understandings not only of literacy, but of knowledge—of what knowl-edge is, how it is produced, and why it matters. What is the role of our relationships—of our understandings of others and ourselves and our world—in our understanding of knowledge?

THINKING VISUALLY: CHAPTER ORGANIZER

Think of this graphic organizer as a flowing river. One side references Kornelsen's life and professional experiences in the field, while the other references the theoretical

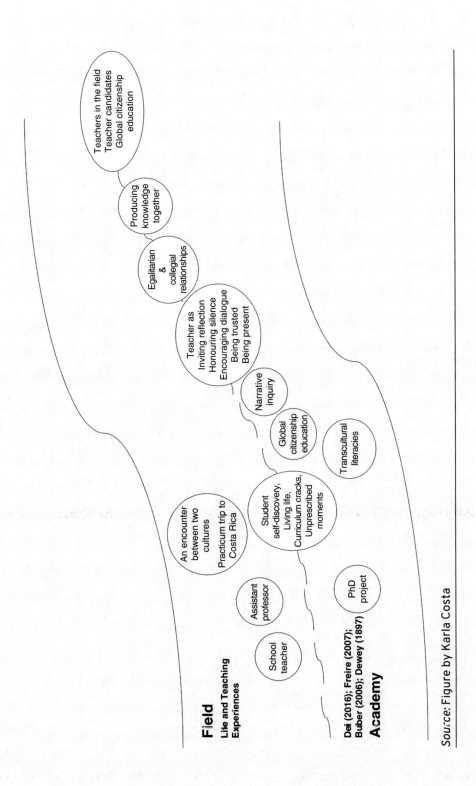

Field

Life and Teaching
Experiences

School
teacher

Assistant
professor

An encounter
between two
cultures
Practicum trip to
Costa Rica

Student
self-discovery,
Living life,
Curriculum cracks,
Unprescribed
moments

Global
citizenship
education

Transcultural
literacies

Narrative
inquiry

Teacher as
Inviting reflection
Honouring silence
Encouraging dialogue
Being trusted
Being present

Egalitarian
&
collegial
relationships

Producing
knowledge
together

Teachers in the field
Teacher candidates
Global citizenship
education

**Dei (2016); Freire (2007);
Buber (2006); Dewey (1897)**

PhD
project

Academy

Source: Figure by Karla Costa

knowledge he has gained from the academy. The chapter follows Kornelsen's journey, with his experiences tagged in their locations (in the field and/or the academy). Of course, it becomes possible to see that the river journey is a mix and interflow of professional theory and knowledge, learned from transcultural contexts, literacies, and relationships. As you read this chapter, you might consider adding other aspects of the journey, or you might create alternative ways to show the connections between these ideas. You might also consider making a visual of your own, highlighting the knowledge you have gained in your own professional journey, and the sources of your theories and experiences.

CHAPTER 4

Transcultural Literacies: Bridging Field and Academy, a Personal Account

Lloyd Kornelsen

Three years ago, after 25 years of teaching high school, I secured a position as an assistant professor, working in a teacher education program at a public university. The transition from field to academy was mostly seamless. My past work life (as professional) informed, contextualized, and grounded my current work (as academic)—the experience of teaching informed the teaching and research of teaching. However, from the beginning, I encountered subtle messages that the knowledge (and rhetoric) acquired through teaching experience was not on par with the knowledge (and rhetoric) more typically produced in and by the academy (e.g., illustrated around the pragmatic issues of granting promotion and tenure [Kornelsen, 2017]). According to Loughran (2004) and Aulls and Shore (2008), this is to be expected: teaching practice is often given low status or little account in teacher education literature and scholarship.

In response, I have been explaining—to myself and others—how and why previous work serves as a necessary and seamless function for my current endeavours, and that the work teachers do in the field informs, advances, and nuances knowledge of teacher education taught in universities—often in unique and indispensable ways. In short, our work in the field is worthy of recognition and on par with knowledge produced in the academy. However, this explaining (justifying?) process has necessarily been reconciliatory: Arguing to have past professional experience respected by members of the academy has meant needing to better understand the perspectives, expectations, and offerings of the academy. It has entailed explaining one to the other—the field to the academy and the academy to the field—as I seek to articulate an equitable (symbiotic?) relationship between the two.

TWO SOLITUDES: FIELD AND ACADEMY

I have not been alone, and the issue is not new. The disparateness in what constitutes and counts for knowledge and knowledge production in education has
been noted in academic literature since at least the 1980s, when numbers of
young scholars in teacher education committed to school and teacher education improvement—oftentimes themselves former school teachers—struggled
to negotiate tenure and promotion (Bullough & Pinnegar, 2001). They saw
the value of teacher self-study for teacher education and school improvement
and recognized the limits to knowledge and modes of research typically and
traditionally rewarded by the academy. Teachers' professional knowledge,
they argued, could be conceived as experiential (or as reflection-in-action,
as Donald Schön [1987] called it)—knowledge that derived from decisions
made and actions taken in the "heat and thick of teaching" (Bullough & Pinnegar, 2001, p. 9), and knowledge that is embodied (Huber, Caine, Huber, &
Steeves, 2013). This form of knowledge is often contrasted with propositional
knowledge, knowledge perceived as created and taught by the academy. Propositional knowledge is considered knowledge *for* practice, theoretical-derived
knowledge transmitted by professors to students (Bullock, 2009). It is knowledge seen as received from elsewhere and conveyed by others, whereas teacher
professional knowledge is "based on how they [teachers] frame and respond
to experience, not in how they enact propositions" (Bullock, 2009, p. 278).[1]

My intent in this chapter is not to supplant the importance of university-based
knowledge production, nor to dispute the value of propositional knowledge for
educating teacher candidates, nor to suggest that these forms of knowledge
do not converge in collaborations and partnerships between schools and universities (Cole & Knowles, 2000). But along with Kincheloe, McLaren, and
Steinberg (2011), I believe that "teachers must join the culture of researchers
if a new level of educational rigour and quality is ever to be achieved" (p. 165).
Because as Bullough and Gitlin (2001) implore, schools and universities, representing two distinct cultures, two different ways of knowing about teaching,
must collaborate for the sake of teacher education. School teachers and members of faculties of education have much to learn from each other because of
their shared concern: good teaching.

It is in this spirit and with this intent that I revisit a teaching experience—
one that revealed pedagogy germane to global citizenship. The objective is to
recount the experience, as remembered and narrated these many years later,
and then interpret its educative signals: first, by drawing on my professional
teaching knowledge; second, by connecting it to scholars like Paulo Freire, John

Dewey, and Martin Buber (education theorists whose writings were required reading in my undergraduate studies and who are still widely read in faculties of education today); and third, by interweaving the two, professional knowledge and education theory/philosophy. In short, I explore how field and academy can dance[2] and work together to enlighten and be enlightened by each other's ways of knowing and coming to know—using an individual case (Jardine, 1992). This attempt at personal reconciliation—between field and academy, both of which have inhabited large parts of my work life—is a testimonial to George Sefa Dei's (2016) imperative: communities that produce knowledge differently need to talk to each other, to become literate of one another. My hope is twofold: (1) that the symbiotic relationships between school and university are elucidated, with regard to the production of knowledge, and (2) that the narrated experiences are ones in which others in similar situations recognize themselves (Jardine, 1992) and find inspiration for their own growth (Syrjala & Estola, 1999).

NARRATIVE INQUIRY AND GLOBAL CITIZENSHIP EDUCATION

First, a few words on narrative inquiry, the rhetorical means by which my experience is conveyed; and global citizenship, the particular teaching challenge in question.[3] Widely documented as uniquely and critically suited for accessing teacher professional knowledge and to the production of teaching knowledge (Bullough & Gitlin, 2001; Carter, 1993; Connelly & Clandinin, 1988, p. 90; Huber, Caine, Huber, & Steeves, 2013; Schnee, 2009), narrative inquiry begins with experiences as expressed in the lived and told stories of individuals. Oftentimes stories serve as a primary portal to experience and understand phenomena. Though it must be remembered, as Clandinin and Connelly (2000) remind us:

> As we tell our stories as inquirers, it is experience, not narrative, that is the driving impulse. We came to narrative inquiry as a way to study experience. For us, narrative is the closest we can come to experience. Our guiding principle in an inquiry is to focus on experience and to follow where it leads. (p. 188)

In my case, the teaching experience that leads, and the stories that follow, happened on a global citizenship practicum trip to Costa Rica in 2003. It brought into sharp relief what past teaching experience (being a witness of, a participant in, and a facilitator of learning) had hinted at and unsettled for years.

The teaching experience that is narrated has to do with teaching for global citizenship. Global citizenship is a contested concept[4] with no agreed upon definition (Shultz & Jorgenson, 2009). However, a review of literature sympathetic to world citizenship (Appiah, 2008; Boulding, 1990; Heater, 2002; Nussbaum, 1997; Schattle, 2008; Todd, 2009, 2015) points to a cluster of three aspirational characteristics. A global citizen is someone who: (1) recognizes a common humanity, and hence appeals to a universal sense of justice; (2) has an open predisposition, and is able to see the world through the lens of people who are different from themselves; and (3) has a sense of agency and responsibility, and hence is able and willing to engage the world thoughtfully, helpfully, and hopefully (Kornelsen, 2014). For the purposes of this discussion, I will assume that the objectives of global citizenship education correspond with these three traits.

THE FIELD: TEACHING FOR GLOBAL CITIZENSHIP AND TEACHER SILENCE

In the spring of 2003, a colleague, Adrienne (all names of practicum participants, including Adrienne, are pseudonyms), and I at the Collegiate at the University of Winnipeg took 13 high school students on a trip to Costa Rica. It was part of an eight-month global citizenship course that was to culminate in a two-week home-stay in the village of Pedrogosso.[5] The night we arrived in Pedrogosso, the schoolhouse where we were to meet our host families was overflowing with people, young and old. It seemed like the whole community had come out to greet us, their visitors from Canada. The students seemed anxious and nervous; several looked scared and overwhelmed. In a short while each would go off into the darkness, on their own with host moms and dads, to live with people they did not know, whose language they did not speak. As their teacher, I felt helpless and powerless—this was a first for me, too. Here we all were in a small schoolhouse in Costa Rica, Spanish-speaking Costa Ricans on one side of the room, English-speaking Canadians on the other, each looking at the foreigners on the other side. What was my role here, as teacher, ethically and pedagogically? I felt at once responsible and immobilized.

A short welcome program was presented, including music, dance, and children performing, followed by individual student-host introductions. The tension in the room was palpable as each student met their host parent onstage. Then something unexpected happened. As our guide/translator was introducing the third student, a large, burly young man, to his host mom, a short, petite, elderly woman, she ran across the stage and gave him a big bracing hug, almost knocking him to the floor. The room broke up in peels of laughter. Everyone laughed: the Costa Ricans and the Canadians, the old and the young. The tension in the room seemed to evaporate; there was a tangible shift in what was being seen and felt—the grimaces and frowns replaced with smiles and laughter, ones that lingered. It felt as though a barrier between them and us, between Costa Ricans and Canadians, had been breached, a transformation of sorts—as though we were now a part of the same group having a good laugh at the same thing, and something was learned.[6]

Almost nine years later, as a part of a PhD research project, I interviewed the practicum participants about their Costa Rica experience. When asked about how the trip had affected their lives, participant responses clustered around three changes evocative of world citizenship: (1) the development of a global perspective and identity; (2) a growing awareness of global interconnectedness, tied to a discriminating respect for diversity and difference; and (3) a heightened sense of agency and global responsibility. Participants linked these changes to experiences like the schoolhouse opening night and other moments of connection and insight realized in daily living with families, in instances unguarded and occasions unscripted (Kornelsen, 2014). The most consequential changes in how they saw themselves and their world, they said, had happened in the course of living their lives in Costa Rica. In other words, they admitted that their most significant learning for global citizenship occurred when their teachers were not around.[7]

It came as no surprise. It confirmed what I had known for a while: Direct instruction has little long-term influence on student learning,[8] especially for those qualities associated with global citizenship. It is knowledge that I had acquired from the "decisions made and actions taken in the heat and thick of teaching," from participating in and witnessing student learning, and from hearing from students years after they graduated: Many of the most transformational changes[9] students undergo, I learned, happen not from the history/social studies being "taught" or because of any particular teaching strategy being employed (Kornelsen, 2006), but from students seeing and understanding one another for the first time—overcoming stereotypes, chauvinisms, misunderstandings, and fears of others—often in classrooms brimming with difference and diversity.

The Costa Rica practicum validated this "knowing." Students' world outlooks were transformed and global citizenship qualities cultivated, not because of any specific thing I did or said as teacher, but through a particular life experience—as evidenced by what they said many years later. But could this be said to be true, generally? From a scholarly point of view it could be argued that my conclusions derived from anecdote and vignette—"an isolated incident and nothing more" (Jardine, 1992, p. 52). How did they fit into, or inform, a theoretical frame?

But I did have a frame—based on knowledge that was valid and reliable. It had emerged through practice. I had been (re)searching teaching and learning for 25 years, between and during classes—in seeking to respond more effectively (ethically and pedagogically) to encounters with students, whether parsing a reading, facilitating a discussion, breaking up a fight, responding to a student suicide, conducting a role-play, or watching students perform democracy (Kornelsen, 2016). At times the queries were phenomenological (asking colleagues about their experience caring for students), pragmatic (looking for reasons why a particular teaching strategy worked in one class and not another), critical (reflecting on the effect and manifestation of teacher power), or existential (thinking about the purpose and meaning of teaching). The knowledge that was produced had a tentative feel, for, as Bullough (2014) says, "Education ... is messy, and highly context sensitive, with outcomes uncertain and proof of accomplishment always indirect and usually long delayed" (p. 189). Much of it was unarticulated and un-scribed; but, as I found out later, it had a frame, a philosophical coherence. This knowledge—embedded and marinated in practice—was remembered, affirmed, and enriched many years later when I read education theorists like Paulo Freire, John Dewey, and Martin Buber. They helped me to understand, interpret, and frame what I knew to be true from practice: that some of the most important things students learn about global citizenship often happen when teachers are not "teaching," as confirmed in the Costa Rica practicum.

THE ACADEMY: TEACHING FOR GLOBAL CITIZENSHIP AND TEACHER SILENCE

The idea that there are limits to what teachers can teach or to what students can learn from teachers is not new: From Aristotle's dim view of didactic teacher-centred forms of instruction ("For do teachers profess that it is their thoughts which are perceived and grasped by the students ... in order that [they] may learn what the teacher thinks?" [Aristotle, *Politics*, p. 54]) to Martin Heidegger's (1954) motif of "let learners learn," to Carl Rogers's

(1969) claim that teachers are at their best when they just let learners learn, scholars have questioned the long-term impact and pedagogic value of teacher-centred instruction. In particular, the theorizing of three philosophers of education—Freire, a critical pedagogue; Dewey, a pragmatist; and Buber, an existentialist and Jewish theologian—shed light on how the most significant things people learn about their world and their relationship to others come not so much from teacher-dominated instruction but from living life. So, back to the schoolhouse in Pedrogosso—how might these philosophers' learning theories explain what happened that night when people laughed?

John Dewey (1897), writing about democracy and education at a time when the American democratic imagination was expanding, contended that life experience was central to learning, arguing that "education ... is a process of living and not a preparation for future living" (p. 6), and that "the process and the goal of education are one and the same thing" (p. 12): living life. Furthermore, he argued that life experience in the social world helps people realize their connection to a larger community and to know who they are in that community (italics are mine):

> The only true education comes through the stimulation of the child's powers by the demands of the social situations in which [they] find [themselves]. Through these demands [they] are stimulated to act as a member of a unity, to *emerge from [their] original narrowness of action and feeling*, and to conceive of [themselves] from the standpoint of the welfare of the group to which [they] belong. (p. 3)

Many years later, Maxine Greene (1995), invoking Dewey, argued that in these contexts it is *disorienting* life experiences that are critical to getting young people to consciously undertake the world, to move "toward what is not yet known. In this search, a refusal of the comfortable is always required, a refusal to remain stuck in everyday-ness" (p. 175). So from a Deweynian perspective, Pedrogosso can be seen as an event where people encountered a disorientating social situation, and through this disorienting social situation, they *emerged from their original narrowness of action and feeling*, and conceived of themselves from the standpoint of the welfare of the group to which they now saw they belonged—and as members of larger (global?) community.

Martin Buber (2006), a theologian and all his life worried about Jewish-Palestinian co-existence, was concerned with communication across differ-ence. He described dialogue as both a kind of communication and a type of relationship: communicating in ways that are open, direct, mutual, and present, and cultivating relationships that are characterized by openness, directness, mutuality, and presence. Genuine dialogue, he said, meant experiencing the other side of the relationship, and thinking in a way that includes "orienting ourselves to the presence of the other person" (p. 33). This, Buber said, was what it is to communicate with a human being, a subject (a *Thou*, and not an *It*). It happens rarely, in unexpected and unguarded occasions. What happened in the schoolhouse could be seen in this way. The response to the hug was an experience of Buberian dialogue: It was unexpected, unguarded, and mutual. People encountered each other's common humanity; Canadians and Costa Ricans (and all Other types that were seen—young, old, white, brown, Latinos, Gringos) *saw* each other—for the first time. People related, not as Others, but as persons, not as *its*, but as *thous*. They were present to each other. The outcome, as expressed by participants years later—feelings of relatedness and commonality—is what Buber would have predicted of *I-thou* encounters.

Paulo Freire (2007), working with illiterate farmers in Brazil to help claim their political power, recognized the interconnectedness of literacy and political empowerment, believing that the goal of education was to help learners be human, people who can name their world and act upon it. A teacher's primary responsibility, he argued, was to help students move from being objects who are alienated from the world (colonized), to being subjects who are participants in the world—from being spectators and those acted upon to being actors. Freire said this process is partly facilitated by teachers helping "to direct (a learner's) observations towards previously inconspicuous phenomena" (p. 82). How this is done varies, but it cannot be accomplished through didactic teaching methods; indeed, they often exacerbate student objectification. According to Freire, means and ends are intimately linked: to help students be "considerers of the world" (p. 139), to help remove the veil, teachers must be considerers together with them, and remember that they are not so much preparing students to live in the world, but are living in the world with them, together, now, as inter-active subjects. From a Freirian perspective, that night in Pedrogosso, students and teachers together encountered a difficult social situation, one rife with power differentials (e.g., students, teachers, "First Worlders," "Third Worlders").[10] The teachers were quiet (they too felt helpless), "considering the world" together with their students, not telling them how to think or interpret what they saw or were experiencing. In the end, nine years later, students remembered occasions like these for their critical unveiling, ones that revealed a common and shared global community.

According to these different theoretical interpretations—critical theory, existentialism, and pragmatism—about how and why learning happened that night in Pedrogosso, the teacher is verbally silent—not unlike what I had learned from my teaching practice. Is it to be concluded, then, that students' most important learning regarding global citizenship is self-discovered, happens in unprescribed moments, and occurs in the cracks of the formal curriculum? Probably. But does it follow that teachers should absent themselves so that students can find themselves and their own way, and thereby grow into paragons of cosmopolitan virtue? In other words, does silence equal absence? Not necessarily—as is evident when field and academy speak to each other.

FIELD AND ACADEMY, PRODUCING KNOWLEDGE TOGETHER: CRITICAL ROLES FOR TEACHERS IN GLOBAL CITIZENSHIP EDUCATION

By mid-career, I had come to realize the teaching limits of pedantic entreaties and didactic deliveries, particularly for cultivating qualities of global citizenship. However, I also knew that teachers were not without great influence and responsibility. I believed that a social studies teacher's primary teaching responsibility was respecting learners as free and independent subjects and helping facilitate critical reflection of the world. A teacher's role was to foster relationships with students that engendered trust and mutuality and to engage course content with enthusiasm and care; and underpinning all good teaching (effective and moral) was commitment, care, and love. My perspective was shaped by 20 years of teaching high school, affected by 20 years of parenting two children, and enlightened by fellow teaching practitioners. However, it was not until working on a PhD, near the end of my high school teaching career, when rereading scholars like Buber, Dewey, and Freire, that I fully understood why—or acquired the imagination and language to confidently make these claims. I return now to the experience in Costa Rica and look at how experiential knowledge, interwoven with insights from educational philosophy, points to three critical responsibilities/roles teachers have in global citizenship education.

For years following the practicum, Adrienne and I replayed the trip, wondering whether, in incidences like the night in Pedrogosso, we had done the right thing. Matters and memories of responsibility lingered. Nine years after Costa Rica, Adrienne reflected:

> I was very aware of these 13 young people I was responsible for.... So it was that awareness always. I mean it was a huge responsibility for me, and I don't think I realized till I got there just how big this was.... So that's probably my strongest impression still, today.

And mine. I remember sleeping only three or four hours a night, worried about the well-being—physical, emotional, educational—of the 13 practicum participants, distressing about doing the right thing. So, even though I had my doubts about a teacher's impact in cultivating global citizenship, our worrying, the decisions we made, and actions we took in the "heat and thick" of the practicum, as well as our musings afterwards, signalled that Adrienne and I believed (whether implicitly or otherwise) that we were playing a necessary and pivotal role. As Sharron Todd (2003) says, "Teachers, as the vehicles through which the pedagogical demand for learning to become is made real for students, cannot escape their role" (p. 31), nor, argue others like Freire (1997) and Van Manen (1990, 2000), their power and responsibility. So, what was our power and for what were we responsible? *Being trusted.*

When asked what or who had been the primary determinant in their decision to participate in the practicum, seven students named a parent; six identified a teacher (or teachers). Dan (a participant) echoed what most of the group said: "I knew this was something that you (and Adrienne) were interested in ... so I knew that it would be something I would be interested in [too]." What this suggests is that one of the primary influences of teachers, perhaps their most affecting pedagogy, derives from a trusting relationship with students, as persons who are seen as trusted elders. In this case, it was a person who inspired involvement and participation in a global citizenship practicum. In particular, as Phillips (1998) says, it is an Elder whose judgment can be trusted for a specific experience's significance. The students were there that night, in Pedrogosso, because of us, their teachers. We were trusted—and implicitly looked to for our responses and judgments (for good or ill), signifying a second responsibility: *being present.*

In *Experience and Education*, Dewey (1938/1997) made this observation:

> Perhaps the greatest of all pedagogical fallacies is the notion that a person learns only the particular thing he is studying at the time. Collateral

learning in the way of formation of enduring attitudes of likes and dislikes, maybe and often is much more important than the spelling lesson or lesson in geography or history that is learned. But these attitudes are fundamentally what count in the future. (p. 48)

The most important things students learn in school, Dewey went on to say, are not the content of the curriculum per se, but are derivative, such as attitudes that affect one's bearing in the world. This affirms what Adrienne and I discovered about what students learned in Costa Rica. Here is Adrienne:

> I went with no expectation in terms of the kids, how much they would actually glean from this experience.... In our debrief after, I was amazed at what came out, stuff that I hadn't noticed or picked up on (at the time): They're very sentient beings, and they picked up a lot of interesting things.

I too was amazed at what "came out." And like Adrienne, I had few specific expectations about what the students would take from the experience. This is not to say we did not have intention or see potential in the experience for students, but whether learning would happen, and explicitly how, we did not know and were not willing to predict. We knew from experience that the greatest learning often happens during times unexpected and in situations uncontrived (not unlike Dewey's conceptions). And during the trip itself, we were mostly too preoccupied with keeping students safe, healthy, and alive to think too much about student learning. But when we came back, we discovered students had learned in ways and at depths not expected or prescribed. Many of the most significant things that students learned emerged from life experience (like their first night in Pedrogosso) and without any conscious pedantry or deliberate planning on Adrienne's part or mine—not unlike what Dewey would have predicted.

However, after revisiting the practicum experience nine years later, I learned that the practicum teachers had had a significant, yet unexpected, influence. Here are two participants, Lily and Jayne:

Lily: The fact that we had your trust, that was huge. That was really important, and it made us more confident in how we interacted with people. Because by you trusting us made us feel like, "Ok, yeah. I'm trustworthy."

Jayne: Adrienne and you treated us like we were one of you when we were there. I'll never forget when we went and stopped at Adrienne's house.... And she talked to us like she was a student with us. She shared some experiences ... there was something about that that was distinct because everything was new to everyone, everybody involved. So much of the experience was seeing our teachers in the same place as we were.

What Jayne and Lily describe here—being trusted, being seen and treated as equals—is not something to which Adrienne and I had given any thought—before, during, or after Costa Rica. It never occurred to us that we had been perceived by the students in that way (as noted above, we were too preoccupied with more pressing concerns). Perhaps it was, as Jayne suggests, derivative of the fact that we were all equals, by virtue of the experience being a significant first for us all, along with the common fears, novelties, and sharings. What is notable in both Jayne's and Lily's responses is the impact of their teachers' "nod," their orientation of trust and equanimity. It was remembered vividly nine years later and felt with consequential significance. It demonstrated how a teacher's trust and bearing of equanimity confers confidence and independence. Yet, at the time, Adrienne and I did not realize the implications of our behaviour.

But a passage from Buber (2006) affirms, enlightens, and reminds. In seeking to convey the essence of dialogue, he says that "for where un-reserve has ruled, even wordlessly, between [people], the word of dialogue has happened sacramentally" (p. 11). He underscores this for teachers:

Only in [their] whole being, in all [their] spontaneity can the educator truly affect the whole being of [their] pupil.... [The educator's] aliveness streams out to [the pupil] and affects [the pupil] most strongly and purely when [the educator has] no thought of affecting them. (p. 125)

Buber says it is through an educator's whole being that students are most affected, implying that teachers are at their affecting best not when exercising their teaching intentions, but when most unself-consciously present. A teacher's whole being includes their enthusiasms and worries but also their convictions, expectations, and judgments—for which teachers are responsible. Their presence has lasting repercussions. So, while Adrienne and I might have been surprised at what "came out," as it was beyond our imaginations, expectations, or plans, Peggy McIntosh (2005) reminds us that "sometimes it is the heartfelt trust of a teacher in the worth of a student ... that produces a faith within the student that he or she is connected to the world in a way that matters, and that the world is worth caring about" (p. 38). A teacher's felt presence implies relationship, and that signals a third teaching responsibility: *being dialogue partners.*

According to Freire (2007), for students to experience and interpret the world they need to be seen as autonomous actors, not as objectified recipients of "teacher talk." They should be treated as partners in dialogue. Dialogical theory, Freire (2007) wrote, "requires that the world be unveiled. No one can, however, unveil the world for another. Although one Subject may initiate the unveiling ... the others must become subjects of this act" (p. 169). In our positions as teachers in Costa Rica, Adrienne and I were mostly silent. We were present primarily in our roles as fellow participants, trip organizers, and sounding boards. Since this was our first time facilitating an international practicum we were often without words (just not knowing what to say), or distracted (troubled with some arising urgency). Students came to their discoveries on their own: encountering new experiences, being open to them, and reflecting on their meaning. No one was there to tell them how to think or experience, or remember for a test. From a critical perspective, they were living and thinking autonomously and freely as subjects. Freire says that for true dialogue to happen, teachers need to have faith and hope—faith in humankind's vocation to become more fully human, and hope in the prospect of a more humane world. Looking back, maybe it was faith in our students' willingness to be open to new worlds, and hope that high school students were capable of unveilings, that motivated Adrienne and me to develop this program in the first place and to stay silent at times when students were unveiling the world for themselves, like that first night in Pedrogosso.

To summarize, when field and academy are brought together in ways where each informs and sheds light on the other—in this case, when investigating the pedagogy of a single event—it becomes clear that teacher silence does not necessarily mean teacher absence. Indeed, teachers can be present in ways that transcend silence and imbue student-teacher relationships with trust, equality, and dialogue—thus playing a vital and critical role in helping students cultivate traits of global citizenship.

QUESTIONS, IMPLICATIONS, AND A CONCLUSION

I examined and interpreted a particular teaching-learning event—a response to a hug in a schoolhouse in Costa Rica—for its educative significance, blending insights acquired in practice with knowledge derived from education theorists and philosophers. An analysis using these two lenses revealed that when educating for global citizenship, a teacher's silent presence might play a significant role in learners' learning. This example (a single event) demonstrates how when two different ways of knowing about teaching are employed to interpret a teaching event, understanding of education is enriched and teaching practice is enlightened. My analysis raises and elucidates several questions and implications for knowledge production, teaching knowledge, and teacher education.

Questions

Reconciliation between field and academy necessarily happens afterwards,[11] as a way of making sense of both practice and theory, and in seeking interpretation and understanding of experience. Each, field and academy, enriches and gives meaning to the other and helps embolden both the practitioner and the theorist (oftentimes the same person). It is important to note that I read all three philosophers, Buber, Dewey, and Freire, in my undergraduate studies and found their writings to be mostly unengaging, dense, and esoteric. It was only much later, after years of teaching, that they made sense and I was able to recognize their interpretive genius and educative insight (as illustrated above), and that they then emboldened and informed my practice. The question, then: Should propositional knowledge—knowledge conceived and described as transmission of theoretical-derived knowledge transferred by professors to students and intended to be knowledge *for* practice—be conceived more as knowledge *of* practice? And if it were, what would be the implications for teacher education programs?

There is some pressure in the academy to situate one's teaching practice and research within a particular philosophical stance or ideological perspective. Yet, in the case described in above, three theoretical interpretations (Buber, Dewey, and Freire—each with a different stance [existential, pragmatic, critical] based on, and derived from, their own unique societal situations and philosophical assumptions) made a claim on mine and enlightened my practice's meaning. If this is the case, how might other questions in education be informed or understood by engaging with multiple philosophies or frames of inquiry? Are we, those of us who endeavour to understand teaching and learning, not all, by necessity, *bricoleurs* (Levi-Strauss, 1966; Kincheloe, 2001)?

Just as one cannot disembody practical teaching knowledge—it is indelibly present in all of what teachers do and see—the same holds true for theory and theorists. Theory cannot be abstracted or divorced from life. Freire, Buber, and Dewey, in their thinking and writing, were deeply affected by (and responded to) what was happening in their respective societies, shaping their educational stance. Are practitioners drawn to that in a theory that theorists have come to know from experience and practice?

Implications

Teaching experience invariably informs, motivates, and explicates current practice; but how exactly does it contribute to a body of knowledge? Teachers have lived questions and issues that animate education, necessarily researching them day in and day out, struggling to teach well. They have a knowing and understanding that may be hard to articulate. Yet it is present in all they do and it offers perspective and insight for questions explored in faculties of education. Faculties of education need to continue examining ways of articulating and recognizing the role of field experience (i.e., school teaching) in education scholarship. This may include exploring the meaning and purpose of scholarship in education contexts. For as critical theorists Kincheloe, McLaren, and Steinberg (2011) write:

> In the conservative educational order of mainstream schooling, knowledge is something that is produced far away from the school by experts in an exalted domain. This must change if critical reform of schooling is to exist. Teachers must have more voice and more respect in the culture of education. (p. 165)

Mine is a single case. There are many former teachers who, like me, work in faculties of education and often write about their past teaching experience, doing so in an academic milieu with its attendant publishing expectations. This compels them to think about those experiences more critically, interpret them more judicially, and write about them more clearly than they otherwise might. They engage with past experience through an academic lens. Consequently, they better come to know their teaching lives and practices. This implies a crucial responsibility for faculties of education: extending the same academic guidance and support to teachers working in the field so they can better articulate and critique the education meaning of their teaching experiences.

Egalitarian and collegial relationships should be fostered between academy and field—between school teachers and university professors. For example, look for meaningful and practical ways of including school teachers in academically oriented education conferences, forums, and colloquia. The dearth of practitioners at events that share research on, and make judgments about, education policy and goings-on in schools and classrooms without input and perspective from lived experience, impoverishes all three—practice, policy, and scholarship (Kornelsen, 2017). According to Sahlberg (2015), one of the reasons Finland continues to rank near the top of PISA scores is because Finnish teachers spend much less time in the classroom than teachers do elsewhere. As a consequence, they have the time, energy, and mental wherewithal to reflect on and write about their practice (Kornelsen, 2017).

With regard to teacher education programs: (1) Candidate teachers should have opportunities to meaningfully take leadership in the classes they teach—opportunities that allow them to fully experience the "heat and thick of teaching" (not just "being observed," or "play acting," or "practising"). It will help them sketch acquired knowledge more fully and confidently into theory and philosophy. (2) Teacher-practitioners should teach courses in educational theory and philosophy—as knowledge from practice and knowledge from the academy indelibly, and often in ways most unexpectedly, inform, enrich, and affirm each other. (3) If the analysis of my single case holds true, faculty instructors and professors are reminded that their silent presence (one that nurtures and honours trust, equality, and dialogue) may be critical for fostering the very dispositions in teacher candidates that teacher candidates will need to cultivate traits of global citizenship in their students. (4) Finally, teachers and teacher educators should remember that when they help different communities become literate of one another, knowledge horizons are broadened. It is a pedagogical practice of and for global citizenship, as people seek the shared and universal amidst a world of difference and diversity.

CONCLUSION

George Sefa Dei (2016) writes that, for the purposes of building global understanding, communities that produce knowledge differently need to become literate of one another. Closer to home, Bullough and Gitlin (2001) argue that for the sake of teacher education, since schools and universities represent two distinct cultures, they should "talk to each other." This chapter, by examining the pedagogical veracity of a single teaching-learning, showed that when these two cultures—school and university—that produce knowledge differently talk to each other, horizons of knowledge and understanding can be extended, and pedagogical practice and thought may be enlightened.

QUESTIONS FOR REFLECTION AND DISCUSSION

1. In this chapter, Kornelsen describes that his research confirmed what he knew from experience: "Students' world outlooks were transformed and global citizenship qualities cultivated, not because of any specific thing I did or said as teacher, but through a particular life experience." As a learner and/or teacher, what have been some of your most powerful life experiences (in or out of school)? What did you learn (and how? from whom?)? How did such an experience shape you? Should schools and teachers do more to facilitate experiences such as the Pedrogosso global citizenship practicum?

2. Kuly (chapter 2) and Kornelsen (this chapter) are concerned about the communicative gap between practice and theory; field and academy. They both shared experiences and perspectives about the roles of school and university cultures in promoting (or not promoting) knowledge that emerges from practice, and practice that is consciously informed by knowledge. In reflecting about that, what kind of spaces and opportunities for dialogue should schools and universities foster in order to promote practices and theories that are informed by each other?

3. "Who we are as individuals reflects who we are as teachers" (Palmer, 1998/2008). Do you agree or disagree with Palmer's statement that, in essence, we teach who we are? Explain. Based on your reading of Kornelsen's chapter, in what ways do you show students, parents, colleagues, and administrators that you can be trusted, be present, and be open to dialogue?

4. Although a vital dimension, the teacher is not the only resource in the learning journey. How might the other students in the classroom, people in the community, and the larger global community enrich your students' experiences of learning? What might make it easier or more challenging to access these learning resources?

5. To what extent is there a "culture of silence" that makes teachers reluctant to share their fears and insecurities (Brookfield, 2006; Palmer, 1998/2008)?

What can be done to reduce this silence so that teachers can express their values, beliefs, ideals, and ideas in a non-threatening environment?

6. To what extent do you agree or disagree with these "essential truths" of skillful teaching proposed by Stephen Brookfield (2006):
    · Be clear about the purpose of your teaching.
    · Reflect on your own learning.
    · Be wary of standardized models and approaches.
    · Expect ambiguity.
    · Remember that perfection is impossible.
    · Research your students' backgrounds.
    · Attend to how students experience learning.
    · Dialogue with your colleagues.
    · Take risks.
    · Don't evaluate only by students' satisfaction.
    · Acknowledge your personality.
    · View yourself as a helper of learning.
    · Expect surprise.

    Based on your reading of Kornelsen's chapter, could you add any more essential truths of teaching?

DEEPEN YOUR INQUIRY: RELATED READINGS AND RESOURCES

Ayers, W. (2001). *To teach: The journey of a teacher.* New York: Teachers College Press.

Batacharya, S., & Wong, Y. L. (2018). *Sharing breadth: Embodied learning and decolonization.* Edmonton: Athabasca University Press.

Bickmore, K., Hayhoe, R., Manion, C., Mundy, K., & Read, R. (2017). *Comparative and international education* (2nd ed.). Toronto and Vancouver: Canadian Scholars Press.

Brookfield, S. (2006). *The skillful teacher: On technique, trust, and responsiveness in the classroom.* San Francisco: Jossey-Bass.

Brookfield, S., & Preskill, S. (1999). *Discussion as a way of teaching: Tools and techniques for democratic classrooms.* San Francisco: Jossey-Bass.

Burke, A., Johnstone, I., & Ward, A. (2018). *Challenging stories: Canadian literature for social justice in the classroom.* Toronto and Vancouver: Canadian Scholars Press.

Campbell, J. (1988). *Joseph Campbell and the power of myth* [Video]. Montauk, NY: Mystic Fire Video.

Egan, K. (2005). *An imaginative approach to teaching.* San Francisco: Jossey-Bass.

Gardiner, H. W., & Kosmitski, C. (2002). *Lives across cultures.* Boston: Allyn & Bacon.

Groen, J., & Kawalikilak, C. (2014). *Pathways of adult learning: Professional and education narratives.* Toronto: Canadian Scholars Press.

Horton, M., & Freire, P. (1990). *We make the road by walking: Conversations on education and social change.* Philadelphia: Temple University Press.

Intrator, S. M. (2002). *Stories of the courage to teach: Honoring the teacher's heart.* San Francisco: Jossey-Bass.

Jarvis, P. (2008). *Globalization, lifelong learning, and the learning society: Sociological perspectives.* New York: Routledge.

Palmer, P. (1998/2008). *The courage to teach: Exploring the inner landscape of a teacher's life.* San Francisco: Jossey-Bass.

Vella, J. (2002). *Learning to listen, learning to teach: The power of dialogue in educating adults* (2nd ed.). San Francisco: John Wiley & Sons.

Winchester, I. (2013). On seeing our deepest intellectual, educational, and practical traditions from a non-Western perspective. *Interchange, 43*(1), 67–69.

Useful Websites

Primary Source: http://www.primarysource.org
Teachers interested in global education can access this website that includes valuable teaching guides and additional educational resources on global education.

Reach the World: www.reachtheworld.org
This website connects K–12 students and teachers with world travellers who explore the globe with the intent to understand knowledge, attitudes, values, and thinking skills that will help them become global citizens.

Teaching to Encourage Transformative Change: http://www.teachingforchange.org
This website helps teachers, parents, and students learn more about timely world issues. Online resources, references to social justice texts, and ideas for encouraging social action are included.

Films to Encourage Transformative Education: http://www.movingimages.ca
Teachers can use film (novel adaptations to cinema), Ted Talks, and documentaries (e.g., the Moving Image series), National Geographic films, and other related films

that highlight global and local issues for learners to reflect upon. In this process, new forms of learning and possibly transformative shifts in thinking may occur.

NOTES

1. Max Van Manen (1990) argues that in a phenomenological sense theory always arrives late, too late to inform praxis in an instrumental way, and so in the daily practice of living we are forever at a loss for theory. This certainly describes many of my teaching experiences. When something worked or when it did not, it was often only upon reflection that I understood why, and the specific teaching act that led to student learning. Some of the most significant transformative learning experiences my students had, had little to do with conscious planning or anticipation on my part.

2. See *Salsa dancing into the social sciences: Research in an age of info-glut* (Luker, 2008).

3. Global citizenship, or citizenship in global contexts, is identified as a central theme in all K–12 social studies curricula in Manitoba—hence it is a teaching expectation for all social studies teachers in the province.

4. Much has been written in critique of world citizenship and world citizenship education. Important issues include: Whose version of global citizenship is being articulated? Is it feasible to practise citizenship at a global level? Is it possible or desirable to cultivate an identity and allegiance that is global? Is it possible to navigate the tension at the core of global citizenship, between universalism and pluralism, without mythicizing or regressing (see Greene, 1995)? Is it possible to educate for perspectives that reconcile two global outlooks, a universal sense of justice and a sympathetic imagination of the different; in other words, for mindsets that are critical yet curious and imaginative at once (see Todd, 2009; Kornelsen, 2014)?

5. High school and university global citizenship practicums are said to be transformative. By having participants experience the intimacies and day-to-day challenges of living life in a foreign culture, three important qualities of global citizenship are cultivated: a *global perspective and identity*; an *awareness of global interconnectedness*, tied to a heightened respect for diversity and difference; and a sense of *agency and responsibility*.

    But they face three critical challenges. First, if participants are not afforded opportunities for critical reflection, North-South practicum experiences may thwart *global-minded perspectives*, as attitudes of dominance, ethnocentrism, and separateness may prevail. Second, ethical issues of power and privilege must be addressed if participants are to experience an authentic sense of *global connectedness*. Third, global citizenship programs need to strike a pedagogical balance between challenge and security if they are to foster a sense of *agency and responsibility* (Kornelsen, 2014).

6. Nine years later Dan remembered the event much as I had (the grandmother's hug and the subsequent laughter and relief in the room). However, he recalled a specific gesture no one else had: his host mom apologizing to him, onstage, for not having coffee, demonstrating an eloquent awareness of what is expected of a host (to have coffee). This gesture raises the issue of how the roles of guest and host shape expectations, assumptions, and perceived outcomes, begging the question of whether we all felt the same thing that night, an instance of human and universal connection. We do not know for certain. The grandmother and the people of Pedrogosso have not spoken. And so it must be remembered that this interpretation of a shared event is that of the guests. It is *their* memory—of an embrace that left *them* feeling less fearful and more connected.

7. See Aoki (2005) for an elegant account of the limits of behavioural ways of measuring and understanding what good teaching "is."

8. Many interpretations could be provided—for example, psychological, sociological, anthropological.

9. When using the term *transformational learning*, Jack Mezirow's (1995) conception of perspective transformation is assumed: becoming critically aware of how and why our presuppositions have come to constrain the way we perceive, understand, and feel about our world; of reformulating these assumptions to permit a more inclusive, discriminating, permeable, and integrative perspective; and of making decisions or otherwise acting on these new undertakings (as cited in Kiely, 2004, p. 6).

10. Freire would have much more to say about the oppressor-oppressed relations represented in the room, as shaped and determined by the neo-colonial economic arrangements between Global North and South. This chapter's interpretation of Freire's interpretation is delimited to the University of Winnipeg Collegiate teacher-student relationships in the room that night.

11. See Grumet (1992) on dialogue.

REFERENCES

Aoki. T. (2005). Layered voices of teaching: The uncannily correct and the elusively true. In R. Irwin & W. Pinar (Eds.), *Curriculum in a new key: The collected works of Ted T. Aoki* (pp. 17–27). Mahwah, NJ: Lawrence Erlbaum Associates.

Appiah, K. A. (2008). Education for global citizenship. In D. L. Coulter & J. R. Weins (Eds.), *Why do we educate? Renewing the conversation* (pp. 83–99). Malden, MA: National Society for the Study of Education.

Aristotle. (H. Rackham, Trans.). *Politics*. Digital Books. Retrieved from http://digitalbookindex.com/search001a.htm

Aulls, M. W., & Shore, B. M. (2008). The experienced teacher and action research. In M. W. Aulls & B. M. Shore (Eds.), *Inquiry in education* (Vol. 1; pp. 69–81). New York: Routledge.

Boulding, E. (1990). *Building a global civic culture: Education for an interdependent world.* Syracuse, NY: Syracuse University Press.

Brookfield, S. (2006). *The skillful teacher: On technique, trust, and responsiveness in the classroom.* San Francisco: Jossey-Bass.

Buber, M. (2006). *Between man and man.* (R. G. Smith, Trans.). London: Kegan Paul.

Bullock, S. (2009). Becoming a teacher educator: The self as basis-for-knowing. *Counterpoints, Making Connections: Self-Study & Social Action, 357,* 269–283.

Bullough, R. V. (2014). Toward reconstructing the narrative of teacher education: A rhetorical analysis of *preparing* teachers. *Journal of Teacher Education, 65*(3), 185–194.

Bullough, R. V., & Gitlin, A. D. (2001). *Becoming a student of teaching: Linking knowledge production and practice of teaching.* New York: Routledge Falmer.

Bullough, R. V., & Pinnegar, S. (2001). Guidelines for quality in autobiographical forms of self-study research. *Educational Researcher, 30*(3), 13–21.

Carter, K. (1993). The place of story in the study of teaching and teacher education. *Educational Researcher, 22*(1), 5–12.

Clandinin, D. J., & Connelly, F. M. (2000). *Narrative inquiry: Experience and story in qualitative research.* San Francisco: Jossey-Bass.

Cole, A. L., & Knowles, G. J. (2000). *Researching teaching: Exploring teacher development through reflexive inquiry.* Needham Heights, MA: Allyn & Bacon.

Connelly, F. M., & Clandinin, D. J. (1988). *Teachers as curriculum planners: Narratives of experience.* New York: Teachers College Press.

Connelly, F. M., & Clandinin, D. J. (1990). Stories of experience and narrative inquiry. *Educational Researcher, 19*(2), 2–14.

Dei, G. J. S. (2016). *Decolonizing education for inclusivity: Implications for literacy education.* Public lecture, September 30, Manitoba Teachers Society, Winnipeg, Manitoba.

Dewey, J. (1897). *My pedagogic creed.* Baltimore: Norman T. A. Munder.

Dewey, J. (1938/1997). *Experience and education* (1st Touchstone ed.). New York: Touchstone.

Freire, P. (1997). *Pedagogy of the heart.* New York: Continuum.

Freire, P. (2007). *Pedagogy of the oppressed* (30th anniversary ed.). New York: Continuum.

Greene, M. (1995). *Releasing the imagination: Essays on education, the arts and social change*. San Francisco: Jossey-Bass.

Grumet, M. R. (1992). Existential and phenomenological foundations of autobiographical methods. In W. F. Pinar & W. M. Reynolds (Eds), *Understanding curriculum as phenomenological and deconstructed text* (pp. 28–43). New York: Teachers College Press.

Heater, D. (2002). *World citizenship: Cosmopolitan thinking and its opponents*. New York: Continuum.

Heidegger, M. (1954). *What is called thinking?* (F. D. Wieck & J. G. Gray, Trans.). New York: Harper & Row.

Huber, J., Caine, V., Huber, M., & Steeves, P. (2013). Narrative inquiry as pedagogy in education: The extraordinary potential of living, telling, retelling, and reliving stories of experience. *Review of Research in Education, 37*(1), 212–242.

Jardine, D. W. (1992). The fecundity of the individual case: Considerations of the pedagogic heart of interpretive work. *Journal of Philosophy of Education, 26*(1), 51–61.

Kiely, R. (2004). A chameleon with a complex: Searching for transformation in international service-learning. *Michigan Journal of Community Service Learning, 10*(4), 5–20.

Kincheloe, J. L. (2001). Describing the bricolage: Conceptualizing a new rigor in qualitative research. *Qualitative Inquiry, 7*(6), 679–692.

Kincheloe, J. L., McLaren, P., & Steinberg, S. R. (2011). Critical pedagogy and qualitative research. In N. K. Denzen & Y. S. Lincoln (Eds.), *The Sage Handbook of Qualitative Research* (pp. 163–177). Thousand Oaks, CA: Sage.

Kornelsen, L. (2006). Teaching with presence. In P. Cranton (Ed.), *Authenticity in teaching* (pp. 73–82). San Francisco: Jossey-Bass.

Kornelsen, L. (2014). *Stories of transformation: Memories of a global citizenship practicum*. Ulm, Germany: The International Centre for Innovation in Education.

Kornelsen, L. (2016). Democracy and the public space: When do students become citizens? A teacher's reflections on a protest at school. *Journal of Educational Thought, 49*(1), 55–69.

Kornelsen, L. (2017). For academy's sake: A practitioner's search for scholarly relevance. In T. Sibbald & V. Hubbard (Eds.), *The academic gateway: Understanding the journey to tenure* (pp. 159–178). Ottawa: University of Ottawa Press.

Levi-Strauss, C. (1966). *The savage mind.* (George Weidenfeld and Nicolson Ltd., Trans.). Chicago: University of Chicago Press.

Loughran, J. J. (2004). A history and context of self-study of teaching and teacher education. In J. J. Loughran, M. L. Hamilton, V. K. Laboskey, & T. Russell (Eds.), *International handbook of self-study of teaching and teacher education practices* (Vol. 1; pp. 7–39). Dordrecht, the Netherlands: Springer.

Luker, K. (2008). *Salsa dancing into the social sciences: Research in an age of info-glut.* Cambridge, MA: Harvard University Press.

McIntosh, P. (2005). Gender perspectives on educating for global citizenship. In N. Noddings (Ed.), *Educating citizens for global awareness* (pp. 22–39). New York: Teachers College Press.

Mezirow, J. (1995). Transformative theory of adult learning. In M. R. Welton (Ed.), *Defence of the lifeworld* (pp. 39–70). New York: SUNY Press.

Nussbaum, M. (1997). *Cultivating humanity.* London: Harvard University Press.

Palmer, P. (1998/2008). *The courage to teach: Exploring the inner landscape of a teacher's life.* San Francisco: Jossey-Bass.

Phillips, A. (1998). Learning from Freud. In A. O. Rorty (Ed.), *Philosophers on education: New historical perspectives* (pp. 411–417). New York: Routledge.

Rogers, C. R. (1969). *Freedom to learn.* Columbus, OH: Charles E. Merrill.

Sahlberg, P. (2015). *Finnish lessons: What can the world learn from Finland?* New York: Teachers College Press.

Schattle, H. (2008). *The practices of global citizenship.* Toronto: Rowman & Littlefield.

Schnee, E. (2009). Writing the personal as research. *Narrative Inquiry, 19* (1), 35–51.

Schön, D. A. (1987). *Educating the reflective teacher.* San Francisco: Jossey-Bass.

Shultz, L., & Jorgenson, S. (2009). *Global citizenship in post-secondary institutions: A review of the literature.* Unpublished manuscript, University of Alberta. Available at http.www.uofaweb.ualberta.ca/uai_globaleducation/pdfs/GCE_literature_review.pdf

Syrjala, L., & Estola, E. (1999). *Telling and retelling stories as a way to construct teachers' identities and to understand teaching.* Paper presented at the European Conference on Educational Research, Lahti, Finland, September 22–25.

Todd, S. (2003). *Learning from the Other: Levinas, psychoanalysis, and ethical possibilities.* Albany: State University of New York Press.

Todd, S. (2009). *Toward an imperfect education: Facing humanity, rethinking cosmopolitanism.* Boulder, CO: Paradigm.

Todd, S. (2015). Creating transformative spaces in education: Facing humanity, facing violence. *Philosophical Inquiry in Education, 23* (1), 53–61.

Van Manen, M. (1990). *Researching lived experience: Human science for an action sensitive pedagogy.* London, ON: Althouse Press.

Van Manen, M. (2000). Moral language and pedagogical experience. *Journal of Curriculum Studies, 32*(2), 315–327.

Transcultural Literacies: Encouraging Transformative and Creative Learning

Educators play a key role in creating a climate where empathetic understandings, authentic learning, and intercultural sensitivity can flourish.
    —*Karen M. Magro*

OPENING THE CONVERSATION: READING NOTES

In this chapter, we are invited to think about how the changes in our communities and world—globalization, immigration, economic inequity, geopolitical tensions, climate issues, technology—challenge us to be more critical, but also more creative in our approaches to literacy, teaching, and learning. Through theory and research, Karen Magro explores the connections between transcultural literacies, critical literacy, and theories of transformative learning. She addresses questions such as: How do we understand, engage, and mobilize the changing dynamics, practices, and contexts of literacy in more complex ways? How do we acknowledge and support the multiple dimensions of literacy learning so that our students may flourish and thrive? What texts, materials, and approaches are teachers using, and what are they learning? What kinds of transcultural spaces and practices should we be creating for creativity?

Magro shares highlights from her research; first, by introducing the theoretical concepts, definitions, and themes that grounded her study, and then, by highlighting interview data collected from six teachers working in secondary schools, alternative high schools, and Adult Learning Centres (ALC) in the city of Winnipeg. Her analysis leads to reflections on the complexity of teachers' roles, and on connecting local and global events. Magro considers how experiences with literature and non-fiction in the classroom create possibilities for re-envisioning education perspectives for teaching and learning in/for a globalized world. In these contexts, students are reading and thinking about/with literary texts, and then associating with, telling, and writing their own stories. The classroom becomes "a psychological and social space," where teachers encourage discussions about themes such as discrimination, racial prejudice, identity, belonging, family, love, trust, exclusion, loneliness, ostracization, and experience. Magro argues that "an interdisciplinary approach that links literature and non-fiction to world issues, psychology, sociology, and the visual arts may have the potential to enrich adult learning."

As you read this chapter, consider the relationships between transcultural, critical, and transformative literacies and learning: What might such a framework make visible and possible in your context—theoretically and pedagogically? Take note of the approaches of the teachers featured in the chapter: What opportunities do they provide for students to share their traditions, stories, and experiences? How do such dialogic and dynamic spaces produce creativity, expand literacy, and connect "thinking, imagining, and participating in a 'global discourse'" to students' local and social environments?

THINKING VISUALLY: CHAPTER ORGANIZER

In this figure, the context is a world affected by the forces of globalization, immigration, and digital connectivity. This context shapes what it means to teach effectively, to be aware of the complexities of learning in a transcultural world, and to think critically and creatively about how curriculum and classrooms can bridge local and global issues and events. While responding to such change can be daunting, the teachers featured in this chapter approach the challenge as an opportunity for creative and transformative learning. Through literature, non-fiction, and students' own stories, transcultural literacy learning emerges as a result of feeling, thinking, imagining, and participating in curricula organized around global discourses and local events.

After reading the chapter, you might return to this figure to reflect, sketch, discuss, or jot down related questions, examples, images, and ideas. What resonated for you? What ideas sparked your own thinking? What questions did the chapter raise for you? How might you map your own context and opportunities and imagine a creative and transformative response?

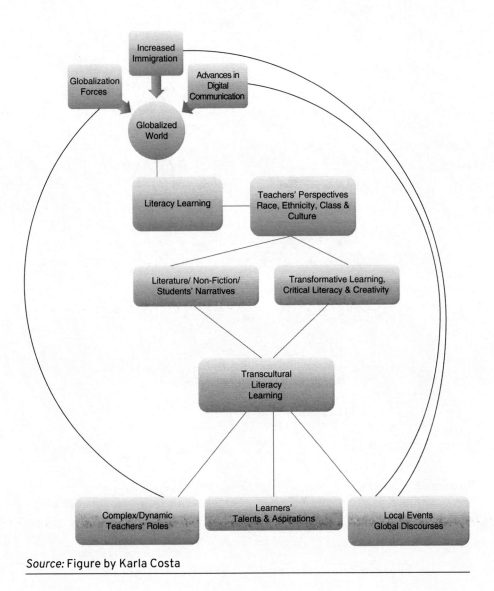

Source: Figure by Karla Costa

CHAPTER 5

Transcultural Literacies: Encouraging Transformative and Creative Learning

Karen M. Magro

Transcultural literacies offer a new way of looking at literacy, language, learning, and education. Relationships among students, teachers, and administrators in educational systems can be viewed with new potential and possibility. In an increasingly globalized world, transcultural literacy learning challenges educators to explore linguistically and culturally diverse pedagogies. Globalization, geopolitical shifts in power, conflict and war, environmental deterioration, perceived economic prosperity, and improved quality of life make Canada a destination for thousands of migrants. There are now about 192 million people living outside their places of birth; countries like Canada are increasingly becoming the final destination for a growing number of migrants, both forced and voluntary (Magro & Ghorayshi, 2011). Indeed, estimates project that one in every three Canadians will be born outside of Canada in the next decade (Government of Canada, 2015). These developments raise important questions for educators: How can we create more effective learning contexts that tap into the rich myriad of experiences that diverse learners bring? How do we build upon an asset model of learning that empowers individuals and groups in creative and productive ways? How might our communities be enriched if we encourage our students' visions and aspirations?

For provinces like Manitoba, immigration and settlement are integral to economic development. Literacy learning is directly linked to identity, belonging, and citizenship. Educators are compelled to create new literacy programs that build upon an asset model of human development and learning that recognizes and affirms the unique experiences and literacy practices of learners from diverse regions of the world. Slimbach (2005) describes trans-cultural learning as

> being rooted in the quest to define shared interests and common values
> across cultural and national borders. At its best, it comes to the forefront
> in transnational efforts to address consequential global issues, such as
> personal prejudice, group violence, environmental protection, human
> rights. (p. 206)

Educators play a key role in creating a climate where empathetic under-standings, authentic learning, and intercultural sensitivity can flourish. In-quiries into social justice and global issues develop from the teacher's strong knowledge base and a deep understanding of complex socio-political issues. Freire's (1970/1997) transformative vision of literacy learning embraces a more expansive and inclusive vision of learning that engages, affirms, and inspires learners. Learning involves both a psychological and social transformation that can take many forms: personal improvement and the realization of per-sonal, educational, and career goals; healthier lives; and more sustainable communities. The curriculum, for Freire (1997), is rooted in learners' aspi-rations, needs, and interests. Students are "co-investigators in dialogue with their teacher" (p. 62). Culturally responsive teachers do not suppress alterna-tive viewpoints expressed by their students; rather, they create opportunities for students to express themselves and gain confidence (Taylor & Cranton, 2012). Short, Day, and Schroeder (2016) write that "the integration of global books across cultures can help students develop conceptual understandings of social issues such as poverty, gender inequality, discrimination, and oppres-sion" (pp. 22–23).

I will be drawing from my own research that explores how teachers inte-grate cultural diversity and social justice themes in teaching English language arts and in related subject areas that include media studies, history, world issues, and psychology (Magro, 2015; Magro & Pierce, 2016). My research explores how powerful texts and transformative teaching practices can help learners explore dynamic intersections of culture, gender, religion, nation, eth-nicity, race, and class. I will be comparing themes that have emerged from the research on transcultural literacies to processes of transformative learning and dimensions of creativity (Mezirow & Associates, 2000; Taylor & Cranton, 2012). Learning processes are non-linear, complex, and influenced by mem-ories, experiences, and emotions. Transformative learning can encourage both personal change and social transformation (Taylor, 2009). Alternative approaches to teaching and learning can serve to bridge the gap between global and local literacies. It is through this nexus of transcultural literacies that competencies can develop. This chapter will also highlight specific psychological, situational, and institutional barriers that erode the development of literacy and learning among youth and adults. In addition to the "Deepen Your Inquiry" section, an appendix featuring useful texts for educators that can promote the development of transcultural literacies is provided at the end of the chapter.

EXPLORING THE TERRAIN OF TRANSCULTURAL LITERACIES

The school can be a haven of creativity and resilience when a climate of respect, appreciation, and intercultural competence is transformed from an ideological construct into everyday actions. Teachers also need to explore their own insights and understandings of culture, literacy, identity, and practice. In his essay "Literacy and the Politics of Difference," Giroux (1993) asserts that central to learning "is the need for students to understand how cultural, racial, ethnic, and ideological differences enhance the possibility for dialogue, trust, and solidarity" and that "literacy must be rewritten in terms that articulate differences with the principles of equality, justice, and freedom rather than with those interests supportive of hierarchies, oppression, and exploitation" (p. 368). A holistic assessment of literacy considers "what children bring to schools, their blended linguistic and cultural stocks of knowledge, the economic infrastructure and social capital in their communities, and [their] emergent life pathways and prospects" (Luke & Elkins, 2002, p. 669).

Perspectives on transcultural literacies have been informed by research by the New London Group (1996) into multimodal literacies (Gee, 1993; Luke & Elkins, 2002; Street, 1984), critical pedagogy (Freire, 1997; Giroux, 1993), and critical literary theory (Greene, 1995; Spivak, 2003). New literacies evolve as individuals interact with their material and social worlds (Gee, 1993). Themes of identity, citizenship, belonging, and social justice are connected to these changes. Cuccioletta (2001/2002) writes that, more than simple multiculturalism that "solidifies difference," transculturalism "acknowledges hybrid identities, cultural fusion, and the interspersion of difference and sameness. It enables individuals to acknowledge that culture is in a state of change—always seeking new terrains of knowing and being" (p. 3). In his work *The Location of Culture*, Bhabha (1994) writes that "we find ourselves in the moment of transit where space and time cross to produce complex figures of difference and identity, past and present, inside and outside, inclusion and exclusion" (p. 26). This liminal space is an opportunity for individuals and societies to rethink assumptions about race, class, gender, and ethnicity. Bhabha (1994) examines the way powerful texts such as Toni Morrison's (1987) *Beloved*, Franz Fanon's (1952) *Black Lives, White Masks*, and Nadine Gordimer's (1990) *My Son's Story* can provide new insights into understanding the way historic memories "haunt" present and future conceptualizations of cultural identity, belonging, and internalized oppression. Transformative teaching involves breaking down these zones along the lines of colonizer and colonized, oppressor and oppressed (Freire, 1997). Newcomer youth and adults, for example, need opportunities to break the "neat trajectories" of pre-existing, potentially explosive contact zones.

In *Cultural Transformations: Youth and Pedagogies of Possibility*, Jocson (2013) provides numerous examples of literacy projects that can positively impact the academic, career, and life trajectories of immigrant and minority youth. Innovative teaching and learning strategies replace conventional ones so that self-expression might take the form of video production, art displays, or spoken word poetry. Learner-initiated projects might investigate social justice issues such as teen suicide, gangs, drug addiction, family fragmentation, poverty, and discrimination. Literacy learning is connected with significant personal learning. A transcultural approach to literacy learning breaks down cultural misconceptions and stereotypes and finds new ways of affirming learners' skills, aspirations, and talents. This is achieved when teachers create a climate of trust and innovation and when they experiment and explore teaching and learning strategies that build on students' skills and talents. Transformative teachers are perceptive, empathic, and appreciative of cultural nuances and differences (Magro & Ghorayshi, 2011). Greene (2007) writes that transformative pedagogies invite individuals to "look through new eyes upon the world around, to listen to new frequencies, to heed shapes and nuances scarcely noticed before" (p. 47). Pedagogy, in this context, is more than curricular content, systems of assessment, and teaching strategies. Jocson (2013) explains that, for students, "pedagogies of possibility" means

> grabbing hold of opportunities that can better shape their academic, career, and life paths. It means accessing available resources inside and outside the school toward self-empowerment and social empowerment....

Pedagogies of possibility are not a set of practices with fixed or technical characteristics. (p. 9)

Positive educational environments "include teachers, parents, and other community members who are also learning alongside [students]" (p. 9). Learning opportunities need to be able to cross ethnic, class, and geographic boundaries. Patel et al. (2013) suggest that, too often, minority and newcomer youth are alienated and left out of the educational process. A transformative shift in thinking about minority youth as individuals needing help or remediation can occur through innovative literacy and mentorship programs that engage rather than alienate youth. Students need to build positive relationships in both the school and community that nurture hope, resilience, and self-esteem. Rather than creating a program for youth and adults to become "acculturated," Patel et al. (2013) emphasize the importance of validating and valuing the prior knowledge, languages, and skills of youth. They describe an innovative interest-driven internship project where newcomer youth participate in professional internships and have peer and mentor conversations about race, values, and social status. Learners have an opportunity to explore different career possibilities in law, business, government, and non-profit organizations. Dei (2010) further explains:

The relevance of race, class, gender, sexual and [dis]ability identity and representation of schooling is that they point to particular embodiments of being, social existence and knowledge production. A school system that fails to tap into youth's myriad identities and/or particular identifications as valuable sources of learning is shortchanging learners. (p. 119)

How inclusive are teachers in developing a literacy program that addresses some of the concerns Dei (2010) raises? What needs to change? Naqvi (2015) suggests that a broader and more inclusive conception of literacy can lead to a cosmopolitan citizenship where universal values, peace, and social justice are goals. Transcultural literacies reflect "traditional cultural norms, values, and beliefs, and emerging new insights gleaned from the introduction to new spaces and places of knowing" (p. 5). A step in this direction involves teachers encouraging their students to be creative in writing and producing their own texts. Naqvi (2015) further considers the way that changing media images, political statements, news reports, interest websites, laws, workplace language, and everyday discourse impact individual lives and social relationships.

Similarly, Guy (2006) explains that media and technology have become a "powerful global communications network" that influences our thoughts, feelings, and behaviours. He writes that conceptions about social class, gender identity, ethnicity, and lifestyle are all influenced by media texts. The concentration of the media has the potential to divert learners away from "critical, socially conscious forms of learning and social action" (p. 64), and "critical media literacy is a necessary step toward addressing the underlying issues of control, homogenization, and conformity" (Guy, 2006, as cited in Magro & Pierce, 2016, p. 193). Teachers can be instrumental in helping students navigate, deconstruct, and synthesize diverse texts (traditional and modern) in ways that enhance communication and critical literacy. Transcultural literacy learning, in essence, celebrates different literacy expressions among individuals and among the language of literacy that includes verbal, graphic, artistic, musical, and dramatic dimensions.

Working with African American and minority youth, Carter (2017) uses texts such as Ta-Nehisi Coates's *Between the World and Me*, Twain's *Huckleberry Finn*, Toni Morrison's *Beloved*, and Edward P. Jones's *The Known World* to explore the journey from slavery to freedom for African Americans. She challenges students to examine "the American Dream" in the context of inequitable social, class, racial, and economic structures in society: "The dream of success for a poor but hopeful young white man of the Revolutionary Era is not a dream very many young Americans—black, Hispanic, American Indian, including many poor white kids—dare to dream today" (p. 29). Prior to reading the texts, Carter's students complete research projects on the racism that exists today. By integrating history, culture, and literature with writing and research opportunities, Carter tries to provide her students with a platform to develop literacy skills with a goal of activating positive life changes. Along these lines, Shipp (2017) challenges teachers "to shift from focusing exclusively on required texts to equally acknowledging the urgent need for consciousness and activism from our students" (p. 40). Potentially, literacy classes can spark students' curiosity to explore and to create new forms of literacy.

Transcultural literacies embrace the importance of understanding and valuing underrepresented narratives. For example, Graham Reynolds's (2016) *Viola Desmond's Canada: A History of Blacks and Racial Segregation in the Promised Land* details the racism that African Canadians faced as they fled the United States in search of a safe haven. This can be compared with the narratives presented in Isabel Wilkerson's (2010) *The Warmth of Other Suns* recounting the "great migration" (1920s–1970s) of African Americans from the southern states to find a better life and the protection of their civil rights in cities such as Chicago, Detroit, and New York. Rosanna Deerchild's (2015) *Calling Down the Sky* is a compilation of poetry that recounts her mother's traumatic experiences in a residential school in northern Manitoba, and in turn, the impact that her experiences had on her children. Along similar lines, Katherena Vermette's (2016) *The Break* features the shifting narratives of Métis and First Nations women coping with personal hardships and tragedies in their lives. Underreported narratives provide individuals with opportunities to challenge cultural stereotypes and misconceptions. In *Teaching Aboriginal Literature: The Discourse of Margins and Mainstreams*, LaRocque (2016) explains that highlighting, appreciating, and exploring the multidimensionality and "kaleidoscope" of Indigenous literature is one way for readers to appreciate "an Indigenous worldview and experience that comes only from the land and the language" (p. 66). Land, family, mythologies, living histories, acts of resistance, and cosmological mysteries emerge as themes in texts by E. Pauline Johnson, Chief Dan George, Thomas King, Richard Wagamese, Tomson Highway, and Maria Campbell. LaRoque observes that

> land-based orally-literate peoples code their information about their world differently from those of us whose discourse is conditioned by written documents.... Appreciating oral literature is also an effective means to appreciate contemporary written Native poetry. For the generation of Native poets who grew up with their mother language, poetry reflects the transition from oral to written literature. (p. 60)

Read, Listen, Tell: Indigenous Stories from Turtle Island (McCall, Reder, Gaertner, & L'Hirondelle Hill, 2017) provides a rich and diverse collection of poems, stories, artistic images, myths, essays, and play excerpts that are grounded in Indigenous knowledges and scholarship. LaRoque (2016) writes that despite the diversity of texts among Indigenous peoples, "there appears to be among Indigenous peoples a fairly remarkable shared understanding of life as a cosmo/ecological whole, enabling the human being to experience life past the sensory confines" (p. 66). More can be done through education, notes LaRocque, to encourage a greater understanding of Indigenous experiences, including experiences of tragedy and trauma. Chimamanda Ngozi

Adichie (2015) recognizes the value of understanding complex and unique narratives:

> Stories matter. Many stories matter. Stories have been used to dispossess and malign, but stories can also be used to empower and to humanize. Stories can break the dignity of a people, but stories can also repair that broken dignity ... when we reject the single story, when we realize that there is never a single story about any place, we regain a kind of paradise. (p. 22)

Adichie's (2015) message has particular relevance for teachers who hope to create a truly culturally inclusive classroom. Stories, notes Kennedy (2018), "confirm us as the human beings we are. We become one through the sharing of our personal tales" (p. 79). Survival through war, famine, disease, and other hardship should encourage empathy, compassion, and insight. Dagnino (2012) emphasizes the values of reading stories written by "transcultural writers" where home is an "imaginary place" (p. 1). These writers have lived neo-nomadic lives that go beyond the "limits of any one culture or national/ ethnic landscape" (p. 1). Works by Ilija Trojanow, Kamila Shamsie, Jhumpa Lahiri, and Michael Ondaatje reflect this interactive and dialogic dynamic between and across cultures. Dagnino (2012) writes that "transculturality offers a new discursive field from which to critically address the cultural impact and creative expressions of global modernity" (p. 8).

DYNAMICS OF IMMIGRATION: NAVIGATING UNFAMILIAR PSYCHOLOGICAL, SOCIAL, AND GEOPOLITICAL TERRAIN

Immigration can be an opportunity for different groups to share their stories, symbols, values, traditions, and experiences. Building on spatial theory and the notion of contact zones (Pratt, 1991), Kostogritz and Tsolidis (2008) consider the potential of transcultural literacies to build bridges to new ways of knowing and creative cultural encounters as opportunities for learning:

> Looking at places as meeting points to explore the enrichment potential of difference.... This would also suggest more numerous and more fluid relationships between people using literacies in multiple ways and contributing to the production of new meanings that would in turn mediate

the construction of new spaces. We need to imagine a new spatiality of literacy, referred to as transcultural literacies. (p. 139)

With growing immigration in North America, there is also greater linguistic diversity. For example, today in Manitoba, more than 100 languages are spoken across the province. Over 27% of newcomers speak Tagalog, the official language of the Philippines. Other languages spoken include Punjabi, Spanish, Mandarin, Arabic, Amharic, Ukrainian, German, and a number of African languages and dialects (Manitoba Immigration Facts, 2014, p. 24). A resurgence of interest in studying Indigenous languages such as Cree, Dene, Michif, Ojibway, Oji-Cree, Dakota, and Inuktitut further attests to the rich linguistic heritage in Manitoba. An asset model of newcomer literacy education would appreciate the potential advantages that this diversity offers. Innovative thinking and the shift away from government to governance that promotes intercultural exchanges and alternative spaces for learning can re-invigorate democratic citizenship.

Newcomers to Canada have traversed different geographical, cultural, and social terrains; teachers, in particular, are central in helping these learners feel welcomed and valued (Magro, 2008; Magro & Ghoryashi, 2011). It is important to acknowledge the unique trajectory of individual immigrant experiences as well. Learning from a transcultural literacy perspective affirms, validates, and integrates the newcomers' life experiences in positive ways. An asset model of literacy builds upon the rich repertoire of languages students may know, their knowledge of living in different geographic contexts, their prior work experiences, and the resilience needed to survive and to surmount crises such as war and the loss of family and friends.

Many newcomers describe multiple "disorienting dilemmas" that involve loss. Navigating an unfamiliar culture, a new language, and a new educational system requires time and the willingness of teachers and community members to be culturally astute and sensitive. It is vital for educators to consider the way emotions, stress, and memories of trauma impact learning (Magro, 2008; Magro & Ghorayshi, 2011; Magro, 2016). Indeed, the first few years of adapting to a new country may be the most stressful for immigrants. Access to education, health care, the employment sector, and other services will increase the likelihood of successful resettlement.

My own research in responding to the educational needs of adult newcomers found that adults are often balancing multiple disorienting dilemmas, such as the loss of one's homeland, professional standing, and family members along with the stress of surviving and trying to succeed in a new and unfamiliar culture (Magro, 2008; Magro & Ghorayshi, 2011). The normal stabilizing influences of family support, cultural connections, and a sense of community integration may have been lost. The importance of a supportive and caring teacher who can listen and provide guidance in helping individuals formulate short- and long-term goals is reflected in the following narrative of Alem, an Ethiopian teacher who resettled in Canada. The "trans" in transcultural literacies suggests a dynamic movement; this occurs when individuals travel and relocate themselves in different countries, cities, and cultural contexts. As a cultural guide, co-learner, and facilitator, the teacher can embrace the rich background of learners in ways that encourage motivation and learning. Alem recalls the impact that caring teachers made in his life:

> After leading a peaceful student demonstration in Ethiopia, I was arrested and imprisoned. I ended up living in a refugee camp for several years and then I was sponsored by the Canadian government [and given refugee status]. I have learned a lot since being in Canada. I have significantly changed from being pessimistic to being more optimistic and open-minded. I am now thinking of Canada as a place of hope whereas before I felt hopeless. My teachers helped me change my thoughts and perceptions about Canada. They were willing to listen to the problems that new immigrants like myself face.... I now see myself as a "moving star" because I am moving one step closer to my life dream of being a teacher in Canada. (Magro, 2008, p. 76)

Poverty, exclusion, discrimination, and lack of resources erode resilience and the motivation to learn and to contribute to society in productive ways. A discussion of innovative literacy learning practices must also consider the factors that erode learning and literacy access. How effective, for example, are the "systems of support" that might help newcomers heal from past trauma and move toward wellness, personally, socially, academically, and economically? A new and holistic vision for learning and literacy would address ways to remove systemic barriers. A transformative literacy vision would encourage opportunity, access, community revitalization, and the valuing of individuals from diverse backgrounds. Narratives of newcomers such as Anne Mahon's (2013) *The Lucky Ones: African Refugees' Stories of Extraordinary Courage* and The Book Project Collective's (2015) *Resilience and Triumph: Immigrant Women Tell Their Stories* can provide educators with insightful narratives that attest to the rich experiences newcomers and refugees bring with them to the educational context.

TRANSCULTURAL LITERACY LEARNING AS A TRANSFORMATIVE LEARNING JOURNEY

Cuccioletta (2001/2002) states that a cultural synthesis and "reinvention" of a new common culture is based on the

> meeting and the intermingling of different people and cultures ... in other words, one's identity is not strictly one-dimensional (the self) but is now defined and more importantly recognized in rapport with the other ... one's identity is not singular but multiple. Each person is a mosaic. (p. 22)

Immigration is a social phenomenon, according to Cuccioletta, and in the process of dialogue, the potential for enrichment, learning opportunities, and a new appreciation of alternative perspectives can be developed. Transculturalism is very different from multiculturalism (Cuccioletta, 2001/2002), which can serve to alienate, undermine, trivialize, and reinforce cultural and ethnic boundaries. Moreover, "the process of recognizing oneself in the other leads inevitably to a cosmopolitan citizenship" (p. 11). This paradigm shift is also a transformative learning journey. Psychological, cultural, geographical, and social borders and boundaries are broken, reconfigured, and re-imagined. It is a hopeful vision and a learning process that involves self-awareness, empathy, and an insight into and appreciation of alternative perspectives. Cuccioletta (2001/2002) writes:

> A cosmopolitan citizenship is a citizenship that recognizes that each person of that nation-state possesses multiple identities that not only link him or her to their own cultural heritage, but also to the culture of the host country, continent, neighborhood, street, etc. (p. 10)

Cuccioletta's observation challenges teachers to consider their own views of citizenship and belonging in a time of change.

The idea of significant personal transformation and openness to new perspectives is at the heart of transformative learning. For Mezirow (1981), social change is rooted in individual perspective transformation. Transformative learning theory can help to inform our understanding of transcultural literacies. There is an emphasis on critical reflection, creative thinking and dialogue, challenging misconceptions, intercultural competence, and developing new perspectives. Transformative learning theory can provide a rich lens to understand and to explore the multi-layered dynamics of literacy and learning (Cranton, 2006; Dirkx, 2011; Mezirow & Associates, 2000; O'Sullivan, 2002; Taylor, 2008; Taylor & Cranton, 2012).

Drawing from both the humanistic and constructivist perspectives of learning, transformative learning is a "deeper level" learning that, as Clark (1993) writes,

> produces more far-reaching changes in the learners than does learning in general, and … these changes have a significant impact on the learner's subsequent experiences. In short, transformational learning shapes people; they are different afterward, in ways both they and others can recognize. (p. 47)

King (2005) further asserts that "the roots of transformative learning are found in the critical reflection of the being and self" (p. 32). In an educational climate of trust, learners can ask difficult questions of themselves and others. "Such questioning may take many forms including discussion, debate, simulations, case studies, journal writing, self-assessment, and problem solving to name a few" (p. 36). O'Sullivan (2002) provides a "core definition" of transformative learning that highlights the link between personal, social, and environmental dimensions:

> Transformative learning involves experiencing a deep, structural shift in the basic premises of thought, feeling, and actions. It is a shift of consciousness that dramatically and permanently alters our way of being in the world. Such a shift involves our understanding of ourselves and self-locations; our relationships with other humans and with the natural world; our understanding of relations of power in interlocking structures of class, race, and gender; our body-awareness; our visions of alternative approaches to living; and our sense of the possibilities for social justice and peace and personal joy. (p. 11)

Mezirow's (1981, 1991; Mezirow & Associates, 2000) theory of transformative learning describes how individuals interpret, construct, validate, and reappraise their experiences. For Mezirow (1981, 1991) learning includes not only the acquisition of new information, but also how we understand, analyze, and interpret our world and how our perceptions can be transformed through reflection and action (Cranton, 2006; Taylor & Cranton, 2012). Learning may involve changes in our existing meanings (the content of our personal model of reality), in premises (how we come to know and to value what we know), and in perspectives or the framework and cultural understandings that are the foundations of our model of reality (Magro, 2001). Individuals can "reframe" their perspective, note Mezirow and Associates (2000), through problem solving, action learning, and critical self-reflection gained from applying insights learned from another person's narrative to their own experiences, or through the exploration of thought and feeling in psychotherapy. Drawing on the work of adult developmental theorists, Mezirow (1991) writes that "learning is understood as the process of using a prior interpretation to construe a new or revised interpretation of the meaning of one's experience in order to guide future action" (p. 162). Life crises such as the death of someone close, divorce, a move, trauma, conflict, or war, and rebuilding one's life in an unfamiliar culture, can create conflict and a disorienting dilemma, self-examination, reflection, and a change or revision in perspective. Through shared dialogue and discussion, individuals explore new roles, gain new skills, and develop action plans. Competence and confidence develop as individuals experiment and explore new ways of thinking and acting. Mezirow's (1981, 1991; Mezirow & Associates, 2000) theory asserts that social changes must first begin with individual change and perspective transformation.

These stages can apply to the psychological and sociocultural sense of dislocation that many youth and adult learners, particularly from minority backgrounds, experience as they search to establish themselves in life. Many newcomers, for example, experience a "cultural disequilibrium" as they learn to build new relationships while they are navigating new legal, social, educational, and cultural terrain. Supportive teachers and counsellors, notes Mezirow (1981), can help learners gain a sense of confidence and competence.

Slimbach (2005) writes that transcultural learning involves thinking "outside the box of one's motherland, seeing many sides of every question without abandoning conviction, and allowing for a chameleon sense of self without losing one's cultural center" (p. 211). He identifies six general skill areas that educators can use as a guide to further individual learner development:

- Perspective consciousness: the ability to question constantly the source of one's cultural assumptions and ethical judgments, leading to the habit of seeing things through the minds and hearts of others.
- Ethnographic skills: the ability to carefully observe social behaviour, manage stress, and establish friendships across cultures while exploring issues of global significance, documenting learning, and analyzing data using relevant concepts.
- Global awareness: basic awareness of transnational conditions and systems, ideologies, and institutions that affect the quality of life of human and non-human populations, along with the choices confronting individuals and nations.
- World learning: direct experience with contrasting political histories, family lifestyles, social groups, arts, religions, and cultural orientations based on extensive, immersed interaction within non–English speaking, non-Americanized environments.
- Foreign language proficiency: a threshold-level facility in the spoken, non-verbal, and written communication systems used by members of at least one other culture.
- Affective development: the capacity to demonstrate personal qualities and standards of the heart (e.g., empathy, inquisitiveness, flexibility, humility, sincerity, good, justice, and joy) within specific intercultural contexts in which one is living and learning (see pp. 206–207).

Transcultural literacies are dynamic, evolving, and interconnected to community, cultural, social, psychological, and geographical contexts. New literacy forms emerge as both formal and informal learning experiences are valued. Literacy is viewed as a "life-widening" process that goes beyond learning in the classroom. Libraries, community centres, nature sites, art galleries, museums, Internet cafes, health centres, and workplaces are also potential spaces and places where informal and formal learning can occur. A focus on the development of literate families, literate communities, and literate societies can also challenge policy makers to examine other indicators of healthy communities that include safety, access to quality schools, proper housing, health care, good nutrition, mental health care, and resources needed to help children and youth with learning challenges. Literacy learning is not just about providing learners with "tools and resources"; rather, it involves creating a learning culture and climate that encourages trust, belonging, and creativity (UNESCO, 2010, p.10).

ENCOURAGING TRANSFORMATIVE LEARNING THROUGH CREATIVE TEACHING

To highlight key themes of transcultural learning and literacy in classroom contexts, I will draw upon my own qualitative research studies that have focused on exploring the roles and responsibilities of secondary English language arts teachers who teach from a social justice and transformative lens. I was also interested in learning more about the specific teaching and learning strategies of English teachers working with culturally diverse adolescents and adults. I wanted to learn more about the way teachers were adapting the curriculum to meet the changing demographics of Manitoba youth and adults. The interview data was collected between 2014 and 2018.

Collectively, the teachers' ideas highlight the following key themes in transcultural literacies: the value of literacy to expand, inform, uplift, and inspire; literacy as multimodal and situated in the complex lives of the learners; the use and application of culturally diverse literature and non-fiction; the value of interdisciplinary approaches to enrich learning; the importance of self-expression and personal empowerment as creative processes in learning; and the recognition that narratives can enrich literacy learning. Social justice themes emerged from the interviews as well. These were connected to understanding the roots of poverty, homelessness, prejudice, gender inequality, and planetary sustainability, and they were integrated into the texts and forms of assessment used by the teachers. Six teachers' perspectives from the larger participant group are presented in this chapter. These teachers specialized in English language arts, biology, art, drama, photography, world issues and history, and psychology (Grades 9–12). The teachers worked in adult learning centres, alternative education schools, and secondary schools in Winnipeg, Manitoba. I met these teachers through local literacy organizations and at workshops I facilitated at different schools, colleges, and adult learning centres.

I wanted to learn more about the texts that the teachers were using and the specific teaching and learning strategies they applied in the classroom. I asked questions such as: How would you describe your role and responsibility as a teacher? Are there particular values, beliefs, and ideals that have guided your practice? Are there preferred teaching and learning strategies that you believe motivate your students? I was particularly interested in teachers' perceptions of the ways race, ethnicity, class, and culture impacted learning. The six teachers' insights in the following section best reflected the themes emerging from the larger group of participants. Pseudonyms are used in all excerpts.

THE TEACHER AS ADVOCATE, ARTIST, AND RESEARCHER

From the framework of transcultural literacies, the teacher's role shifts from being a "manager" or "instructor" to a challenger, an advocate, a co-learner, an artist, a resource person, a co-investigator, and a facilitator (Magro, 2015). While the teachers that I interviewed did not necessarily use the terms "transcultural" and "transformative" in expressing their approaches to literacy learning, many of their ideas and their approaches to curriculum development and assessment reflected key themes of transcultural literacies. In addition, the educators' insights into learning processes reflected significant dynamics found in the research literature on transformative learning theory (Magro, 2015; Mezirow & Associates, 2000; Taylor, 2008).

Anna-Marie teaches Grade 12 biology, psychology, art, and English at an adult learning centre in the north of Winnipeg. She has worked in this position for 10 years and continues to find her work very rewarding. About 300 to 400 students are enrolled in the Grades 11 and 12 alternative program. In addition to English, her students speak a range of languages that include Mende, Kono, Farsi, Cree, Spanish, and Arabic. Anne-Marie's most recent students are from smaller communities in northern Manitoba. Others are newcomer and refugee adult learners coming from Syria, southern Sudan, and Iraq. Many of her students are coming from lower socio-economic backgrounds. The students see the completion of their Grade 12 diploma as a necessary step in advancing their education and careers. Some of Anne-Marie's students are single parents who are trying to balance education with part-time work. We discussed some of the psychological and situational barriers that her students face:

> Some of my students have never experienced success. They have difficult lives and I try to encourage them to have confidence in themselves. One student from a northern community is living in a hotel room here in Winnipeg. He felt isolated and depressed. I encouraged him to continue his education; I told him how talented he was in writing and in art. This

student told me that no one had ever spoken to him in this way. Adult learners are very perceptive and gifted, but they need more opportunities and resources to become successful. Part of my job is helping my students make sense of their learning experiences and move ahead with their lives. Connection and meaning, I would say, are the two most important parts of learning.

Anne-Marie conceptualizes her role as a challenger, researcher, role model, facilitator, and guide. She approaches teaching from an interdisciplinary perspective and when opportunities to make links arise, she challenges her students to make meaningful connections with varied texts. "I am not expecting my students to recite information. Sometimes students expect a 'linear' or more conservative style of teaching, but I try to engage them in different ways."

Creative teaching, from Anne-Marie's perspective, involves engagement (for teachers and students), challenge, curiosity, and exploration: "There should be a sense of enjoyment in learning for both students and teachers." Anne-Marie described showing her students Francisco Goya's 1814 painting *The Third of May 1808* as a way of introducing the themes of war and resistance:

> Paintings tell a story. Goya's work is a powerful commentary about the tragedy of war. It is also about resistance and courage. It makes some of my students feel uncomfortable, but I challenge them to look more deeply at the underlying narrative. I connected this art with Ishmael Beah's *A Long Way Gone: Memoirs of a Boy Soldier.* We read this book out loud together as a class. The students are often amazed to read about Ishmael's journey from despair to hope. I encourage them to connect the theme of courage and resilience to their own lives. Ishmael started a new life and in many ways, the adult learners are starting a new life in coming back to school. You have to use texts that are powerful and meaningful. Richard Wagamese's *Embers* contains poetry and visual images; his autobiographical works are also very relevant to my students' lives. Love, loss, shame, racism, courage, and gratitude are highlighted in his books.

Anne-Marie noted that the philosophy of her adult learning centre is based upon David Bouchard's "Circle of Courage." Emotional and social skills such as belonging, achievement, autonomy, and altruism are integrated in each subject area. Anne-Marie explained that part of her role as a teacher is to help students coming from culturally diverse backgrounds to understand each other and to appreciate the different experiences they have encountered. "While the students take a separate Aboriginal education course, I integrate essays and narratives linked to Truth and Reconciliation themes. I want to take away misconceptions that newcomers in particular may have about Indigenous people." Social justice themes related to equity and discrimination, she noted, emerge in many of the short stories by Rohinton Mistry and reflective essays by Richard Wagamese. Anne-Marie mentioned that while her students find reading books such as Aldous Huxley's (1934) *Brave New World* very challenging, they love discussing topics related to genetic engineering, the future, and personality being shaped by society. She integrates poetry, myths and legends, novels, and art. There is a balance of teacher-directed and student-centred teaching so that, while Anne-Marie will guide the students in reading texts such as *A Long Way Gone*, her students also have opportunities to select their own novel and related text.

> We looked at myths and legends of transformation and I showed my students prints from Norval Morrisseau. Many of his paintings portray Anishinabe stories of creation. The students then found their own creation myth and they drew their own interpretation of the myth as a painting.

When asked what the most important qualities of an educator are, Anne-Marie identified "patience, flexibility, motivation, and a love for engaging learners from many backgrounds."

Justine, a senior high English language arts and media studies teacher at a large secondary school, views her role as an advocate and a challenger. While the classroom can potentially be a place for students to develop self-efficacy and personal empowerment, Justine explained that students can also learn about competition, unequal self-worth, and relational aggression. She hopes to create a psychological and social space in her classes where individual talents can be nurtured:

> Part of being a critical educator is seeing that there is not a single definition of hope, social justice, or equity. It is not so much about covering content as it is about the depth of understanding. Learning to me

involves a process of challenging my students to look at the complexity of issues from an intersection of race, identity, culture, and experience. In my Grade 12 classes, I use a lot of non-fiction essays that address social inequities. I use international short stories to encourage cultural awareness. We do not use art and poetry enough in teaching. I challenge my students to create a visual poem and symbol book representing key themes of the stories that impacted [them the] most. I want students to leave my class having read stories set in the Middle East, Africa, and Asia. The curriculum framework has to be ever evolving; otherwise, adults will lose valuable opportunities to learn.

Justine emphasized the importance of reading and reflecting upon powerful texts to encourage critical thinking about social justice issues such as discrimination and racial prejudice:

My students find Sherman Alexie's *The Absolutely True Diary of a Part-Time Indian* riveting. Alexie shows how trauma is part of the "normal" experience for many Indigenous people. This is a book that can help non-Indigenous students develop greater empathy for the experiences of First Nation youth living "in between worlds"—the reserve, and the larger city here they need to adapt [to] quickly in order to survive. Students who have experienced hardship and discrimination can also relate to Alexie's character Junior. He is sensitive, witty, and artistic, despite the pain of losing close family members to suicide and tragic events. The novel is a hopeful novel in many ways and you can examine many specific social justice issues: discrimination, poverty, the impact of alcoholism on the family, the impact of colonial oppression and residential schools, and the struggle of being accepted when you are "different." I like books that examine complexity. The world is only going to improve if people have a positive vision.

Justine's emphasis on helping her students make personal connections to literature and non-fiction illustrates Mezirow and Associates' (2000) concept of "narrative reframing" or "applying a reflective insight from someone else's narrative to one's own experience" (p. 23). Interdisciplinary links between English language arts, politics, sociology, Indigenous issues, and psychology are further explored in a context of "deeper" level learning (Magro, 2015). The emphasis on encouraging students to reflect more deeply on texts reinforces

Jarvis's (2006) observation of the transformative potential of fiction and related texts to

> offer scope for imagining alternatives—different resolutions to familiar
> problems, alternative lifestyles, and moral choice ... and the process of
> trying different viewpoints is part of the formulation of a new perspec-
> tive. Textual study by its very nature, challenges certain commonly held
> beliefs about knowledge and the making of meaning. (p. 77)

Lou teaches Grades 10, 11, and 12 English language arts at an alternative education school. She describes herself as an advocate and a "challenger
of misconceptions." She explains that so many of her students struggle with
low self-esteem, negative body image, and mental health challenges such as
depression: "So many youth at our school have been traumatized, and I see
myself as a challenger of their own misconceptions that they have about themselves. I want them to reverse their negative self-image and see themselves as
vital and vibrant."

Lou begins her classes by reading aloud inspiring books such as *A Child
Called "It": One Child's Courage to Survive* by Dave Peltzer (1995), *Runaway:
Diary of a Street Kid* by Evelyn Lau (1996), *Persepolis: The Story of a Childhood* by Marjane Satrapi (2003), *Running the Rift* by Naomi Benaron (2010),
and *Wonder* by R. J. Palacio (2012). She integrates short films like *The River*
by Ericka MacPherson and Katherena Vermette (2016). This powerful short
film presents an Indigenous perspective on the experience of searching for a
loved one who has disappeared. Lou explained that the texts and resources in
her classroom reflected her students' interests in psychology, science fiction,
speeches, classics, young adult fiction, advertising, true stories, crime, and
overcoming hardships in life. After reading, or after viewing a film, Lou will
invite her students to write about their thoughts in their individual notebooks.
She explained:

> Creativity to me is change and effective teaching is being open to my
> students' insights and observations. I see myself as a positive role model
> who the students can trust. In sharing my reading interests with my
> students, I am hoping that they can be inspired to read more. I also
> use writing prompts and questions. After we read *Running the Rift*, I
> asked my students: "What is the thing/person/experience that saved
> you or that could save you?" Rather than teach writing style from a

formulaic position, I observe what the students are responding to and writing about in their notebooks. I comment, have conversations, and ask questions. I might say: "This looks like a poem here, or this could become a great tribute."

Lou noted that teaching English language arts texts can be a form of expression and healing if students are given more opportunities to read, to reflect, to discuss, and to communicate their understandings in a supportive context. Her ideas reinforce Young's (2009) conceptualization of a creative classroom as one that includes "time for students to brainstorm, envision, dream, and think impossible thoughts" (p. 75). As a role model, guide, coach, and mentor, Lou helps her students "translate" their dreams into productive accomplishments. Problem-solving skills, experiential learning, resilience, and creativity can be enhanced when texts are used in an imaginative and impactful way. Texts become a vehicle to illuminate experiences; they are a catalyst that can open a dialogue where students inform and are informed by texts (LaRocque, 2016). She also emphasized that more could be done to reduce institutional barriers that prevent youth who are going through a crisis from seeking out counselling and education. Transgendered youth, and youth and adult learners with mental health challenges, could benefit from more resources. And, she pointed out, "Teachers also need ongoing professional development to keep up with the new literacy strategies. You have to be a lifelong learner to be effective."

NEW LANDSCAPES FOR LITERACY LEARNING: CONNECTING THE LOCAL AND GLOBAL

Transcultural literacies also encourage an understanding of local and global events. Naqvi (2015) writes that "identity-shaping issues having to do with global events and political upheavals and our students' awareness and understanding about these events is crucial" (p. 5). In the face of geopolitical events, planetary devastation, and ongoing war and conflict in many world zones, students need to feel a sense of optimism, that given their resources and education, they can act to make a positive change in their lives and in the larger community.

Steven, a Grade 12 history and English teacher who works at a high school where over 70 languages are spoken, explained the importance of encouraging students to read a range of texts that focus on social justice themes such as exclusion, loneliness, discrimination, and ostracization. He teaches English, history, and psychology. In his classes, Steven poses questions that challenge students to think critically about connections between local and global events. What are the similarities in patterns of colonialization, for example, that have taken place in large parts of Africa, North America, and Australia? What happens to Indigenous peoples when their languages, cultures, belief systems, and lifestyles are dismantled? How does that impact identity and belonging? How might this link to their experiences here in Winnipeg? He believes that discussions and research opportunities can bring to light "disruptive knowledge" so that students begin to challenge accepted beliefs and to recognize alternative possibilities. His observation reinforces Kelly's (2012) insight that students can show their capacity to imagine as they craft visions and take actions toward social change:

> Teaching English language arts has the potential to be transformative if teachers are knowledgeable and willing to take risks. Teaching from a social justice frame to me involves identifying the contradictions and hypocrisy in our society. Students can see these contradictions. You are helping them understand their world. There is a depth and richness in literature that is ideal for exploring social concerns such as crime, poverty, and unjust situations. Adult learners can identify with the *outsider* theme. You can see from the bookcases in my classroom that my students read *Night* (Elie Wiesel), *I Know Why the Caged Bird Sings* (Maya Angelou), *The Road* (Cormac McCarthy), *1984* (George Orwell), and *The Alchemist* (Paulo Coelho). These books are disrupting but in a positive way.

Literacy learning has the potential to be transformative, notes Jarvis (2006), when there is a "critical dialogue—a dialogue with the text itself, between the students, with imagined possibilities, and with teachers and critics" (p. 71). Steven spoke of a recent book review written by a Grade 12 student who compared the experiences of racism that Ta-Nehisi Coates (2015) recounts in his memoir *Between the World and Me* and James Baldwin's (1955/2012) modern classic *Notes of a Native Son*. Steven explained that

> in *Notes of a Native Son*, Baldwin recounts his experiences in Europe and his sense of ambivalence toward Western cultures that oppressed and enslaved his ancestors, while Coates's memoir is saying that racial

injustices and misconceptions are still part of everyday life for many in America. Baldwin, decades earlier (in 1955), was searching for meaning in a world that held misconceptions about Black people. Students can examine two texts from different time periods to assess the change in racial divisions in our society. We can apply this to minority groups who are stigmatized in Canada as well. What has changed among [Indigenous peoples] in terms of human rights, access to health care, education, family life, and personal and career fulfillment? There are too many young [Indigenous] adolescent students growing up without a sense of hope; they have known only chaos and fragmentation.

Themes that highlight identity, belonging, and family fragmentation can become a catalyst for students to discuss and to write about their own life experiences. Steven emphasized that students find it interesting to examine the way characters (some fictional, some real) cope with challenges and tragedies in life: "The challenge we have is to take steps to break down racial barriers and misconceptions." There is an emphasis on engaging students' emotions. In encouraging students to appreciate different cultural perspectives and experiences, Steven is helping his students think more critically. Mezirow and Associates (2000) write that "subjective reframing involves an intensive and difficult emotional struggle as old perspectives become challenged and transformed" (p. 23).

Evan, a secondary English and psychology teacher at an adult learning centre, views himself as an advocate and co-investigator. He recognizes that for many adult learners, returning to complete a high school certificate is a difficult challenge. Adult learners are often balancing family responsibilities with work and study. His classes include students from First Nations, Métis, and Inuit backgrounds and many students from war-affected countries. Evan emphasized that being an effective teacher requires patience and resilience: "I am not prone to despair and I believe I have a commitment to justice." When I met with Evan, his students were analyzing films such as *Rabbit-Proof Fence* and *Othello* from the perspective of race, identity, and experience. He emphasized: "We need to work with parents more and provide better learning and employment opportunities for newcomer children and youth in our communities." Evan views himself more as an advocate who would like to help adult learners integrate practical work-based skills with innovative academic courses.

Cynthia, an English and geography teacher at a community college in Winnipeg, emphasizes the value of experiential learning projects. Through innovative strategies, she hopes that her students will gain a deeper understanding of human nature through literature. In studying William Shakespeare's *Romeo and Juliet*, Cynthia's students are challenged to compare different film adaptations of the play. They are asked to rewrite scenes from the play using contemporary language. In addition, they are challenged to write connections between the themes of love, trust, and family to their own experiences. Found poems, artistic collages, and new ways of "remixing" Shakespeare's ideas and language into new texts are also encouraged. Inspired by Rachel Carson's (1962) *Silent Spring*, her students created a photography exhibit called "A Sense of Wonder" as a way to capture the beauty of nature in their neighbourhood. Photographs of birds, flowers, and trees were then sold as part of an effort to raise money for a school in India. Gruenewald (2003) emphasizes the importance of place-based learning as a way to encourage exploration, inquiry, and action. O'Sullivan (2002) suggests that all educational institutions have a responsibility to play a role in fostering a community's sense of place:

> This is accomplished by having, as part of the curriculum, studies of the "bioregion." Bioregional study would encompass study of the land, the history of the community that has occupied a region, and histories of the people in a bioregion. Educating for the purpose of cultivating a sense of histories of an area enables people to have loyalties and commitment to the place of their dwelling.... Educating for a sense of place not only has a history to give, it also has a history to make. (p. 9)

Learning and literacy processes, from this perspective, are linked to inquiry, discovery, and personal and social awareness.

DISCUSSION: ENCOURAGING A SYMPHONY OF PERSPECTIVES

Shipp (2017) writes that "our curriculum, our rituals and routines, and our purpose in the classroom [need] to be rooted in something deeper. We [need] spiritually, culturally relevant, and intellectual connections to the texts being used in class" (p. 35). The theoretical and practical insights in this chapter highlight the way literacy learning can potentially enlighten and broaden learners' perspectives. Literacy learning is not solely a technical process; rather, it involves an opportunity to explore power structures and social conventions that are culturally situated. A diverse selection of texts that reflect historical, personal, and cultural themes connected to equity, social justice, oppression, the environment, and overcoming obstacles could provide a foundation for critical literacy development. Jones (2006) writes that "all texts are embedded with multiple meanings and one way to examine some of those meanings is to peel away the layers through the consideration of perspective, positioning, and power" (p. 79). Anne-Marie, Lou, Justine, Steven, Evan, and Cynthia encouraged their students to find meaning in a text by exploring the power structures and societal patterns in other texts, including the texts of their own experiences. These educators also encouraged learners to go beyond "deconstructing a text" to using a text as a vehicle to write poetry, create artistic representations, dramatize scenarios, conduct research, and reframe problems from multiple perspectives through letters and diary entries. Creative learning is experimental, notes Tsai (2013); "it questions the starting points and opens up the outcome of curriculum" (p. 34). The meaning and interpretation of texts is created not just by the writers but by the readers; reading is not a passive process but rather a potentially transformative one that can build empathy and compassion (Greene, 1995). Personal agency, imaginative ways of knowing, discussion, experiential learning, and self-direction were encouraged. The six teachers emphasized that the curriculum must be dynamic, evolving, and grounded in ways that value and validate learners' existing talents and experiences.

This study also suggests an interdisciplinary approach that links literature and non-fiction to world issues, psychology, sociology, and the visual arts may have the potential to enrich adult learning. These creative approaches reinforce Dozier's (2017) observation that "works of art, including paintings and photography, encourage reflection, analysis, and evaluate thinking skills that build success for students in both academic and workplace environments" (p. 27). Building on the importance of integrating philosophy, music, and visual arts in teaching, Kazemak & Rigg (1997) write that "the imagination is indispensable for knowing the world. It and its often-attendants of creativity, love, beauty and tradition allow us to re-vision the world, seeing it anew" (p. 136). The transformative power of artistic expression through poetry, music, dance, drama, and painting has "the capacity to give people a voice and change their perception of themselves and their place in the world.... Art transforms audiences as well as artists" (Jarvis & Burr, 2011, p. 167). While not stating that their approach to literacy learning was transformative or transcultural, the educators' views did acknowledge that learning involved affective, imaginative, creative, and cognitive dimensions (Dirkx, 2006). A goal in transcultural learning, notes Slimbach (2005), is to "open windows to reality outside our-selves" (p. 214). Literacy involves deeper-level connections and dialogue with individuals who have different histories and experiences.

Hadaway (2011) writes that "there has never been a more opportune mo-ment than now to use literature as a bridge to understanding in our global village, to reach across the national, cultural, and religious differences that often divide us" (p. 5). Transformative types of learning experiences are more likely to occur when individuals possess emotional intelligence qualities such as empathy, cultural competencies, and an openness to new ideas (Mezirow & Associates, 2000). It is also important to recognize that, ultimately, the will-ingness to learn rests within the learners themselves. Knowing this, it is still vital for teachers to create a climate conducive to learning. Dei (2010) reminds us that a meaning-centred curriculum and a "pedagogy of language libera-tion" (p. 120) would empower youth and adults to tell their stories and to learn more about their heritage, history, and culture in interconnected ways. Johnson-Bailey & Alfred (2006) synthesize their practical teaching approach for encouraging transformative learning:

> Each class we teach has varied instructional modes (printed materials, audio, WebCt components, video presentations, guest lecturer, collab-orative and individual projects) and a range of other ways in which stu-dents can participate.... Perhaps the most often used and most successful building block in our transformational teaching is the use of dialogue, an informal conversational approach.... It has been our experience that multiple voices, whether as discourse or free flowing ... produce a sym-phony of ideas and lay groundwork that supports an environment where change is possible. (p. 47)

In a transformative approach to literacy learning, it is also vital for students not only to research the informational content of a particular topic (e.g., child soldiers, poverty, racism) but to examine the emotional content of a theme they are researching. How do learners feel about particular issues and topics?

CONCLUSION: RE-IMAGINING LEARNING FOR A GLOBAL ERA

Context shapes educational practice, and the ideas presented in this chap-ter suggest that the changes reflect diverse demographic shifts. Teachers are challenged to reflect upon and to examine their assumptions about identity, belonging, citizenship, and literacy learning. Transcultural literacies embrace a diversity of approaches to textual practices that encourage a creative re-imagining of texts and discourses, identities, histories, and culture (Luke, 2004). Slimbach (2005) writes that transcultural journeys of learning involve the capacity to "put oneself in another's shoes—to apprehend their point of view and felt experiences is prerequisite to finally taking responsibility as citizens of the global community" (p. 218). The economic, political, and cultural challenges we face as a world today place a greater urgency on educational systems to provide innovative programs that embrace new spaces for learning. The integration of world literary and non-fiction works in the adult literacy curriculum can provide adult learners with opportunities to "immerse themselves in multiple cultures/geographies/territories ... and identities" (Dagnino, 2012, p. 1). This opportunity can further open up new possibilities for thinking, imagining, and participating in a "global discourse" that is also connected to their local and social environments.

Collectively, the educators' perspectives in this chapter suggest a need to move beyond a linear conceptualization of literacy into a new paradigm that crosses boundaries, disciplines, and skill specialization areas. Future studies could also explore specific dispositions of educators that are more likely to encourage transcultural literacies and transformative types of learning. How might a teacher's optimism, creativity, curiosity, openness to new and different ideas, problem-solving abilities, willingness to tolerate ambiguity, and resilience impact the facilitation of learning? What resources and opportunities need to be provided and encouraged for educators to develop and learn more about transformative approaches to teaching and learning?

The ideas presented in this chapter provide pathways for educational transformation that seek to break down psychological, situational, and institutional barriers, and create contexts where youth and adults can develop literacy skills that tap into talent, creativity, and resilience. Wagamese (2011) writes that "we need to hear stories of healing, not just relentless retellings of pain" (p. 31). Yet, as educators, we cannot underestimate the way factors like these impact motivation and literacy learning: unsafe housing, family fragmentation, a lack of access to justice and social services, financial hardship, mental and physical health challenges, trauma, experiences of racism, and other myriad forms of discrimination. These barriers can create a context of chaos, anxiety, and hopelessness. A greater effort is needed by policy makers and educational leaders to work with parents, teachers, and community leaders to address these challenges; a transformative approach to educational change is a critical part of multi-layered solutions. A committed effort on the part of researchers, practitioners, program planners, and educational policy makers is needed to address these challenges. Future studies that link themes from transcultural literacies to transformative processes of learning would further enrich this emerging field.

Appendix: Recommended Texts to Encourage Global Awareness and Transcultural Literacies

Alexie, S. (2007). *The absolutely true diary of a part-time Indian.* New York and Boston: Little, Brown, and Company.

Alexie's richly illustrated novel is based in part on his own experiences growing up on an isolated reserve near Spokane, Washington. Junior, the narrator of the novel, shares his struggles with identity, internalized feelings of inferiority, discrimination, poverty, and family fragmentation. He must also come to terms with his gifted sister's suicide. Junior describes the strong bond of love that he has for his family and the fragile hope he has of rising above his impoverished circumstances to become a cartoonist and artist. Students could read Deborah Ellis's (2013) *Looks Like Daylight: Voices of Indigenous Kids*, Richard Wagamese's (2008) *One Native Life*, and Thomas King's (2012) *The Inconvenient Indian* as related texts.

Baldwin, J. (1955/2012). *Notes of a native son.* Boston: Beacon Press.

Baldwin's compelling collection of essays portrays life in Harlem, the growing civil rights movement, the continual struggle for social justice, and the racism and discrimination that many African American people, including Baldwin, experienced. Baldwin emphasizes that despite the hardships he encountered, there is hope to lead one's life with dignity, purpose, and with the possibility of activating positive social change. Themes of identity, belonging, and overcoming obstacles can be highlighted in this text. Related texts include the documentary film *I Am not Your Negro* (2017), Cornel West's (2015) *The Radical King*, Maya Angelou's (1993/2017) *Life Doesn't Frighten Me (with paintings by Jean-Michel Basquiat)*, and *Black Voices: An Anthology of African-American Literature* (edited by A. Chapman, 2001).

Beah, I. (2009). *A long way gone : Memoirs of a boy soldier.* New York: Farrar, Straus, and Giroux.

This riveting memoir recounts Ishmael Beah's journey from being a child soldier to becoming an advocate for children's rights and peace. Beah's narrative is a story of redemption and forgiveness. While Beah grew up as a gentle boy with a loving family, his life quickly turns into a nightmare when he is picked up by government rebels and forced to commit acts of violence as a child soldier. He is rescued by UNICEF and, throughout his recovery, Beah learns to forgive himself and regain his humanity. Themes such as forgiveness, redemption, and personal transformation, and issues related to war and peace-building, can be explored. Beah's (2014) *Radiance of Tomorrow* and Mende Nazer's (2003) *Slave* would be excellent complementary texts to explore in a unit centring around the impact of war on children.

Bradbury, R. (2005). *Short stories (100 of Bradbury's most celebrated tales)*. New York: William Morrow.

Bradbury's science fiction stories are more relevant than ever as individuals grapple with the impact of totalitarian governments, alienation, environmental devastation, surveillance and privacy, freedom and responsibility, artificial intelligence, robotics, and virtual worlds. Bradbury's works can be compared with the vision of humanity presented in the work of Ursula Le Guin, George Orwell, and Aldous Huxley.

Carson, R. (1962/2004). *Silent Spring*. New York: Houghton Mifflin.

In a post–World War II world of technological advancements, little thought and critical insight was given to the way people and the natural world could be adversely impacted. Carson's groundbreaking book examines the dangers of DDT and other pesticides. Her writing became a catalyst to the development of government agencies, like the EPA (Environmental Protection Agency), and the rise of activist organizations such as Green Peace and the Sierra Club. *Silent Spring* continues to be a timely cautionary tale that urges readers to honour and protect our fragile planet. Technological "advances" cannot be at the expense of environmental devastation. Carson's book can be used with a myriad of non-fiction and fiction texts centring on the theme of the environment and reverence for all living things.

Class Divide. (2016). Directed by Marc Levin. HBO Documentary Films (75 min.).

Same street but different destination. Levin explores the impact of gentrification and increasing economic disparity in New York's West Chelsea neighbourhood. Poverty, social class, injustice, and unequal access to education are explored through the voices of students and other residents from the neighbourhood.

Continued

This film brilliantly shows the way education intersects with immigration, employ-ment, affordable housing, and income inequality. Interviews with students from different cultural and economic backgrounds poignantly reveal that all children have dreams, hopes, and aspirations to succeed and create a better life. The film sends the message that all our children deserve respect, dignity, and the oppor-tunity to realize their potential.

Coates, T. (2015). *Between the world and me*. New York: Spiegel and Grau.

Coates's letter to his son vividly describes the challenges faced by African American youth and men who live in the historical shadows of slavery, segrega-tion, and unjust incarceration. How does a young man carve a positive sense of self and how can one envision the possibility of a brighter future "when the en-tire narrative of this country [the United States] argues against the truth of who you are"? Coates urges his son to "never forget that for 250 years black people were born into chains—whole generations followed by more generations who knew nothing but chains" (p. 70). Parallels between Coates and the works of James Baldwin could be researched. In addition, this text can be used to complement works such as Teresa Cardenas's (1998/2006) *Letters to My Mother* and Edwidge Danticat's (1995) *Krik Krak*. These texts examine the complex relationships of par-ents and children as they navigate the intersection of race, culture, history, and ancestral legacies.

Coelho, P. (1988). *The alchemist*. New York: Harper Collins.

Brazilian writer Paulo Coelho centres his novel on Santiago, the Andalusian shepherd boy who travels from his homeland in search of a treasure buried in the Pyramids. Along the way, Santiago meets guides, including the alchemist, all of whom direct the shepherd on his spiritual quest. The importance of hav-ing dreams, the power of mentors in our lives, and significant personal learning journeys are themes that emerge from this book. This book can be explored with complementary texts such as Herman Hesse's (1922) *Siddhartha* and Cormac McCarthy's (2006) *The Road*.

Deerchild, R. (2015). *Calling down the sky*. Markham, ON: BookLand Press.

Rosanna Deerchild's poetry is both heartbreaking and hopeful. Many of the poems capture poignant memories that Deerchild has of her mother at different times in their lives. The poems also reflect her mother's experiences in residential school. Deerchild elaborates on the devastating history of the residential schools and the intergenerational trauma that prevented so many from realizing their full potential. The poems honour her mother's courage and spiritual strength. Bev Sellars's (2013) *They Called Me Number One*, Katherena Vermette's (2016) *The Break*, and Tanya Tagala's (2017) *Seven Fallen Feathers* could enrich students' exploration of the lives of Indigenous girls and women. For cross-cultural connections, *Maya Angelou: The Complete Poetry* (2015) could be explored.

Morrisseau, N.

For further explorations of the work of Norval Morrisseau, the website www .norvalmorrisseau.com can direct learners to additional resources.

Palacio, R. J. (2012). *Wonder.* New York: Penguin.

Born with an extreme facial abnormality that causes him to be isolated and ridiculed by others, the protagonist of Palacio's novel gains confidence and self-acceptance as he begins to see himself as someone with intelligence, compassion, and the capacity to love and inspire others. Themes related to body image, identity, discrimination, the importance of empathy for others, family and community, and the journey toward personal empowerment can be woven in with related texts. Laurie Halse Anderson's (1999) *Speak* and David Peltzer's (1995) *A Child Called "It"* are complementary texts that encourage readers to look beyond "difference."

Pazira, N. (2005). *A bed of red flowers: In search of my Afghanistan.* New York: Simon & Schuster.

Now living in Canada, journalist and filmmaker Nelofer Pazira describes the journey she took with her family as they were forced to flee Afghanistan as a result of years of conflict and war. In her memoir, Pazira describes the beauty and joy of Afghanistan before the Soviets invaded in the 1980s. Human rights violations that include the denial of free speech and women's rights, and the ability of individuals to overcome adversity, emerge in this powerful book. Suffering, courage, belonging, family, cultural heritage, and the impacts of war that can dislocate and destroy individuals, families, and the environment are themes that emerge from Pazira's memoir. This book could be used in conjunction with Gayle Tzemach Lemmon's (2011) *The Dressmaker of Khair Khana*, Khaled Hosseini's (2007) *A Thousand*

Continued

Splendid Suns, and *I am Nujood, Age 10 and Divorced* by Nujood Ali, with Delphine Minoui (2010).

Robertson, D. A., & Henderson, S. B. (2011). *Sugar falls: A residential school experience*. Winnipeg: Highwater Press.

This graphic novel is based on the true story of Betty Ross, an Elder from Cross Lake First Nation. The main character, Daniel, interviews Betsy, his friend's grandmother. Abandoned as a child, Betsy was adopted into a loving family. However, her peaceful childhood was shattered when she was taken away to a residential school. Betsy's heart-wrenching narrative describes her traumatic experiences at the residential school, where she encountered neglect, abuse, and other indignities. Betsy draws upon the loving memories of her father as she regains courage, resilience, and determination. This book can be used in conjunction with Robertson and Henderson's (2010) *Seven Generations* series and *Betty: The Helen Betty Osborne Story* (2015). These texts illuminate important Indigenous themes that relate to residential school experiences, intergenerational trauma, missing and murdered Indigenous girls and women, racism and injustice, and the resilience of the human spirit. With bold illustrations, Robertson's graphic novels beautifully bring to life timely issues that can help youth, and indeed all Canadians, understand important aspects of our country's history. Christy Jordon Fenton and Margaret Pokiak's (2010) *Fatty Legs* and Gord Downie and Jeff Lemire's (2016) *Secret Path* are also excellent complementary texts that are appropriate for both middle years and senior high school students.

Satrapi, M. (2003). *Persepolis*. New York: Pantheon.

Satrapi's graphic novel is based on the author's own childhood growing up during the Islamic Revolution in Iran. With wit, honesty, and elegance, Satrapi describes the story of her life from ages six to fourteen. During this time, she witnessed the overthrow of the Shah's regime, the dominance of the Islamic Revolution, and the tragic impact of the war with Iran. Widespread human rights violations and ongoing war forced Satrapi and her family to seek a new life in Europe. Satrapi's main protagonist, Marjane, presents a compelling portrait of childhood life being intricately connected with events of history. Themes related to resilience, courage, and overcoming obstacles could be explored, and comparisons with other graphic novels such as *Maus* (1991) by Art Spiegelman could be made.

Wagamese, R. (2016). *Embers: One Ojibway's meditations*. Toronto: Douglas & McIntyre.

This beautifully illustrated volume by Richard Wagamese includes the author's personal reflections on the universe. Wagamese draws life lessons from his ancestral heritage to write about the importance of stillness, harmony, trust, reverence, persistence, gratitude, and joy. This book nicely complements Wagamese's *One Story, One Song* (2011) and *One Native Life* (2008). Learners can reflect on existential themes such as life journeys and life lessons, honouring others, cherishing the environment, and courage amid adversity.

QUESTIONS FOR REFLECTION AND DISCUSSION

1. "The idea of significant personal transformation and openness to new perspectives is at the heart of transformational learning." How open are you to exploring new cultures and experiences? How open are you to expanding your beliefs and practices? Can you describe a significant personal learning experience that may have led you to revise your beliefs and actions?

2. How are transcultural literacies defined in this chapter?

3. How are learning and literacy development linked to culture, ethnicity, experience, age, and so on?

4. What opportunities and challenges might teachers and students face in transcultural learning spaces?

5. This chapter explores some of the roles and responsibilities of educators. Think about your role and responsibility as a teacher. How would you describe the specific responsibilities connected with the following roles:
    - advocate
    - co-learner
    - co-inquirer
    - challenger
    - researcher
    - navigator
    - resource person
    - manager

· artist
· director

Which role(s) best describe your teaching style and approach?

6. Can you find any common threads that link the educators' approaches to teaching and learning?

7. In your view, what barriers stand in the way of "literacy for all"?

8. Are you familiar with any of the texts that the teachers used in this chapter? How might a particular text, piece of music, painting, photograph, digital media resource, or film be a catalyst for transcultural literacies? Can you provide some examples?

DEEPEN YOUR INQUIRY: RELATED READINGS AND RESOURCES

Ali, N. (with D. Minoui). (2010). *I am Nujood, age 10 and divorced.* New York: Three Rivers Press.

Al-Solaylee, K. (2016). *Brown: What being brown in the world today means (to everyone).* New York: Harper Collins.

Beach, R., Campano, G., Edmiston, B., & Borgmann, M. (2010). *Literacy tools in the classroom: Teaching through critical inquiry, Grades 5–12.* New York: Teachers College Press, National Writing Project.

Beach, R., Johnston, A., & Thein, A. H. (2015). *Identity-focused ELA teaching: A curriculum framework for diverse learners and contexts.* New York: Routledge.

Blohm, J. M., & Lapinsky, T. (2006). *Kids like me: Voices of the immigrant experience.* Yarmouth, MN: Intercultural Press.

Burr, J. C. (2017). Springsteen, spoken word, and social justice: Engaging students in activism through songs and poetry. *English Journal, 106*(6), 61–66.

Burwell, C. (2017). Game changes: Making new meanings and new media with video games. *English Journal, 106*(6), 41–47.

Campano, G. (2007). *Immigrant students and literacy: Reading, writing, and remembering.* New York: Teachers College Press.

Carey-Webb, A. (2001). *Literature and lives: A response-based, cultural studies approach to teaching English.* Urbana, IL: NCTE.

Christensen, L. (2009). *Teaching for joy and justice: Re-imagining the language arts classroom.* Milwaukee: Rethinking Schools Publication.

Dimaline, C. (2017). *The marrow thieves.* Toronto: Cormorant Books.

Duke, N. K., et al. (2006). Authentic literacy activities for developing comprehension and writing. *The Reading Teacher, 60(*4), 344–355.

Egan, K., & Judson, G. (2016). *Imagination and the engaged learner: Cognitive tools for the classroom.* New York: Teachers College Press.

Eichler, K. (2006). Creative communication frames: Discovering similarities between writing and art. Available at http://www.readwritethink.org/lessons

Ekphrasis: Using art to inspire poetry. Available at www.readwritethink.org

ePals. www.epals.com/#/connections. (Teachers and students can connect, communicate, and embark upon collaborative learning projects through pen-pal letters from students [and teachers] around the world.)

Finkle, S. L., & Lilly, T. (2008). *Middle ground: Exploring selected literature from and about the Middle East.* Urbana, IL: NCTE.

Giovanni, N. (Ed.). (2008). *Hip hop speaks to children: A celebration of poetry with a beat.* Naperville, IL: Sourcebooks Inc.

Greenberg, J. (2008). *Side by side: New poems inspired by art from around the world.* New York: Abrams.

Highway, T. (2017). *From oral to written: A celebration of Indigenous literature in Canada, 1980–2010.* J. Abel (Ed.). Vancouver, BC: Talon Books.

Hillyard, S. (2016). *English through drama: Creative activities for inclusive ELT classes.* New York: Helbling Languages.

Janks, H. (2014). *Doing critical literacy: Texts and activities for students and teachers.* New York and London: Routledge.

Jocson, K. (2008). *Youth poets: Empowering literacies in and out of schools.* New York: Peter Lang.

Johnson, A. B., Augustus, L., & Agiro, C. P. (2012). Beyond bullying: Pairing classics and media literacy. *English Journal, 101*(6), 56–63.

King Jr., M. L. (2005). C. West (Ed.). *The radical King.* Boston: Beacon Press.

Koch, K., & Farrell, K. (2000). *Talking to the sun: An illustrated anthology of poems for young people.* New York: Metropolitan Museum of Art.

Lahiri, J. (1999). *Interpreter of maladies.* Boston: Houghton Mifflin Harcourt. (A collection of short stories to broaden transcultural awareness).

Learn Around the World. http://learnaroundtheworld.com/. (This website helps learners embark upon a virtual expedition of the world. Photographs, maps, trip logs, and other artifacts are presented.)

Leland, C., Lewison, M., & Harste, J. (2013). *Teaching children's literature: It's critical!* New York: Routledge.

Life Is Living. www.lifeisliving.org

MacDonald, K., & McCarthy, M. (2018, August 17). Turning poetry into photos. *The New York Times.* Available at https://www.nytimes.com/2018/08/17us/how-poems

Metropolitan Museum of Art. https://www/metmuseum.org/learn/education/lessonplans. (PDF files on creative ways of teaching world art from an interdisciplinary perspective).

National Geographic. (2016). *Every human has rights: A photographic declaration for kids.* Washington, DC: National Geographic. Available at www.nationalgeographic.com

Read, Write, Think. http://www.readwritethink.org. (Using picture books to explore identity, stereotyping, and discrimination).

Short, K. G., Day, D., & Schroeder, J. (2016). *Teaching globally: Reading the world through literature.* Portland, MN: Stenhouse Publishers.

Sternberg, R. J., Jarvin, L., & Grigorenko, E. L. (2015). *Wisdom, intelligence, creativity, and success.* New York: Skyhorse Publishing.

Teaching for Change. www.teachingforchange.org/. (Teaching for Change is a website for teachers and parents who are interested in building upon a social justice perspective in education. World issues and global citizenship ideas are presented.)

UNESCO lesson plans in global citizenship and peace education. www.unesco.org.

Zaidi, R., & Rowsell, J. (Eds). (2017). *Literacy lives in transcultural times.* London: Routledge.

REFERENCES

Adichie, C. N. (2016). The danger of a single story. In L. Blass, M. Vargo, & I. Wisnieska (Eds.), *21st century reading: Creativity and thinking and reading with TedTalks.* Boston: National Geographic/Cengage Learning.

Alexie, S. (2007). *The absolutely true diary of a part-time Indian.* New York and Boston: Little, Brown and Company.

Baldwin, J. (1955/2012). *Notes of a native son.* Boston: Beacon Press.

Beah, I. (2007). *A long way gone: Memoirs of a boy soldier.* New York: Farrar, Strauss, and Giroux.

Bhabha, H. K. (1994). *The location of culture.* London: Routledge.

Carter, M. (2017). Beyond the dream, the journey: American novels that track the path from slavery to freedom. *English Journal, 106*(4), 29–34.

Clark, C. (1993). Transformational learning. In S. Merriam (Ed.), *An update on adult learning theory* (pp. 46–56). *New Directions for Adult and Continuing Education, 57*(1), 46–58. San Francisco: Jossey-Bass.

Coates, T. (2015). *Between the world and me.* New York: Spiegel and Grau.

Cranton, P. (2006). *Understanding and promoting transformative learning.* San Francisco: Jossey-Bass.

Cuccioletta, D. (2001/2002). Multiculturalism or transculturalism: Toward a cosmopolitan citizenship. *London Journal of Canadian Studies, 17*, 1–11.

Dagnino, A. (2012). Global mobility, transcultural literature, and multiple modes of modernity. *Transcultural Studies, 1*(2), 1–14.

Deerchild, R. (2015). *Calling down the sky.* Markham, ON: Bookland Press.

Dei, G. J. (2010). The possibilities of new/counter and alternative visions of schooling. *English Quarterly, 41*(3–4), 113–132.

Dirkx, J. 2006. Engaging emotions in adult learning: A Jungian perspective on emotion and transformative learning. In E. Taylor (Ed.), *Teaching for change: Fostering transformative learning in the classroom* (pp. 15–26). San Francisco: Jossey-Bass.

Dirkx, J. (2011). The meaning and role of emotions in adult learning. In S. B. Merriam & A. P. Grace (Eds.), *The Jossey-Bass reader on contemporary issues in adult education* (pp. 349–362). Malabar, FL: Krieger.

Dozier, L. (2017). Art as text: Seeing beyond the obvious. *English Journal, 106*(6), 29–34.

Freire, P. (1997). *Pedagogy of the oppressed.* New York: Continuum. (Originally published in 1970).

Gee, J. P. (1993). Postmodernism and literacies. In C. Lankshear & P. L. McLaren (Eds.), *Critical literacy: Politics, praxis, and the postmodern* (pp. 271–296). New York: Albany State University.

Giroux, H. (1993). Literacy and the politics of difference. In C. Lankshear & P. L. McLaren (Eds.), *Critical literacy: Politics, praxis, and the postmodern* (pp. 367–378). Albany: State University of New York.

Government of Canada. (2015). Immigration, Refugees, and Citizenship Canada: Facts and Figures. Ottawa: Government of Canada. Retrieved from www.Cic.gc.ca/english/resources/statistics/menu-fact.asp

Greene, M. (1995). *Releasing the imagination: Essays on education, the arts, and social change.* San Francisco: Jossey-Bass.

Greene, M. (2007). Toward a pedagogy of thought and a pedagogy of imagination. Available at http://www.maxinegreene.org/articles

Gruenewald, D. A. (2003). The best of both worlds: A critical pedagogy of place. *Educational Researcher, 32*(4), 3–12.

Guy, T. (2006). Adult education and the mass media in the age of globalization. In S. B. Merriam, B. C. Courtnay, & R. M. Cerveroi (Eds.), *Global issues and adult education: Perspectives from Latin America, Southern Africa, and the United States* (pp.64–77). San Francisco: Jossey-Bass.

Hadaway, N. L. (2011). Building global awareness with international literature. *English Quarterly, 42*(3/4), 5–20.

Jarvis, C. (2006). Using fiction for transformation. In E. Taylor (Ed.), *Teaching for change: Fostering transformative learning in the classroom. New Directions for Adult and Continuing Education, 109*, 69–78. San Francisco: Jossey-Bass.

Jarvis, C., & Burr, V. (2011). The transformative potential of popular television: The case of Buffy the Vampire Slayer. *Journal of Transformative Education, 9*(3),165–182.

Jocson, K. M. (2013). *Cultural transformations: Youth and pedagogies of possibility.* Cambridge, MA: Harvard University Press.

Johnson-Bailey, J., & Alfred, M. (2006). Transformational teaching and the practices of Black women educators. In E. Taylor (Ed.), *Teaching for change: Fostering transformative learning in the classroom. New Directions for Adult and Continuing Education, 109*(1), 49–58. San Francisco: Jossey-Bass.

Jones, S. (2006). *Girls, social class, and literacy: What teachers do can make a difference.* Portsmouth, NY: Heinemann.

Kazemak, F. E., & Rigg, P. (1997). "… the sense of soul … goes hand in hand with an aesthetic response": Art in Adult Literacy Education. *Adult Basic Education, 7*(3), 133–144.

Kelly, D. (2012). Teaching for social justice: Translating an anti-oppression approach into practice. *Our Schools/Our Selves* (Winter 2012), 135–154.

Kennedy, R. (2018). Raven healing. In M. Greenwood, S. de Leeuw, & N. M. Lindsay (Eds.), *Determinants of Indigenous Peoples' health: Beyond the social* (2nd ed.; pp. 73–79). Toronto: Canadian Scholars Press.

King, K. (2005). *Bringing transformative learning to life.* Malabar, FL: Krieger.

Kostogritz, A., & Tsolidis, G. (2008). Transcultural literacy: Between the local and the global. *Pedagogy, Culture, and Society, 16*(2), 1–24.

LaRocque, E. (2016). Teaching Aboriginal literature: The discourse of margins and mainstreams. In D. Reder & L. M. Morra (Eds.), *Learn, Teach, Challenge: Approaching Indigenous Literatures* (pp. 55–72). Waterloo, ON: Wilfrid Laurier University Press.

Luke, A. (2004). At last: The trouble with English. *Research in the Teaching of English, 39,* 85–95.

Luke, A., & Elkins, J. (2002). Toward a critical, worldly literacy. *Journal of Adolescent & Adult Literacy, 45*(8) ,668–673.

Magro, K. (2001). Perspectives and theories of adult learning. In D. Poonwassie and A. Poonwassie (Eds.), *Fundamentals of adult education* (pp. 76–99). Toronto: Thompson Educational Publishing.

Magro, K. (2008). Exploring the experiences and challenges of adults from war-affected backgrounds: New directions for literacy educators. *Adult Basic Education and Literacy Journal, 2*(1), 24–33.

Magro, K. (2015). Teaching for social justice and peace education: Promising pathways for transformative learning. *Peace Research: The Canadian Journal of Peace and Conflict Studies, 47*(1/2), 109–142.

Magro, K., & Ghorayshi, P. (2011). *Adult refugees and newcomers in the inner city of Winnipeg: Promising pathways for transformative learning.* Canadian Centre for Policy Alternatives, 1–30.

Magro, K., & Pierce, K. (2016). Creative approaches to literacy learning: A transformative vision for education in the 21st century. In D. Ambrose & R. J. Sternberg (Eds.), *Creative intelligence in the 21st century: Grappling with enormous problems and huge opportunities* (pp. 191–210). Rotterdam, the Netherlands: Sense Publishers.

Mahon, A. (2013). *The lucky ones: African refugees' stories of extraordinary courage.* Winnipeg: Great Plains Publications.

Manitoba Immigration Facts. (2014). PDF Reports. Retrieved from www.gov .mb.ca/labour/immigration/publication.html

McCall, S., Reder, D., Gaertner, D., & L'Hirondelle Hill, G. (Eds.). (2017). *Read, listen, tell: Indigenous stories from Turtle Island.* Waterloo, ON: Wilfrid Laurier University Press.

Merriam, S. B., & Kim, Y. S. (2011). Non-Western perspectives on learning and knowing. In S. B. Merriam & A. P. Grace (Eds.), *The Jossey-Bass reader on contemporary issues in adult education* (pp. 378–390). Malabar, FL: Krieger.

Mezirow, J. (1981). A critical theory of adult learning and education. *Adult Education Quarterly, 32*(1), 3–24.

Mezirow, J. (1991). *Transformative dimensions of adult learning.* San Francisco: Jossey-Bass.

Mezirow, J., & Associates. (2000). *Learning as transformation: Critical perspectives on a theory in progress.* San Francisco: Jossey-Bass.

Naqvi, R. (2015). Literacy in transcultural and cosmopolitan times: A call for change. Calgary: Werklund School of Education.

New London Group. (1996). A pedagogy of multiliteracies: Designing social futures. *Harvard Educational Review, 31*(3), 60–93.

O'Sullivan, E. (2002). The project and vision of transformative education: Integral transformative learning. In E. O'Sullivan, A. Morrel, & M. A. O'Connor (Eds.), *Expanding the boundaries of transformative learning* (pp. 1–12). London: Palgrave Press.

Patel, L., & Gurn, A., with Dodd, M., Pai, S., Norvilus, V., Yang, E., & Ares, R. S. (2013). Imaging and re-imaging internships: Immigrant youth, community-based research, and cultural transformation. In K. Jocson (Ed.), *Cultural transformations: Youth and pedagogies of possibility* (pp. 97–114). Cambridge, MA: Harvard Education Press.

Pratt, M. L. (1991). Arts of the contact zone (Keynote address to the Modern Language Association). *Profession*, 33–40.

Reynolds, G. (with W. Robson). (2016). *Viola Desmond's Canada: A history of Blacks and racial segregation in the promised land*. Halifax & Winnipeg: Fernwood Publishing.

Shipp, L. (2017). Revolutionizing the English classroom through consciousness, justice, and self-awareness. *English Journal, 106*(4), 35–40.

Short, K. G., Day, D., and Schroeder, J. (2016). *Teaching globally: Reading the world through literature*. Portland, MN: Stenhouse Publishers.

Sinclair, N. J., & Cariou, W. (Eds.) (2011). *Manitowapow: Aboriginal writings from the land of water*. Winnipeg: Highwater Press.

Slimbach, R. (2005). The transcultural journey. *The Interdisciplinary Journal of Study Abroad, 1*(2), 205–230.

Sobel, D. (1996). *Beyond ecophobia: Reclaiming the heart in nature education*. Great Barrington, MA: The Orion Society and The Myrin Institute.

Spivak, G. (2003). *Death of a discipline*. New York: Columbia.

Street, B. (1984). *Literacy in theory and practice*. New York: Cambridge University Press.

Taylor, E. W. (2008). Transformative learning theory. In S. B. Merriam (Ed.), *Third update on adult learning theory* (pp. 5–16). *New Directions for Adult and Continuing Education, 119*. San Francisco: Jossey-Bass.

Taylor, E. W. (2009). Fostering transformative learning. In J. Mezirow & E. W. Taylor (Eds.), *Transformative learning in practice: Insights from community, workplace, and higher education*. San Francisco: Jossey-Bass.

Taylor, E. W., & Cranton, P. (Eds.). (2012). *The handbook of transformative learning.* San Francisco: Jossey-Bass.

The Book Project Collective. (2015). *Resilience and triumph: Immigrant women tell their stories.* Toronto: Story Press.

Tsai, K. C. (2013). Two channels of learning: Transformative learning and creative learning. *American International Journal of Contemporary Research, 3*(1), 32–37.

UNESCO. (2010). *3rd Global Report on adult learning and education: The impact of adult learning and education on health and well-being, employment and the labour market; and social, civic, and community life.* Hamburg, Germany: UNESCO Institute for Lifelong Learning.

Wagamese, R. (2011). *One story, one song.* Toronto: Douglas & McIntyre.

Wilkerson, I. (2010). *The warmth of other suns.* New York: Random House.

Young, L. P. (2009). Imagine creating rubrics that develop creativity. *English Journal, 99*(2), 74–79.

Transcultural Literacies as Provocations to Understand the Other: Ethically Responding to Local/Global Questions

Reading literary transcultural texts in K–12 and post-secondary classrooms cultivates a sensitivity and sensibility to the textured nature of human identities. The imaginative power of this orientation has the potential to fracture taken-for-granted ways of understanding and to re-envision a world that honours the diversity of human life and solidarity.

—*Burcu Yaman Ntelioglou and Tim Skuce*

OPENING THE CONVERSATION: READING NOTES

The transcultural nature of our classrooms, schools, communities, and world creates a need for us to respond to urgent and pressing local/global concerns that raise questions of difference and the ethical responsibility to hear the other. As educators, it is not new to us—or the field—to conceive of curriculum beyond official documents: as a venture, an inquiry, an existential quest that calls for a relationality among self, other, and the world.

In this chapter, authors Burcu Yaman Ntelioglou and Tim Skuce invite us to consider how transcultural literacies present opportunities to experience curriculum as a double encounter. Envisioning curriculum as a double encounter calls for experiences with difference and otherness that require humility, respect, vulnerability, openness, and empathy, as well as a willingness to bear witness to pain and suffering. The double encounter calls us to let go of ideas, assumptions, and beliefs that stand in the way of hearing the voice of the other, which, in turn, may forever change what we have known, understood, and held dear. The double encounter is an ongoing transformation, venturing out into other worlds and returning to see our world and ourselves in new ways.

In classrooms, double encounters can be experienced through expanding the people, discourses, artifacts, experiences, stories, issues, perspectives, and ideas included in the curriculum. As Magro discussed in the preceding chapter, multicultural literature opens up spaces for reflexive, critical, and creative possibilities. In this chapter, Yaman Ntelioglou and Skuce examine excerpts from Richard Wagamese's (1994) novel *Keeper'n Me* to explore the notion of double encounter and the moral and ethical bonds that are fostered with the other through more complicated conversations of difference and otherness in the classroom. Central to this exploration, they inquire into larger questions about the self/other, I/Thou relationship. Their intention is to encourage educators and students to be open to and opened by encounters with others in and beyond the bounds of schools, to foster social commitment, and to re-envision and renew relational understandings of self/other/world.

As you read this chapter, you might make connections to the ideas and examples in earlier chapters: How might you apply the notion of the double encounter to Kuly's story about Alice (chapter 2)? What connections might you make to the teacher candidates' discussion of their unexpected moments in Afterschool U (chapter 3)? How might you add the theoretical and philosophical perspectives highlighted in this chapter to think about the students' experiences in Pedrogosso (chapter 4)? In what ways do the questions about difference and otherness in this chapter speak to the challenges and possibilities articulated by Dei (chapter 1)?

THINKING VISUALLY: CHAPTER ORGANIZER

In this figure, interconnected circles show the movement and relatedness of four concepts: transcultural contexts, curriculum as complicated conversations, inter-listening, and transcultural literacies. Transcultural contexts are marked by ethical local/global questions and moral dilemmas. When the difficult issues and questions of our contemporary communities and world are invited to become curriculum, they inspire complicated conversations, engaging existential questions about ourselves, our relationships to others, and our world (e.g., Who am I in relationship to you? How do you see me? How then, does my perception of myself change?). This attunement becomes possible through inter-listening, an approach to listening that leads learners into genuine conversations, allowing the familiar to become unfamiliar as seen through the perspective of the other. Inter-listening develops sensitivity to the desires of belongingness, and to practices of transcultural literacies. The ability to hear the voices of others breaks down stereotypes and misconceptions, transforming curriculum experiences into double encounters: an encounter of learning with the other and thus, an encounter of learning about one's self.

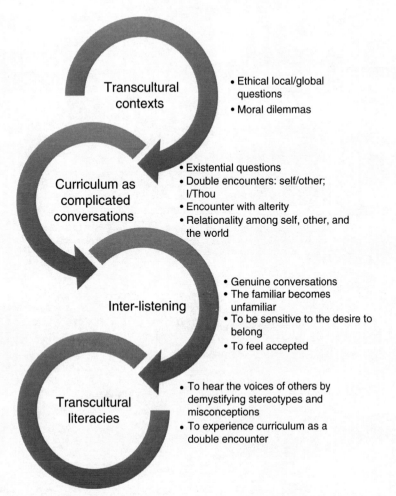

Transcultural contexts
- Ethical local/global questions
- Moral dilemmas

Curriculum as complicated conversations
- Existential questions
- Double encounters: self/other; I/Thou
- Encounter with alterity
- Relationality among self, other, and the world

Inter-listening
- Genuine conversations
- The familiar becomes unfamiliar
- To be sensitive to the desire to belong
- To feel accepted

Transcultural literacies
- To hear the voices of others by demystifying stereotypes and misconceptions
- To experience curriculum as a double encounter

Source: Figure by Karla Costa

CHAPTER 6

Transcultural Literacies as Provocations to Understand the Other: Ethically Responding to Local/Global Questions

Burcu Yaman Ntelioglou and Tim Skuce

> One time we're busy getting up a neighbourhood game of cowboys and Indians. Except back then it was "cowboys and itchybums"—kids bein' kids and all. Naturally being the only itchybum in the crowd my role was easily cast. No one could understand why I broke into tears that day. No one could understand why I dropped my little guns and holster and ran indoors and up to my room, and I, in turn, couldn't understand why everyone at the supper table that night broke into uncontrollable laughter when I was asked about it and I explained, "'Cause I don't know how to be an Indian!" (Wagamese, 1994, p. 19)

Garnet Raven, the fictional boy in Richard Wagamese's (1994) transcultural text, *Keeper'n Me*, who experienced this troubling childhood encounter, is marginalized and subjected to taken-for-granted understandings about his cultures, traditions, and identities. Garnet's encounter—his interaction with the other kids—is fraught with suffering and the recognition that he is framed within a stereotypical gaze. Garnet is cast as an "itchybum," an identity that is unknown to him. In his own words, he does not "know how to be an Indian!" This transcultural novel follows Garnet's existential journey while exposing important ethical questions about what it takes to live in solidarity in transcultural times.

Given today's transcultural context, we are persistently confronted with pressing ethical local/global questions and moral dilemmas, as evidenced in the excerpt above. These ethical questions demand us, all citizens, to address past and present injustices toward Indigenous peoples, displacement and suffering of refugees and immigrants, and environmental degradation. A current priority for Canada is the Truth and Reconciliation Commission's Calls to Action (2015), which explicitly highlight that reconciliation is a responsibility for all citizens: "Reconciliation is not merely an Aboriginal problem, it is a Canadian one. Virtually all aspects of Canadian society may need to be reconsidered" (p. vi).

Our intention in this chapter is to examine how transcultural literacies provide an invitation to venture into existential questions. The authors of this chapter are faculty members in a department of curriculum and pedagogy where our responsibilities include teaching pre-service candidates and graduate students. We address three questions in our teaching and research: (i) How might we understand and enact curriculum in transcultural times?; (ii) How do we cultivate ethical judgments in ourselves and our students (K–12 students, pre-service teacher candidates, and graduate students) to bring into question our and their taken-for-granted ways of knowing and being and to consider new possibilities for self, other, and the world?; and (iii) How are we to respond to difference in transcultural times in a way that life together honours the frailty and vulnerability of all lives?

Our pedagogical commitment, to borrow Gert Biesta's (2014) words, is to "open up existential possibilities for students, that is, possibilities in and through which students can explore what it might mean to exist as subjects in the world" (p. 3). This pedagogical goal is supported in the curriculum documents that we teach. For example, the Manitoba English language arts (ELA) curriculum clearly articulates this goal by stating:

> If Manitoba students are to understand, develop, and deepen their sense of identity/self, draw upon and harness multiple ways of knowing, thinking, and doing, and live well together in an interconnected world, students need many opportunities to explore questions and concerns about themselves and the world. (Manitoba Education, 2017)

Similarly, the social studies curriculum, the framework for all K–12 classrooms, stresses the importance of taking up existential questions of self, other, and the world:

> Diversity of perspectives, beliefs and values, disagreement and dissension are part of living in a democratic society. Furthermore, discussion

and debate concerning ethical or existential questions ... make learning
more personally meaningful. (Manitoba Education, Citizen and Youth,
2003, p. 6)

Even though in the provincial curriculum documents for the subjects we
teach (English language arts, social studies, English as an additional language, drama, curriculum inquiry, etc.) the vitality in engaging in existential questions is explicitly stated, our pre-service and graduate students in the
Faculty of Education often struggle to see why questions of identities and
subjectivities matter when they are learning to teach. Under the weight of
a dominant ethos that presses educators toward covering the curriculum in
the form of predetermined goals, objectives, and outcomes, teacher candidates
express an urgent desire for a tool kit, a collection of methods that are universally applicable, secure, and risk free, and that promise success for all students.
In common educational parlance, this reveals itself in the search for "best
practices," the scientific claim of universal method. Biesta (2014) critiques
this desire for education to be strong and certain. He points to the beautiful
risk of the "weakness" of education. The "weakness" is that when we venture
into profound questions of existence, identity, and ethics, we ought not expect certain, universal, prepackaged answers from our students and ourselves.
Rather, "weakness" refers to keeping the subject matter open to questions and
susceptible to additional interpretations—affording the possibility of understanding and being understood differently. Risk is present because "students
are not to be seen as objects to be molded and disciplined, but as subjects of
action and responsibility" (Biesta, 2014, p. 1). Risk is present when we put our
own understandings in play with others. We risk, at times, altering and even
shattering our own previously held understandings of a topic and understand
it anew. If we take the risk out of education, Biesta argues, "there is a real
chance that we take out education altogether" (p. 1). Education is not simply
the transmission of inert knowledge or information. In transcultural times,
the educative moment calls for a dynamic and ongoing quest of responding
to the ever emerging and pressing questions of our current contexts. Marjorie
Orellana (2017) poignantly describes the hopes for transculturality in literacy
practices with her question:

What kind of literacy practices could facilitate helping people find
their loyalties and forge their identities not in a kinship group, village,
nation-state, religious or political affiliation, race or ethnicity but as

citizens of the world, taking collective responsibility for that world and everything in it? (p. ix)

Thus, transcultural literacy practices require us, educators and students, to take responsibility as citizens of the world by forging new loyalties and identities beyond what we already know. We have come to understand ourselves and the world through our families, countries, nations, religions, ethnic backgrounds, etc. But as citizens of the world in transcultural times, there is an ethical urgency to enlarge our understandings in relations with all others. Transcultural literacies provide spaces that can help us see new possibilities and imagine new future relationships.

THEORETICAL FRAMEWORK

Globalization, migration, and digital technologies have intensified transculturality. The etymology of the Latin origin word *trans* is defined as "across, over, beyond" ("Trans," n.d.). Therefore, we understand transculturality as "moving across, over and beyond single cultures." Transculturality takes culture beyond national borders, referring to the hybridity, interactions, and interdependencies of cultures and identities. Nussbaum (2002) asserts that one cannot determine or control where one is born, whether in Afghanistan, Canada, France, India, Senegal, Vietnam, or elsewhere. Nussbaum stresses that the goal of education is to cultivate ethical responsibility that extends beyond a singular or homogenized national identity, to a global sensibility to act responsibly as a citizen of the world.

What does the embodiment of transculturality look like for educators? How do we practice transcultural literacies? The theoretical framework that we draw upon to answer these two important questions is the notion of "reconceptualization of the curriculum" which calls for the inquiry into the self/ other as examined by Aoki et al. (2005), Biesta (2014), Gadamer (2004), Lipari (2014), Pinar (2004/2012), and Smith (1999). Transcultural literacy practices invite the fostering of an ethical relationality among educators, students, and curriculum topics. In alliance with the goals of transcultural literacies, the reconceptualist theory of curriculum necessitates placing educators and students at the centre of the quest of understanding the other and the world. The reconceptualist theory of curriculum (Grumet, 1988, 1992/2015; Pinar, 2004/2012) emphasizes studying ourselves and our experiences of being in the world as an invitation to perceive them freshly, "washing away the film of habit and dust collected over time" (Grumet, 1988, p. 81) so that we might see them anew. The stereotypical way of seeing the other and the world, such as the framing of Garnet as "itchybum" shared in the introduction, is an example of the "film of habit and dust collected over time." Reconceptualist curriculum invites us to examine these stereotypical representations and become aware of our own prejudices through inquiry into the self, so that we can wash away these taken-for-granted assumptions.

McClintock (1971) suggests that the existential quest as defined in curriculum documents is the ongoing inquiry into the self. Yet, this is not a private project, no soloist venture. It necessitates encounters with others. We stress the importance of taking a questioning stance to our positionality when we conceptualize curriculum in this way. It is the recognition of the unfamiliar through the eyes and voice of the other that makes new understandings possible. Encounters with the other rupture our preformed, assumed understandings of ourselves and the world.

Reconceptualist curriculum moves away from instrumentalist views of teaching and learning, and puts the examination of the self in relation with the other as the educational project. Pinar and Grumet (1976/2015) write: "What is missing is the study of the student's point of view from the student's point of view. What is missing is the portrayal of the self from the point of view of the self" (pp. 22–23). The practice of what transcultural literacies aim to create is a space for the voice of the other to be heard and the self to be examined. We are employing Hans-Georg Gadamer's (2004) notion of the I/Thou relationship in order to more explicitly describe the practice of being in an ethical relationship with the other. Gadamer outlines three possible ways of being in relation with the other. The first and second ways, which we describe next, reflect how people often approach their relationships with difference. However, Gadamer's third way of being in relation with the other, which we explore later in this chapter, represents for us what transculturality desires to achieve.

Gadamer (2004) differentiates three ways that the Thou is experienced: as an object, as a person, and as a partner in a mutual relationship (see pp. 367–368). Monica Vilhauer (2010) problematizes the first relationship, that of experiencing the other as an object, by stating that the I approaches the Thou "as a 'thing' stands at a distance from [its] object ... so that it [the I] may objectively categorize its qualities, calculate its movements ... to anticipate the thing's future behavior to develop some control, mastery, or dominance over it" (p. 77). In education, this limited, confining casting of the other as an object could take the form of enacting judgments about individual students predicated on a presumed fixed social category, such as a black student, EAL student, disabled student, Indigenous student—as if this category were the sole determinant of who the student is. The second problem when Thou is experienced as an object in this way is that we cannot learn about the other when we assume to already know. We fail to achieve an enlarged understanding of ourselves as well as the other. Gadamer (2004) accentuates the ethical commitment to hearing the voice of the other, explaining that "the other should never be used as a means but always as an end to himself" (p. 78). Similarly, Vilhauer (2010) states that perceiving the other as a means to an end disregards the dignity of the other and negates the moral bond.

A second way Thou is experienced and understood is that the Thou is acknowledged as a person, yet the understanding is still a form of "self-relatedness" (p. 367). In Gadamer's (2004) words, "One claims to know the other's claim from [their] point of view and even to understand the other better than the other understands [themselves]" (p. 367). This second way that claims "I know what you mean" is a shortcoming. Vilhauer (2010) contends that taking the other seriously entails "treating what [the other] has to say as a potential truth that could transform what we think or act, rather than as a mere attitude, a subjective reflection" (p. 79). The self-relatedness here is best illustrated with the common expression "putting ourselves in the shoes of the other." Nel Noddings (1984/2003) troubles the experiencing of the other in this second way. She suggests we not seek to answer the question "How would I feel in such a situation?" (p. 30). On the contrary, to hear the voice of the other, we should be ready to risk our preunderstandings and "set aside [our] temptation to analyze and to plan" (p. 30). Gadamer (2004) cautions us that "the dialectical of charitable or welfare work operates in this way, penetrating all relationships between [human beings] as a reflective form of the effort to dominate" (p. 368). Unless we recognize that we are all imbued with prejudices, we will deny legitimacy to the voice of the other. Thus, this second way of experiencing the I/Thou destroys the moral bond between self and other.

The third way the I/Thou relationship is experienced is the most ethical form of encountering the other. This is a profoundly relational state that embodies a comportment of openness that orients one to the art of strengthening the voice of the other. Through dialogic and dialectic encounter, the speaker, the listener, and the subject matter/worldview are transformed. Maurice

Merleau-Ponty (1962) describes the reciprocity required in dialogic experience as follows:

> We are collaborators for each other in consummate reciprocity. Our perspectives merge into each other and we co-exist through a common world. In the present dialogue, I am freed from myself, for the other person's thoughts are certainly his; they are not of my making, though I do grasp them the moment they come into being, or even anticipate them. (p. 49)

The third way honours reciprocity and results in a *double encounter* in which we hear the voice of the other in its otherness and let the voice of the other decentre our own previously held understandings. Lisbeth Lipari (2014) elucidates this notion of the double encounter with the simile of "shedding, like a snake's skin, our old views and certainties about our world" (p. 188). With the double encounter, we venture out into the world with the other, and return back anew. This venturing results in renewed understandings of the other as well as renewed understandings of ourselves.

INTERPRETIVE ANALYSIS

We investigate Wagamese's (1994) *Keeper'n Me* to examine the multiplicities of the I/Thou, self/other relationships in this text. Garnet Raven encounters multiple others, both animate and inanimate, throughout the novel, such as his encounters with Lonnie, Delma, the letter from his brother Stanley, his mother, the Keeper, and the land, which we explore in this section. Each of these encounters poses existential questions and presents new possibilities for enlarged understandings of self and other for Garnet. It is these enlarged understandings that inform Garnet's process of becoming more attuned and open. Chris Higgins (2011) describes this kind of openness by saying that "opening one's mind proceeds only through the slow and sometimes painful process of extending, refining, and demanding one's generalisations, not through jettisoning them" (p. 131). Through familial relationships and complicated conversations with others, Garnet reconstitutes his history, making meaning of past, present, and possible futures.

Keeper'n Me follows the pathway of Garnet's life from a young child taken unwillingly from his home on an Ojibway Indian reserve, unbeknownst to his parents, by government officials following a deeply racist and unethical federal law. The story depicts Garnet's childhood and adolescence as he experiences an unending string of foster homes. His restlessness and sense of impermanence are reflected in his compulsion to be constantly on the move from place to place. As an adult in prison, Garnet receives a letter from his brother Stanley, from whom he had been separated since he was a young boy. At Stanley's request, Garnet returns to the White Dog Reservation, a place foreign and forgotten to him because he had been severed from his home at age three. Upon returning to the reserve, he is able to unlearn his restlessness and relearn how to reside in a place, a space where he navigates once-familiar territories with the help of the teachings of the Keeper, a respected holder of the traditions and history of the White Dog Reservation.

One of Garnet's significant relations with the other explored in the novel is with the Keeper. This relationship spawns multiple double encounters. The Keeper's pedagogical orientation is attuned and present to Garnet. He does not offer predetermined answers or options, but rather creates opportunities for Garnet to venture with existential questions so that he can arrive at renewed understandings. Through the Keeper's guidance, Garnet finds belongingness as he discovers his people's ways of being and living. In the following excerpt, which extends the quotation that opened this chapter, Garnet describes his experience of unlearning and relearning:

> One time we're busy getting up a neighbourhood game of cowboys and Indians. Except back then it was "cowboys and itchybums"—kids bein' kids and all. Naturally being the only itchybum in the crowd my role was easily cast. No one could understand why I broke into tears that day. No one could understand why I dropped my little guns and holster and ran indoors and up to my room, and I, in turn, couldn't understand why everyone at the supper table that night broke into uncontrollable laughter when I was asked about it and I explained, "'Cause I don't know how to be an Indian!" That's how it was for me growing up. I was embarrassed about being an Indian and I was afraid that if I ever met a real one I wouldn't know what to do or say. So I started to try to fit into that white world as best as I could. I decided that I would try to learn to be anything other than what I was. I didn't want to be compared to any of the images that I had of my own people, of myself. But this brown skin of mine was always a pretty good clue to most people that there

must have been a redskin or two creeping around my mama's woodpile. So at various times I was Hawaiian, Polynesian, Mexican or Chinese. Anything but Indian. Those people on the street that day still haunted me. Of course, if I got cornered on evidence then I became any one of four famous kinds of Indian. I was either Apache, Sioux, Cherokee, Comanche. Everyone had heard of those Indians. I mean, if you absolutely had to be an Indian, at least be one that everyone had heard of. Embarrassed as I was at the time I sure didn't want to be Passamaquoddy, Flathead, Dogrib or Ojibway. Aiming for the romantic was my game plan. (pp. 19–20)

The image of children playing often conjures their innocence as they joyfully interact, becoming lost in their participation. Roles are unabashedly assumed for some, while others feel strange or lost. In the seemingly innocent play described in the excerpt above, Garnet's recalled encounter instantiates an overwhelming sense of estrangement, of alienation. He is thrust into a predefined role, a taken-for-grantedness: "After all, it's just playing."

The notion of innocence is emblematic. Gadamer (2004) suggests that long before we critically self-examine ourselves, we inherit other people's stories. The pejorative "itchybums" illustrates how language can also be shaped by dominant ideologies. In the encounter, Garnet was positioned as the best candidate to play the role. In his words, "naturally being the only itchybum in the crowd," his role was easily cast. This positioning brings him into existential questioning such as David Jardine (in Jardine, Friesen, & Clifford, 2006) describes: "First is the question posed, not by us but to us" (p. 91). Garnet's explanation of why he extricates himself points to an internalized oppression: "'Cause I don't know how to be an Indian!" As Gadamer (2004) suggests, we are already imbued with certain ways of understanding ourselves and others. We are always already formed by systemic dominant narratives. Jonathan Lear (2006) points to this phenomenon as "acquir[ing] a capacity for self-regulation by monitoring one's acts in relation to an internal judge" governed by dominant discourses (pp. 85–86). Stanley Porter (in Robinson & Porter, 2011) suggests that "understanding is never without presuppositions of preformed prejudices, for there is no neutral or unbiased starting place from which to begin to understand. There is only the place and situation in which we always already find ourselves" (p. 60). In this view, we are always already embedded within a historicity that exposes and imposes particular narratives. Similarly,

Judith Butler's (2015) notion of performativity suggests that through an utterance we are thrust into existence, and choice comes after.

As Garnet continues to move from place to place, he settles for an extended period in Toronto, where he befriends Lonnie Flowers. Lonnie is charismatic and possesses a forthright demeanour that challenges Garnet to be himself for the first time. In Garnet's words: "I remember thinking that this was the first time I'd ever hit it off with someone without having to run a game on them. It didn't seem to matter to Lonnie Flowers that I was Indian and it sure didn't matter to me that he was black" (pp. 27–28). Garnet develops a close friendship with Lonnie and feels accepted as a family member. Though Lonnie and his family lovingly embrace Garnet, they also provoke him to seek out his own family and Indigenous heritage, and they encourage him to foster a sense of belonging and self-identity. When Garnet's brother Stanley finally tracks him down, he explains how Garnet was taken from his family as a young child, how their family searched for him for many years, and how Children's Aid had denied them any information. Stanley pleads with Garnet to return home. Lonnie and his family's supportive spirit and profound sense of care for his well-being provide a disruption—a provocation inspired by encouraging Garnet to seek out his biological family and cultural heritage.

"Gonna have to face it someday, my man," Lonnie said, pointing back over his shoulder with his thumb. "Can't run away from who you really are all your life, y'know."

"Who's runnin', man? I'm doin' what I want with my life, okay? Besides, what have those dudes got to say that would matter to me anyway?"

"Never know till you find out, will ya?"

"Find out what?"

"Shit, man, I don't know. Indian stuff. What it's like out there livin' Indian, man. Maybe the brothers came up the same as you or maybe they know somethin' about it all you ain't ever figured out. I don't know."

"I don't know either, man. All I know is that I've been around this town now about a year and a half which is longer'n I ever stayed anywhere and I don't wanna be anywhere else. I don't wanna be anywhere or anybody else, okay? You got a problem with that?"

"Ain't never a problem, you know that. I'm just sayin' this 'cause I think you be missin' out on sumpthin' important, that's all, man. Thass all. Don't be goin' all Arapaho on me, brother."

"Fine. That's it then."

"S'it, man."

"Okay."

"Okay."

But it wasn't it really. The more I thought about that conversation the more I started to see the truth in it. (p. 35)

Scholars such as Gadamer (2004) and Lipari (2014) describe the power of the dialectic in I/Thou and self/other relationships. This dialogic encounter has the potential to elicit a provocation that is capable of opening us up to previously hidden understandings of our lives. These genuine conversations with trusted others have the capacity to make the familiar strange to us. Lonnie's role in this conversation with Garnet is significant. In the experience of dialogue, Lonnie is attuned to Garnet's yearning to belong. The story is narrated by Garnet, and the reader is not privy to Lonnie's innermost thoughts as they pertain to Garnet. However, Lonnie's capacities to hear and his compassion are revealed to the reader through Garnet's recollection of their interactions. Lipari (2014) suggests that compassion is listening "that suspends the willfulness of self and foreknowledge in order to receive the singularities of the alterity of the other" (p. 185). Garnet, as evidenced by his persistent avoidance, assumes multiple masks to avoid addressing his own familial connections and disconnections. Lonnie is attuned to these masks and challenges Garnet to confront them. Yet he does not subsume Garnet. He does not assume to know him as the other. He recognizes Garnet's struggles to understand his own family and ancestral history. Lonnie is sensitive to Garnet's desire to belong. Lonnie acknowledges that Garnet attaches this desire to belong to Lonnie's family. Lonnie does not deny the love and belonging Garnet feels toward Lonnie's family, yet he also challenges him to seek and understand his own history—a history of forced separation that resulted in a negation of historical belonging. Nor does Lonnie attempt to determine or dictate what Garnet should be thinking and doing. He is able to appreciate "opaqueness" and to honour Garnet's otherness. It is perhaps Lonnie's own marginal status as a black man that enables his attunement toward the other. The notion of being "Indian" does not exist in a fixed or static group identity.

Garnet's understandings of the way he has lived his life—that is, persisting in denying his Indigenous ancestry—become manifest in multiple masks he wears to hide his heritage. Lonnie brings into question Garnet's belongingness. Lonnie's sister Delma also challenges Garnet to confront his resistance to explore his past and inquire into his roots:

> "You look like a man needsa home," Delma said. "You always did look that way. Can't be movin' around forever. You gotta find yourself some roots and it's sad to say … but they ain't with us. Your roots are callin' you right now and if you run from this you'll be runnin' from ev'rythin' forever'n ever." (p. 41)

These conversations with Lonnie and Delma are encounters that act as catalysts for Garnet to seek out understandings of home—with self and other. He says: "I'd found myself and for all I knew there was no goin' back" (p. 36). These words, in part, prompt Garnet to contact Stanley and precipitate his return home to White Dog. When he arrives, he embraces his mother, despite his initial hesitancy as a natural consequence of years of separation. He describes how he lost himself in his mother's heartbeat. Describing this embrace, Garnet conveys a deep, embodied feeling of knowing, of familial recognition of self and other:

> We stood there sobbing away, hugging tighter and tighter still. And then as the tears began to quiet down the magic happened. Our breathing got slower and deeper. Still locked in that hug I started to be able to feel the rhythm of her heartbeat against the empty side of my chest. My attention got focused on it and I felt its barrrrumpa, barrrrumpa echoing through me. And bit by bit as I lost myself in that heartbeat, any doubt I ever had about this woman being my mother began to disappear. My speeding brain got quieter and quieter and I felt more and more relaxed and safe and sheltered and warm until I began to realize that I'd felt this same way somewhere back in my past. I don't know what it was but something somewhere deep inside me recognized that heartbeat. (pp. 77–78)

After their reunion, Garnet learns from his mother the anguish and torment that had been inflicted on the family as a result of Garnet and his siblings being forcefully apprehended by government officials during the Sixties Scoop. This apprehension had severe and lasting implications for a young child of three. In Garnet's words, "When I was three I disappeared. I disappeared into foster homes and never made it back until I was twenty-five" (p. 12).

Garnet's mother and grandmother found out why the children had gone missing in a detached, officious correspondence the following day. Garnet's mother recollects this traumatizing experience:

> We di'n' know what to do. We come home that day an' your granny was runnin' around all crazy lookin' for you kids. We searched the bush and called for you all that night. Was round noon next day when they came with their letter'n tol' us what was goin' on. We di'n' understand. Your dad, he never did. We di'n' know nothin' 'bout their system then, di'n' know we coulda fought it. We jus' thought we failed you all. (p. 81)

Upon Garnet's return to the reservation, he first meets the Keeper at the family gathering. This relationship, over time, emerges as a caring pedagogical relationship. The Keeper is a long-time friend of Garnet's mother. The two had met in the same residential school. The Keeper acknowledges that if one is going to learn, there needs to be willingness on the part of the learner. The encounter with the other in this case is the encounter with the land. The Keeper describes this reciprocal relationship: "The land's like that. Let yourself be part of it an' it's always gonna give you back a part of yourself you never knew you had. Good friend that land" (p. 238).

Through Garnet's double encounters with multiple others—Lonnie, Delma, the letter from his brother Stanley, his mother, the Keeper, and the land—he cultivates an attunement and openness to self, other, and the world. Each of these double encounters brings into question his own historicity, making the familiar unfamiliar. Through these relationships, he is confronted with his finitude and the corresponding suffering induced by his limited understandings of himself, the other, and the world. He is willing to greet and embrace the other's difference. This brings forth the relevance of a moral bond in the double encounter that Gadamer's third I/Thou relationship points to. When we examine the relations of self/other and the notion of the double encounter with pre-service teachers or K–12 students, we find that stories of transcultural identities such as Garnet's stories in *Keeper'n Me* create an opening up to other ways of understanding the world.

CONCLUSION AND EDUCATIONAL SIGNIFICANCE

Transcultural literacies offer possibilities to embrace difference, to hear the voices of others by demystifying stereotypes and misconceptions. Reading literary transcultural texts in K–12 and post-secondary classrooms cultivates a sensitivity and sensibility to the textured nature of human identities. The imaginative power of this orientation has the potential to fracture taken-for-granted ways of understanding and to re-envision a world that honours the diversity of human life and solidarity.

Educere, the Latin root for the word *education*, means to lead the young out into the world to study their educational experiences and return with renewed understandings. The third I/Thou relationship, the double encounter, as Gadamer suggests, is the recognition and humility that acknowledges our limits and fosters enlarged understandings of ways of being in the world. This relationality in the third I/Thou has been the central focus of this chapter, and also of our teaching. Once one comes to an understanding of the other, it calls for an ethical praxis. Garnet's multiple encounters, which we drew on in our analysis of the novel *Keeper'n Me*, illustrate the radical openness we invite our teacher candidates to embody.

In today's world, urgent and pressing ethical questions concerning diversity in transcultural times call for a collective ethical response. Gadamer (2007) declares that one must foster a hermeneutic virtue, and that

> if we do not realise that it is essential first of all to understand the other person, if we are ever to see whether in the end perhaps something like the solidarity of humanity as a whole may be possible, especially in relation to our living together and surviving together—if we do not do this, then we will never be able to accomplish the essential tasks of humanity, whether on a small scale or large. (p. 119)

Implications for Classrooms

As educators, we have a responsibility to invite our students to engage in ethical questions concerning pressing local/global issues. We would like educators to consider the Truth and Reconciliation Commission's Calls to Action (2015) that point to the urgency of the need for renewed understandings about the practice of teaching and learning:

> Students must be able to make ethical judgments about the actions of their ancestors while recognizing that the moral sensibilities of the past may be quite different from their own in present times. They must be able to make informed decisions about what responsibilities society has

to address historical injustices. Thus, we will ensure that tomorrow's citizens are both knowledgeable and caring about the injustices of the past, as these relate to their own futures. (p. 240)

Engaging in existential questions requires a certain kind of practice. Every classroom is unique, with particular students, contexts, and relationships; therefore there is no universal list of strategies to simply implement. However, it is our intention that this chapter orients teachers, teacher candidates, and K–12 students to a way of comporting ourselves with the other. We propose educators consider the following as a mode of praxis:

Use transcultural texts to inquire into difference: We invite teachers and teacher candidates to engage in reading and collaborative analysis of transcultural literacy texts (novels, film, art, poetry, short stories, lyrics, theatre, etc.) in order to travel across borders that are geographic as well as socially constructed, such as gender, language, culture, race. Encounters with difference across borders provoke educators and students to examine transcultural identities whose lives are very different from their own. As Orellana (2017) suggests, the experience of transcultural literacies helps us understand the ways of seeing the world and imagining the world anew:

> The power of literacy is not just that it allows words and ideas to travel across time and space and to move across borders that sometimes keep people out. It is that words can travel between minds and hearts. They can open our hearts and minds, taking us into the experience of people whose lives are very different from our own. They can help us to see new possibilities and to imagine the world as we want it to be, not just as it is now. (Orellana, 2017, p. ix)

Be open to take up existential questions: In line with the articulated curriculum goals to explore existential questions, we encourage educators to cultivate an openness to put at risk their own previously held understandings about themselves, others, and the world. This comportment of openness is what Biesta (2014) describes as the notion of the beautiful risk of the weakness of education. It is this "weakness" instead of "a strong and fixed predetermined learning outcome" that provides space for creative and generative possibilities for enlarged understandings to see things otherwise and imagine the world anew.

Do not fear your own limited understandings pertaining to an unfamiliar topic: At times teachers fear, avoid, and turn away from complex and unfamiliar topics. Regardless of what we know of something, we are always limited and finite in our understandings. Instead of turning away from these topics, it is important to carry ourselves with the humility of not knowing. The comportment of learning to dwell on these topics is through bringing forth our own and our students' lived experiences of the topic, putting these understandings into question as a way to foster new understandings. Understanding begins when we put forth our understandings in play with others. The call to *study* is to seek the plurality of the voices on the topic. This can be done through examination of transcultural novels, films, and discourses from multiple disciplines, as well as invitations to dialogue with knowledgeable others. Transcultural literacies expose the multiplicity of voices honouring the commitment to co-creation of knowledge in our classrooms.

Create opportunities for the voice of the other to be heard through cultivating complicated conversations in the classroom: Complicated conversation (Pinar, 2004/2012; Pinar & Grumet, 1976/2015) is the meeting place where the voices of individuals with different histories and experiences are invited to share perspectives and challenge taken-for-granted understandings of the topic of inquiry. Complicated conversation as a method of engaging curriculum provides an opportunity for a double encounter: first, an encounter with the stranger—someone/something *other*; and second, an encounter with one's own finitude and historicity. It is in and through our complicated conversations with others that we as teachers may confront challenges to our previously held understandings. For example, in the novel *Keeper'n Me*, through Garnet's complicated conversations with multiple others—Lonnie, Delma, his brother Stanley, his mother, the Keeper, and the land—he is able to overcome his initial resistance to the idea of exploring his Indigenous connections. In a poignant complicated conversation with Lonnie, Garnet comes to recognize his initial resistance and decides to open himself to the risk of venturing to seek his Indigenous connections and heritage: "The more I thought about that conversation the more I started to see the truth in it" (p. 35). This quote for us points to the possibility of hearing the voice of the other through complicated conversations. This is the relational space of reciprocity needed to take up pressing ethical questions in our worlds inside and outside the classroom.

QUESTIONS FOR REFLECTION AND DISCUSSION

1. How can transcultural literacies unsettle familiar, taken-for-granted assumptions about self, other, and the world? How might we understand and enact curriculum in transcultural times?

2. How do we cultivate ethical judgments in ourselves and our students (K–12 students, teacher candidates, and graduate students) to bring into question our and their taken-for-granted ways of knowing and being, and to consider new possibilities for self, other, and the world?

3. How can we best respond to difference in a way that honours the fragility and vulnerability of all lives?

4. How can reading be an act of transformation for the reader(s)? Can you give an example of how a book or another text of some kind (e.g., oral story, film, art, photography, short story) has created a double encounter for you?

DEEPEN YOUR INQUIRY: RELATED READINGS AND RESOURCES

Aoki, T. T., Pinar, W., & Irwin, R. L. (2005). *Curriculum in a new key: The collected works of Ted T. Aoki*. Mahwah, NJ: Lawrence Erlbaum.

Biesta, G. J. (2014). *The beautiful risk of education (Interventions: Education, philosophy, and culture)*. Boulder, CO: Paradigm.

Hubbard, T. (Director). (2017). *Birth of a family* [Film]. Canada: National Film Board.

Justice, D. H. (2018). *Why Indigenous literatures matter*. Waterloo, ON: Wilfrid Laurier Press.

Luke, A. (2017). No grand narrative in sight: On double consciousness and critical literacy. *Literacy Research: Theory, Method, and Practice, 66*, 157–182.

Pinar, W. (2009). *The worldliness of a cosmopolitan education: Passionate lives in public service*. New York: Routledge.

Reder, D., & Morra, L. M. (Eds.). (2016). *Learn, teach, challenge: Approaching Indigenous literatures*. Waterloo, ON: Wilfrid Laurier University Press.

Smith, D. G. (2006). *Trying to teach in a season of great untruth: Globalization, empire and the crisis of pedagogy*. Rotterdam, the Netherlands: Sense Publishers.

Wagamese, R. (2012). *Indian horse*. Toronto: Douglas & McIntyre.

Wagamese, R. (2014). *Medicine walk*. Toronto: McClelland & Stewart.

REFERENCES

Aoki, T. T., Pinar, W., & Irwin, R. L. (2005). *Curriculum in a new key: The collected works of Ted T. Aoki*. Mahwah, NJ: Lawrence Erlbaum.

Biesta, G. J. (2014). *The beautiful risk of education (Interventions: Education, philosophy, and culture)*. Boulder, CO: Paradigm.

Butler, J. (2015). *Notes towards a performative theory of assembly*. Cambridge, MA: Harvard University Press.

Gadamer, H.-G. (2004). *Truth and method*. New York: Seabury Press.

Gadamer, H.-G. (2007). *Gadamer reader: A bouquet of later writings*. Evanston, IL: Northwestern University Press.

Grumet, M. R. (1988). *Bitter milk*. Amherst, MA: University of Massachusetts Press.

Grumet, M. R. (1992/2015). Existential and phenomenological foundations of autobiographical methods. In W. F. Pinar & W. M. Reynolds (Eds.), *Understanding curriculum as phenomenological and deconstructed text* (2nd ed.; pp. 28–43). New York: Teachers College Press.

Higgins, C. (2011). *The good life of teaching: An ethics of professional practice*. West Sussex, UK: Blackwell.

Jardine, D. W., Friesen, S., & Clifford, P. (2006). *Curriculum in abundance*. Mahwah, NJ: Lawrence Erlbaum.

Lear, J. (2006). *Radical hope*. Cambridge, MA: Harvard University Press.

Lipari, L. (2014). *Listening, thinking, being: Toward an ethics of attunement*. University Park, PA: Pennsylvania State University Press.

Manitoba Education. (2017). *Draft English language arts document to support initial implementation*. Winnipeg: Manitoba Education.

Manitoba Education, Citizenship and Youth. (2003). *Kindergarten to Grade 8 social studies Manitoba curriculum framework of outcomes*. Winnipeg: Manitoba Education.

McClintock, R. (1971). Toward a place for study in a world of instruction. *Teachers College Record, 73*(2), 161–205.

Merleau-Ponty, M. (1962). *Phenomenology of perception*. London: Routledge.

Noddings, N. (1984/2003). *A feminist approach to ethics and moral education* (2nd ed.). Berkeley: University of California Press.

Nussbaum, M. (2002). Education for citizenship in an era of global connection. *Studies in Philosophy and Education, 21*(4–5), 289–303.

Orellana, M. F. (2017). Foreword. In R. Zaidi and J. Rowsell (Eds.), *Literacy lives in transcultural times* (pp. viii–x). London, UK: Routledge.

Pinar, W. (2004/2012). *What is curriculum theory?* (2nd ed.). New York: Routledge.

Pinar, W., & Grumet, M. (1976/2015). *Toward a poor curriculum* (3rd ed.). Kingston, NY: Educational International Press.

Robinson, J. C., & Porter, S. E. (2011). *Hermeneutics: An introduction to interpretive theory.* Oxford, UK: Oxford University Press.

Smith, D. G. (1999). *Pedagon: Interdisciplinary essays in the human sciences, pedagogy, and culture.* New York: Peter Lang.

Trans. (n.d.). *The Online Etymology Dictionary.* Retrieved from https://www.etymonline.com/word/trans-

Truth and Reconciliation Commission of Canada. (2015). Calls to action. Winnipeg: Truth and Reconciliation Commission of Canada.

Vilhauer, M. (2010). *Gadamer's ethics of play: Hermeneutics and the other.* Plymouth, UK: Lexington Books.

Wagamese, R. (1994/2016). *Keeper'n Me.* Brantford, ON: W. Ross MacDonald School Resource Services Library.

Transcultural Literacies: Deconstructing the Colonization of Schools and Rebuilding an Education System for All of Us

As we talk about transcultural literacy, we are talking about the need to return to
the beginning, to honour the original stories of all peoples.
—*David B. Anderson*

OPENING THE CONVERSATION: READING NOTES

In their report on the residential school system in Canada, the Truth and Reconciliation Commission (TRC, 2015) is clear that the future of Canada "requires that a new vision, based on a commitment to mutual respect, be developed" (TRC, 2015, p. vi). In that spirit, David Anderson provides a model for us, calling on us as transcultural educators to be committed to a vision of *Kenanow*, of learning and teaching about "all of us" or "all of us who are here."

Our educational system, our schools, our communities, and our country are at a pivotal juncture. In this moment, we have a "rare second chance to seize a lost opportunity for reconciliation" (TRC, 2015, p. 7). Globally, "Canada's place as a prosperous, just, and inclusive democracy ... is at stake" (TRC, 2015, p. 7). Transcultural literacies are key to the work of reconciliation locally and globally: to building new and respectful relationships "between Aboriginal and non-Aboriginal peoples in this country," to deepening our understandings of what it means to live and work together in "awareness of the past, acknowledgement of the harm that has been inflicted, atonement for the causes, and action to change behaviour" (TRC, 2015, pp. 6–7).

As we commit to this work as leaders in our schools and communities, David Anderson urges us to be vigilant: to examine the language and concepts we use and accept as "normal" in curriculum and in teaching, to question the assumptions we make in the materials we choose, and to explore the expectations we have for our students.

Within a framework of transcultural literacies, he calls for educators to continue to expand, deepen, and diversify the knowledges that we share with our students so they can be reconnected with the stories and histories of all our ancestors. As Nichola Too-kome Batzel (2012) reminds us:

> Whether you are from the North, South, East, or West there is value in considering where we have come from as much as where we are going. As our ancestors did, we must make decisions thinking about the place we stand and the place we imagine, and let this guide how we act toward one another and our children. It is important to connect to each other and to our land and ask: How do we support and acknowledge each other? How do we balance our relationships? How do we hear the voices in our home? There are many beautiful stories around us. Do you hear them? Take a moment to breathe, sit, and listen. You will be amazed by what you see and hear. (p. 339)

How do we hear the voices in our students, schools, and communities? Anderson draws on the concept of *Mino Bimadiziwin* (the good life) to show how our beliefs and choices impact each other's lives and the world. In this way, he reflects on the negative impacts of humankind on the earth, and asks about the responsibility of educational policies in this process. Anderson questions what teachers are, or are not, teaching when they follow a curriculum that assumes and imposes "the only way to think about things." From a transcultural literacies perspective, Anderson suggests that the *Kenanow* learning model provides a way forward, a vision for teaching and learning through the Teachings of Seven Grandfathers. Anderson emphasizes that in order to build and to live *Mino Bimadiziwin* in a sustainable world (for now, and for future generations), education must focus on building relationships through actively listening to everyone's stories and committing to living together in respect, honesty, truth, love, bravery, wisdom, and humility. In this way, change is possible; transcultural literacies can produce new assumptions about, and different attitudes toward, "knowledge, society, the environment, and care."

REFERENCES

Batzel, N. T. (2012). Our stories belong here too: Manitoba Inuk. In N. J. Sinclair & W. Cariou (Eds.), *Manitowapow: Aboriginal writings from the land of water* (pp. 338–343). Winnipeg: Portage & Main Press.

Truth and Reconciliation Commission of Canada. (2015). *Final report of the Truth and Reconciliation Commission of Canada, Volume 1: Summary*. Toronto: James Lorimer & Company Ltd.

THINKING VISUALLY: CHAPTER ORGANIZER

In this image, the circle is inclusive, a learning model where "all of us" are recognized, and have a place to tell our stories about:

- our origins
- the frames of mind that we value and that shape us
- the teachings we have received
- how we learn who we are, our literacies
- the artifacts that are important to us
- the mediators who have participated and continue to move in our lives
- the Creation stories we know and tell
- the languages we speak

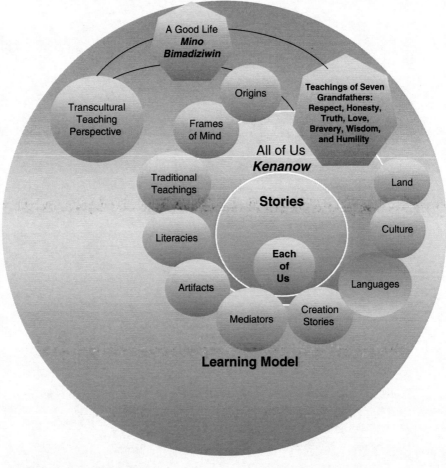

Source: Figure by Karla Costa

- how we live and understand our culture
- how we learn in relationship to the land

Bringing our stories together (as groups, communities, nations, the world) makes "All of Us": *Kenanow*. A transcultural teaching perspective emerges, then, from the concept of *Kenanow*, a learning model that includes the Teachings of the Seven Grandfathers, learning to live together in *Mino Bimadiziwin*, a relationship of respect for and responsibility to one another and the earth. As you read this chapter, consider how such a vision and commitment can be a transformative force in curriculum, teaching, and learning: What are the implications for what we teach, how we teach, with whom we teach, where we teach? In what ways do we need to re-envision our relationships with our students, and with parents, Elders, and knowledge keepers?

CHAPTER 7

Transcultural Literacies: Deconstructing the Colonization of Schools and Rebuilding an Education System for All of Us

David B. Anderson (Wahwahbiginojii)

Tansi, Edlánét'e, Boozhoo. Wahwahbiginojii Nindizhnikahz, Mukwa N'dodem, Dene/Anishinabe Indow, Atikokan Indoonjibaa, Niizho Mide Inini.

> We all have stories within us. Sometimes we hold them gingerly, sometimes des-
> perately, sometimes as gently as an infant, and it is only through sharing our sto-
> ries that it is possible "to know, recognize, and understand each other."
> —Wagamese, 2011, p. 81

It is about *Kenanow.*

As Thomas King (2003) has told us, "The truth about stories is, that's all we are" (p. 2). Transcultural literacies provide a framework from which we can begin to learn about the knowledge, skills, and lives of people from all over this world. Within this framework, we are able to acknowledge that there is more than one story about the His/story[1] of humankind and we can begin to teach the many/stories of humankind. As educators on this land, the land we know as Turtle Island, we can honour the People of this land by utilizing the stories and teachings they have shared with us in our quest to learn about *Kenanow*. Understanding and implementing the Teachings of the Seven Grandfathers will guide us as we provide learning opportunities for our students to learn about and to respect all of us. This teaching, shared by the Anishinabe,[2] guides us in our life (in my own education and talking with Elders and Language Keepers, I have discovered that there is no real word for "work" in

Anishinabe/Ojibway, as in "I have to go to work today." Instead, the Elders use the word *Bimadiziwin* [Anishinabemowin] or *Pimatisiwin* [Ininimowin] and talk about life). The teachings of respect, honesty, truth, love, bravery, wisdom, and humility were given to guide us in our lives. If we are honest about our history, if we are brave enough to tell our stories, if we are respectful of others, if we truly love this land and our relatives, and if we are humble enough to acknowledge that there are other stories, then perhaps our students will begin to love each other, and be brave enough to share the truth of their lives, so that they can be truly wise in their learning.

Transcultural literacy learning involves living with all of Creation here on Mother Earth. We begin by honouring all our ancestors, those who have lived and walked this land/planet since the beginning of time. Each of us has a Creation Story (Deloria Jr., 1992), and although there are many different Creation Stories, each one tells us that human beings were created last, after the sky, the earth, the water, and the plants, as well as after our brothers, the four-legged, the swimmers, the crawlers, and the winged ones. What is significant in their similarities is that these Creation Stories tell us that there is but one Creator who gave each people a set of instructions to live an honourable, respectful, and caring life. How we have come to live with "all of Creation" is the His/story of humankind. The question for educators is "How do we plan to live on this fragile planet in the future?" The answer lies in teaching the truth about our His/story so we can make informed, responsible decisions about how we will live with all of Creation in the future. The truth about our education system is that we do not teach the stories of others. Our task as educators, then, is to learn not only the truth about His/story, but also, the truth about ourselves, as well as each other (Katz & Lamoureux, 2018). Learning about the relationships among the many nations, and about how respect was shown or not shown to each other, will enable *Kenanow* to deliver an honest, respectful education program. Along these lines, Tagalik (2018) reminds us that "Indigenous knowledge systems are holistic in nature and grounded in an 'all-encompassing holistic view of an interconnected world'" (p. 94). This "holistic view of the world is a natural and intuitive view implying connectedness, reciprocity, and relationality—the big picture perspective" (p. 93). She explains the difference between holistic and non-holistic thinking with an analogy of travelling directions:

> We Western thinkers tend to travel off toward a destination with a specific direction in mind. If asked how to get to a place, we narrowly

describe a directional route or just use GPS points. Louis [the Inuit Elder] presents directions from the perspective of looking down on the land to be travelled through. He describes geographical features, including links to unusual land forms, flora, snowdrift patterns, animal trails, and atmospheric conditions. He uses place names that carry information about the way the land looks or the way it has been used over generations. His directions paint a mind picture that enables the traveler to build relationships with the environment. When connected in this way, these relationships will last through a lifetime. (pp. 93–94)

We now continue with Our/stories. One story/prophecy is the Prophesy of the Seven Fires (Benton Banai, 1988). This teaching told us that others would be coming to share this land with us, and we know that many nations were ready when they came. The first settlers who landed on Turtle Island were welcomed with feasts and gifts, as is our traditional way. The people also offered the first Two-Rowed Wampum, an Indigenous Treaty, as an agreement that we would share this land with you, and we will live side by side on the land. Through the lens of transcultural literacies, we can examine This/story and the events that subsequently occurred. Utilizing the concepts presented by Vygotsky (1978) and Gardner (1983), we can talk about the frames of mind of the people involved. We can examine the His/story as recorded in school textbooks, but we also need to ask how each culture saw themselves, and each other, and how they perceived the relationships that were being initiated. The Two-Rowed Wampum offered by the Anishinabe and Haudenosaunee was a treaty to indicate that our ancestors did not want to impose their culture on the newcomers, and that they did not want the newcomers to impose their culture on the original people. However, as we look at what was in the mind of the newcomer, and what was in the mind of the Anishinabe, we begin to see that there was an immense gulf in understanding this treaty and the impact it had on the people involved. What was the "frame of mind" of those who came to this land? How did they see us? What was the "frame of mind" of the Indigenous people who welcomed these newcomers?

In order to answer these questions, more questions arise. First, do we remember who we are as the Indigenous Peoples of Turtle Island? Second, through what lens are we to learn about other cultures? Ours or theirs? Third, how are we to honestly teach the truth in the His/story books, that is, the truth about colonization, about empiricism, about capitalism, and about what we now celebrate as democracy? How are we going to teach our story to others?

What is it we want our students to know about ourselves and of others? And finally, what will be our vision of the future of humankind?

These questions are examined here as I attempt to outline a philosophy that is still held sacred by Indigenous Peoples around the world, namely, we are all in this together. We are here with the water, the air, the other creatures of the earth, the plants, the soil. If we human beings, the last to be created, do not begin to understand and to learn from those who came before us, then we will continue to jeopardize the future of our grandchildren's grandchildren. It is up to all of us to learn, to accept, to celebrate, and to honour our neighbours. Using the framework of what I have been calling the Anishinabe Three Rs—Respect, Responsibility, and Relationship—we can begin by showing respect for the lives of our brothers and sisters; we can accept responsibility and humble ourselves to take only what is needed, and we can also try to understand that we are in a relationship with each other. Using this framework and the understanding of these teachings will help everyone together to share the vast gifts Mother Earth has provided, and everyone can benefit and live *Mino Bimadiziwin*, a good life.

From an Indigenous perspective, transcultural literacies call on every educator to accept their responsibility to learn, to include, and to teach about the people of this earth. It is up to every educator and every Faculty of Education to ensure that all teachers have an understanding that what we currently teach in our schools is taught from the point of view of one dominant culture. This point of view favours a Eurocentric viewpoint and in many ways is biased, racist, intolerant, and ignorant of the knowledge inherent in other cultures. When we teach from only one way and favour one dominant segment of the world's population, we do this to the detriment of everyone. A variety of examples will be provided to demonstrate how curriculum and knowledge are biased toward a Eurocentric, Western philosophy, and the language and textbooks teachers use in schools today place the majority of humankind, and specifically Indigenous Peoples, as second-class citizens.

I offer the readers, policy makers, teachers, and students a challenge. The challenge is to honestly examine the basic assumptions made in the current education system. I want everyone to challenge what we assume is the "correct" knowledge, the "facts" and perspectives that we teach from, and determine if we truly honour other cultures. When we challenge these assumptions, we will see that in reality the knowledge we teach in today's schools is truly a narrow view of His/Her/story, and a biased view of the world. When we challenge these assumptions, we may begin to see how we have denigrated other cultures, and then we can begin to teach in a respectful, responsible way. We need to examine what we are doing and truly identify what this tells us about how we are teaching our students.

To help with this discussion, I present teachings that I have received that are the foundation for my own teaching and life. These teachings are from the Anishinabe tradition and the Midewewin Lodge that has been my home for the past several years.

ORIGIN STORIES/WHOSE STORIES?

I was born in the area now defined by Treaty #3 (the Anishinabe territory in northwest Ontario, west of Thunder Bay, in the area of Quetico Park). My mother was born in the area now defined by Treaty #11 (Denedah, the land of the Dene People, and specifically, on the shores of Great Bear Lake), and I currently live in the area of the Treaty #5 Elders and Ancestors (northern Manitoba, in the land of the Cree, Oji-Cree, and Dene). As I introduce myself and my connections to the land and my ancestors, I share an understanding that is inherent in the Anishinabe. This understanding is that we are all of this land, we are this land, and it is the land that makes us who we are. This understanding is embedded in our teachings, our stories, our way of life, our culture and traditions, and is what we were given as Anishinabe, as Dene, as Haudenosaunee, in our original teachings. I was born in the town of Atikokan (in Anishinabemowin, "land of caribou bones"). Since the beginning of time it has been the home of the caribou, moose, elk, sturgeon, trout, pickerel, eagle, blue jay, and raven, the boreal forest and the white pine. However, in the 1940s, Atikokan became an economic boomtown because someone found that under the rock was a deposit of iron ore. A lake was drained, a town was built, and iron ore was mined, refined, and carried away to be used to produce steel. When the iron ore was all taken, the land was abandoned, and left to return to its natural state. The local people were also abandoned to find other meaningful and gainful employment. This is but one small example of the capitalism, colonialism, and resource-based economy that was brought to this land. It is an example of the conflicts of philosophy, traditions, economics, and relationships among the peoples who now live on this land and those who have been here since the beginning of time.

This is just part of my story. If, as King (2003) tells us, "all we are" is our stories, then why do we not know more stories about other cultures, and truth-fully, why do we not know the real stories about this dominant culture? As we talk about transcultural literacies, we are talking about the need to return to the beginning, to honour the original stories of all peoples.

From the original teachings received by the Anishinabe, our ancestors knew that the earth was round, that there were others with whom we shared this planet. They knew the earth travelled around the sun, and the moon travelled around the earth. They knew that we are all connected to all of Creation, and that as the last to be created, human beings were to live with and learn from all those who came before them. We were no better than any other of the Creator's creatures. Our original teachings provide us with a way of life, a philosophy, and a worldview that has sustained us since the beginning of time. All of this is to say that our ancestors here on Turtle Island were intelligent, knowledgeable, lived a sustainable life, and passed on this knowledge throughout the centuries to their children and their children's children.

The Prophesy of the Seven Fires (Benton Banai, 1988) told us that we were going to be joined by people from across the water, that they would be coming here to live among us. We were to prepare ourselves for their coming, and over time, a series of events would unfold and would come to change us. Our ancestors were not given specific details about exactly what would happen, but at the end of the Seventh Fire it would be up to all of us to decide how we were going to live together and what we would do together to ensure that there would be a place for our grandchildren's grandchildren. Our ancestors prepared for the time when many others would come to this land. When Columbus first landed in the Caribbean (in the Bahamas, 1492), the Arawak, and the Kalinago (also known as the Island Carib People), were prepared with feasts and gifts for these strangers. When the strangers first encountered our ancestors, what did they think, and what was their frame of mind? We know that Columbus thought them to be heathens, primitive, and ignorant of civilized ways. We know that although the Wampanoag welcomed and assisted the Pilgrims in adapting to the new land, the relationships and Treaty that were established were not honoured by the Christian Brethren. They were not interested in learning about us. As His/story shows us, it appears they were more interested in gold, commerce, and profit. This was not a promising start to transcultural literacies.

As we entered the 21st century, we were in the time of the Seventh Fire, or as told in another Nation's story, the Eighth Fire. Today, we are faced with the negative impact humans have had on our Mother Earth, and on each other. Again, thinking about the frame of mind in which we operate our schools, we need to ask the important questions. Current curriculum dictates that we are to teach this His/story, but whose His/story, and whose truth? His/story books teach us about the rise of Western civilization. Do we teach our students that from the time the Greek and the Roman civilizations began to expand their nations, there have been as few as 20 years in which one "civilized" nation has not been at war with another "civilized" nation, all so that one nation can dominate another "lesser" nation? Western science and technologies have created weapons of mass destruction and developed technological advances that have reshaped our climate and our lives. The His/story of Western civilization is a His/story of using Mother Earth as a capitalist dream, a profit machine to be used and abused without conscious thought about the consequences. As the noble examples of capitalism have demonstrated (note, for instance, Rockefeller, Carnegie, Trump, and many more who have made billions of dollars on the backs of workers as they have pursued the American Dream), the current climate changes, the polluted rivers and waters, the decimated fields, are all inevitable consequences of this pursuit of profit. Although these financial icons of capitalism have amassed unheard-of wealth for themselves and their families, in their wake they have left a scarred earth; they have destroyed countless lives, and leave an uncertain future for all of our grandchildren. Modern-day environmental crises, observes Richmond (2018), "are in fact outcomes of the historic and ongoing cultural and environmental dispossession of First Nation peoples" (p. 180). More dialogue is needed, she writes, to explore the multi-faceted relationship between Indigenous Peoples and the land, and its impact on social determinants of health, "including social relationships, spirituality, and access to medicines" (p. 180). Richmond (2018) explains:

> In the past century, the Anishinabe have been dispossessed of their traditional lands due to a number of environmentally exploitive industries, including the arrival of the white trappers, the development of the Canadian Pacific Railway, logging on the Pic River and St. Mary's River, the production of steel at Sault Ste. Marie, and the mining of the Hemlo gold deposit. Among the many other colonial developments, these particular industries have significantly undermined the Anishinabe's traditional use of the land. (p. 176)

So the question for educators is: Do we teach the reality of Western civilization and capitalism? Or do we ignore the realities of the so-called free market economy (land grabs, slavery, union busting, company towns, as well as abuse and deceit after Métis scrip was issued)? This litany of unspoken reality is presented in order to be honest with ourselves and our neighbours as we continue the discussion regarding transcultural literacies. In this time of the Seventh/Eighth Fire, it is time for all of us to reflect on who we are, how we are going to live together on Mother Earth, and how we are going to respect the teachings we were all given. This requires an honesty, humility, and truth regarding the actual stories of this land. As educators, it is up to us to determine what we want to teach our children about the differences in the meaning and importance of our original teachings, what we have come to be as human beings, and what we want our students to learn so they can be responsible and prepared to leave what their children's children will need for a good life. Richmond (2018) highlights an Anishinabe Elder's teaching on the strong spiritual connection to the land: "There is a respect that we need to show the land and its relatedness to us. We are the land. If the land is sick, then it isn't very long before we're going to get sick" (p. 172). In her conversations with Anishinabe Elders, Richmond highlighted several themes: the symbiotic relationship between people and the land must be honoured and respected; physical, emotional, and spiritual health is directly tied to the way people care for the land; knowledge cannot be learned "only by talking about it ... to really understand knowledge, it must be practiced" (p. 178); and the health of future generations depends upon the reverence for life that people practise each day.

SO WHAT DO WE NEED TO ASK OURSELVES?

As an educator in Canada, I have been working with curricula that make basic assumptions about the majority society, *including* the assumption that this majority society has the right to impose its will and knowledge on all others. Here are some basic assumptions that we can challenge.

First, what year is it? At this point, it's 2019. But according to whom? For millions of people around the world there are other ways to measure the passage of time. For some it is the year 4352, for others it is 992. So what year is it? As educators in Canada, the calendar says that it is 2019 and does not acknowledge that this date is imposed on the rest of the world because of the dominant nature of Western civilization. Are we aware that others in the world see the world and time differently? So what should we be teaching our students?

Next, when does the new year start? For millions of people in India the eve of Diwali is the start of the Lunar Year. Or, not until the Earth awakens in the spring according to most Nations on Turtle Island, Canada. But according to the Julian calendar, New Year's Eve is December 31 and the new year starts January 1.

Another question is: How many seasons are there? Our school textbooks and Google handouts all tell us there are four seasons. The question is: according to whom? The Dene acknowledge five seasons, the Muskegowuk six seasons, and for other nations, eight seasons. If you are living on a tropical island in the Pacific such as Fiji, then two seasons. Who says we should teach four seasons? Why are we not teaching about how others see and interact with the world?

Should we be giving pencils to four-year-old children and expecting them to write their names? In the Anishinabe tradition, and all other Indigenous traditions, children are taught to watch and listen, to be patient, to learn their language, to know about stories, to see how things are done, and then they will engage when they are ready. When a young person is ready, they are given the tools to accomplish tasks the adults are doing. They are brought into the way of life through experiences, through language, through observation, and through cognitive processes of thinking and reasoning. When we give children pencils and ask them to write their names before they have a deep understanding of words and language, are we helping them or are we setting them up for failure?

As we ask ourselves these questions, and look at Indigenous Peoples around the world, we can begin to learn that there are different traditions, different histories, and different visions of how we are to live. We see that the lives of other peoples are not honoured in our His/story books because, according to these approved texts, the real His/story is the His/story of Western civilization. We learn of the great conquerors, explorers, and heroes who lived among the "primitive" peoples of the world and used their military force to impose their will on "the savages." We have by abeyance, convention, or the right of might accepted Western civilization as the "right way," and by this exclusion, the only way. When we honestly examine this "right way," we learn it is really the White Way. Colonialism began when Persians and Greeks fought for land, and continued through the Holy Wars as Christians fought the "Infidels." By the 14th century, Western civilization had established its power and presence through its Doctrine of Discovery, using its weapons of mass destruction and its will to impose its power over all "non-Christian" lands, and giving itself the authority to civilize the world by whatever means necessary. It is this dominant vision that is being taught in schools today: that

Western civilization is the culmination of all that is good about humankind. The knowledge of Indigenous Peoples is largely ignored. So how do we get to *Kenanow*?

WHY DO WE THINK THERE IS ONLY ONE STORY?

For educators, it is our task and responsibility to know that people have different understandings, different knowledges, and different ways of seeing the world. Manu Aluli Meyer (2001) explains that in her homeland of Hawaii, she grew up with a sense of the ocean that defined her being Hawaiian. In her story, she tells of a Harvard professor who asks, Do Hawaiians have an epistemology? The professor based this question on the writings of Descartes, *Cogito, ergo sum*, which translates to "I think, therefore I am." This statement elucidates the reified nature of Euro-Western thinking. As Meyer (2001) tells us in her story, she *is* because she is *of the land*. She is human because she is made up of the land, the ocean, the air, and the sky. Her life, her spirit, exists because she is part of all of Creation. Her story (Her/story) presents an Indigenous way of looking at the world, another way of analyzing who we are in the world, and how we are to be. Western thought, with its reification of the Doctrine of Discovery and *Terra Nullius*,[3] are not the only way. As she questions the dominant nature of her chosen academic field and philosophy, Meyer addresses the need for all of us to learn about all of us.

While Western thought (Euro-American thinking) predominates in much of the world, it is not the only way of thinking. While American media dominates throughout the world, there are other ways of seeing the world. As we consider transcultural literacies, we are asking ourselves: How are we to teach and to learn about other cultures? Faced with the realities of great and powerful egocentric cultural societies, some may even ask, why even bother?

HIS/STORY OR OUR STORY?

In our classrooms today, we have students from many different parts of the world. It is only in remote, isolated communities where this might not be true, but with the transient nature of the teaching profession in Canada's North,[4] this is not necessarily the case.

Onaubinisay, Elder Jim Dumont, has asked, "Have we lost our Indigenous mind?" (2002). Elder Dumont teaches us that the Indigenous mind thinks differently, sees differently, and responds differently from other minds. He outlines an Anishinabe way of being and thinking. In Anishinabe terms, our mind consists of our Indigenous intelligence, centredness, consciousness, total responsiveness, connectedness to the whole, connectedness to all of Creation, and living the values (Teachings of the Seven Grandfathers) by seeing, relating, knowing, and doing. This continuum is our life, and our way of thinking and being is embedded in what we know as Indigenous Peoples. He is asking us as Indigenous Peoples and educators who have grown up in a time of colonization, in a reserve/reservation system that has removed us from our traditional connections to the land, to work to create an educational environment that respects our Indigenous minds.

Lev Vygotsky (1978) provides academic support for Onaubinisay's teachings. In his work *Mind in Society*, Vygotsky (1978) outlines similar concepts associated with knowledge that is the basis for all cultures. Along with Howard Gardner (1983), they suggest that the development of "mind" is what cultures do. The way each of us perceives, processes, and utilizes knowledge is different and dependent on the culture in which we are raised. How we think and how we communicate is as important as the cultural artifacts that are seen to be the culture. Too often cultural artifacts are used to create the stereotype for a culture. Even in our textbooks, it often appears that all First Nations Peoples wear a headdress, or live in a teepee, and ride horses on the plains. Without respectful knowledge, and given these stereotypes, it is easy to come to the conclusion that all First Nations Peoples were hunters and gatherers and "just" roamed this land. Artifacts like the canoe, the kayak, and even our bows and arrows, along with the headdress of the Chiefs of the Plains and Prairies, are taken as representative of all "Indians," and it is difficult to teach beyond what easily becomes an accepted stereotype. It is more difficult to teach that Indigenous tools are not just cultural artifacts. Each Nation has its own tools, and these vary greatly across the continent. Each tool has been designed and engineered specifically for the culture, and thus we can learn a great deal about Indigenous cultures through their cultural tools and artifacts. As we learn about different cultures, we should be looking at the tools that were essential to that culture. As we learn about the tools of a society, we will be able to better understand the purposes for which they were designed and to honour the peoples who designed them.

If it is our goal that our students should know the people who live on this land, then we need to allow them to learn about the hundreds of different cultures and languages, and about how our ancestors lived on this land and how they thought. If it is our goal to have our students understand the original teachings given to humankind, and how different cultures have grown and developed, then our education system must provide each student the opportunity to access the information, knowledge, and wisdom that are the foundations for the many different Nations that continue to live around this fragile earth.

Vygotsky (1978) provides us with a framework for this exploration of language, tools, and cultural mediators. Language is key to each culture and frames how and what we think about. In most Indigenous languages of North America, there is no *he* and *she* as in many of the Romance languages. The languages of Turtle Island categorize beings as "living" and "not living." Gender (male or female) is not the significant indicator and is not an important issue. Being alive is what is important. As I noted earlier, neither is there a word for "work" as in "I have to go to work and do my job." There is only life, specifically, *Mino Bimadiziwin*, as in, "When I get up in the morning, I celebrate this life and do what I need to do for myself and my family" to follow the good life.

Another linguistic feature is that Indigenous languages do not have or use the comparative or superlative: good, better, best. In our Indigenous languages, there just "is." The languages all reflect a state of being. For Indigenous Peoples around the world, there is never a question of who is more important, who is better, or who is best. What is important is that each of us be alive and live in a good way.

These linguistic examples have important and powerful implications for the study of transcultural literacies. If the one doing the "studying/learning" has embedded in their psyche that there is a good, better, best, and is not aware that those being studied/learned about do not, then a major conflict in both understanding and relationship will quickly cause misunderstanding. Add the academic imperative from the one doing the studying that there is a right way and a wrong way, a thought deeply engrained in the field of research, and the one(s) being studied/learned about will quickly be seen as inferior, primitive, second class, and therefore, misunderstood. Our task as educators is to help all our students learn to see through someone else's eyes. Tomson Highway (2018) writes of the impression made when audiences first viewed the work of Ojibway visual artist Norval Morrisseau in 1962:

> Up to this point, the non-Indigenous world had been under the impression that we were a people without a history, a religion, a philosophy, a mythology, a theology, a soul, a dream, or even a language.... Now here at his gallery in downtown Toronto, white society was being ushered

into the world of magic that is Indigenous mythology, a dream world inhabited by the most extraordinary beings and events. The Trickster (Wesakechak in Cree, Nanabush in Ojibwa, Glooscap in Mi'kmaq, Raven, Coyote, and so on), the Windigo (in Ojibwa, Weetigo in Cree), the Little People (Memekwesiwak in Cree, Memequasit in Ojibwa), the Son of Ayash, the Woman of the Rolling Head, Oh-ma-ma-ma (the Great Mother Goddess).... The Non-Indigenous world was astonished.... Here was a narrative tradition that went back to the beginnings of human consciousness not only in North America but on this planet. (p. xxiii)

Highway emphasizes that when people begin to tell their own stories, "in their own voices and from their own perspectives," something wonderful can happen. Poetry, biography, oral narratives, painting, music, and works of fiction told from an Indigenous perspective can enrich, empower, and heal so that future generations "can contribute in a manner so significant and so positive to the life of their country that they will help transform it into one that is even better than it is today" (p. xxxi).

SO WHAT SHOULD WE BE TEACHING OUR STUDENTS?

In light of the Truth and Reconciliation Commission hearings, we should start with some basic truths. North and South America are the homes of over 350 different First Nations, and have been since the beginning of time (in 1492 there were 500 Nations, but through genocide, colonization and modernity, many of these Nations have been exterminated). Africa is a continent of over 1,000 different Nations of peoples, each with their own languages, traditions, and ways of living a good life. Through the process of colonization by the "civilized" countries of England, France, Belgium, Portugal, Spain, and Germany, all three continents have been divided, segmented, and brutalized by the colonizers. In doing so, over 100 different countries have been created in Africa, none of which follow the traditional lands of the peoples who have been in Africa since the beginning of time. This simple fact has created the many conflicts that have arisen and that continue in this post-colonial time. Similarly, in North and South America, countries and states and provinces have segmented the many nations of this land, separating the people from their traditional lands. To be clear, colonization is the process whereby one

culture, through violence, slavery, economics, and religious doctrines, dominates, subordinates, subjects, and enslaves other cultures to ensure the superiority of their own. In a truthful teaching of world His/story, the examples of
colonization should not be celebrated, but understood in their time period.
Columbus was not a hero. Cortez was not an honourable man. Captain Cook
had no respect for the "savages" he met as he sailed around the world.

So let us return to Thomas King. It is all about stories, the many stories of
humankind across the many different lands. If we are truly to understand and
to respect each other, then we must include the stories from different peoples
in our teachings. We can learn to see how others see and understand what
others understand through story.

We can start with Creation Stories, stories that provide a framework
for our ways of being and seeing. What can we learn from Spider Woman
(Lakota), Sky Woman (Haudenosaunee), or Eve, the woman created from the
rib of a man (Jewish/Muslim/Christian)? Each of these stories sets the world
in motion and places each of us in relation to each other and all of Creation.
We can learn humility and respect for our elder brothers and sisters when we
learn that Sky Woman would have died had it not been for the Winged Ones
who helped her land, and the Water Beings who provided her a place to land.

Creation Stories are not just great literature; they are imagination, relationship, language, and culture. If we are to respect transcultural literacies,
we need to begin with Everyone's Story. As Bawdwaywidun Banaise (Benton
Banai, 1988) tells us, "All Creation Stories are true." He reminds us that every
Creation Story sets the foundation for our understandings as a culture, and
as we learn and respect each other, knowing the Creation Stories allows for a
common language and the possibility to walk our paths together.

Names are equally important, and learning that others see what we see but
have different names and stories will add to our understanding of each other.
This thinking includes place names, the names of the stars and constellations,
the Four Directions, the seasons, the moons, and the foods we eat. We can
all "see" the seven stars in the north sky, but what are the teachings/stories
that different people tell? These seven stars are called by a number of different
names, including the Great Bear, the Big Dipper, and the Plough.[5] And different cultures have different stories that explain these seven stars. However,
what "story" is taught in schools? Which explanation is given precedence, and
which are termed "myth" or "legend"? Another example, as described earlier, is the assertion that there are four seasons—summer, fall, winter, and

spring—when that is only one of many ways to see the world. There is no "right" answer and it is not a matter of who is "right"; it is a matter of how we see the world, how we interact with all of Creation, and how we interact with each other.

So what is it we are afraid of? Is it the learning? Are we afraid to learn about other cultures? Are we afraid that theirs might be better than ours? Are we afraid that our brains might hurt or explode if we learn too much? Besides telling us that all we are is stories, Thomas King (2003) also asked, "What is it about us that you don't like?" which can be applied to any "other than White" culture. It is up to all of us to stop being afraid, and to begin being honest and respectful of others.

It is about *Kenanow*. As human beings living in a diverse, interdependent, and integrated world, our students need to hear about truth, honesty, bravery, and respect. They need to learn about love, humility, and the wisdom of others with whom we share this planet. There are classrooms now where children have embraced Save the Children and We Day. There are schools, like the Met School, embracing the challenge of integrated learning and the freedom to learn. There are schools where science, technology, mathematics, and engineering from across cultures are being taught. There are schools where the step-by-step grade system has been eliminated and students are learning at their own paces, and being successful with others, both younger and older. It has taken some time for some schools to implement Ivan Illich's (1971) ideas regarding de-schooling, but today there are schools and classrooms without walls,[6] where students work together on the land to learn how the environment is interdependent, and to learn how human beings are dependent on all of Creation.

This is our challenge: to teach all of us about all of us. In today's economic climate, where 10% of the world's population are consuming 80% of the world's resources, where less than 1% of the world's population hold 95% of the world's wealth, we need to change our assumptions about knowledge, society, the environment, and care. A return to the Anishinabe Three Rs—Respect, Responsibility, and Relationship—needs to occur in every classroom, in every school, with every student. Do you accept this challenge? Let's work together for our children, and our children's children, all around this beautiful world.

Miigwech, Maa Sii Chōk, Ekosi

QUESTIONS FOR REFLECTION AND DISCUSSION

1. Anderson critiques "basic assumptions" about knowledge systems that we should challenge. Do you agree with his critique? Can you think of other examples of assumptions and beliefs that often go unchallenged? As an educator, what can you do to encourage a critical inquiry into unquestioned beliefs, norms, and assumptions?

2. Take a few minutes to freewrite in response to one or both of these quotes from the chapter: What are your thoughts? What might this look like in your context? What transformation could these ideas bring, if they were enacted? What would that take?

    > "As educators, it is up to us to determine ... what we want our students to learn so they can be responsible and prepared to leave what their children's children will need for a good life."

    > "Teaching to subvert and to transform cannot be an idealistic thought. So how can we do even more disrupting of the status quo in classrooms, school spaces, or other social settings?"

3. What makes us feel we belong to a place? What makes a person feel they belong to a community/family/school/university? Can you identify two or three factors that would lead a person to feel alienated or isolated?

4. Anderson writes, "Creation Stories are not just great literature, they are imagination, relationship, language, and culture. If we are to respect transcultural literacies, we need to begin with Everyone's Story." Take a few minutes to read, then respond with a symbolic sketch inspired by "The Haudenosaunee Creation Story" (Oneida Indian Nation), available at http://www.oneidaindiannation.com/the-haudenosaunee-creation-story/.

5. You can find an image of Daphne Odjig's mural *The Indian in Transition* (1978) online. What do you notice? What story(ies) do you think it is telling? Then read the description provided by curator Lee-Ann Martin (as cited by Bailey, 2011):

    > *The Indian in Transition* takes the viewer on an historical odyssey that begins before the arrival of Europeans, continues through the devastation and destruction of Aboriginal cultures, and ends

on an expression of rejuvenation and hope. Odjig's story unfolds with the figure on the left playing the drum, which symbolizes strong Aboriginal cultural traditions, while overhead is a protective Thunderbird.

Then a boat arrives filled with pale-skinned people. The boat's bow becomes a serpent, a bad omen in Anishnabe mythology.

Next, Odjig depicts Aboriginal people trapped in a vortex of political, social, economic and cultural change. Four ethereal figures rise above the fallen cross and broken drums against a background of a bureaucratic symbol of authority.

To the right, a figure, protectively sheltering the sacred drum, struggles free, under the protection of the Thunderbird and the eye of Mother Earth depicted in the top left. Odjig ends the story as it began, with a message of hope and mutual understanding for the future. (See "Daphne Odjig" in *Herizons* magazine, Spring 2011, available at: http://www.herizons.ca/node/481)

6. What stories contribute most to your understandings of who you are? Jot them down as they come to mind. They may be stories that you have heard from family members, friends, grandparents, Elders; they may be stories you have learned at home, school, a place of worship; they may be stories you associate with certain activities or events; you might also think about stories you have read (or have had read to you).

7. Identify two or three ideas from this chapter that you wish to think about further, read more about, discuss with someone, or apply to your own teaching.

DEEPEN YOUR INQUIRY: RELATED READINGS AND RESOURCES

Anzaldúa, G. (2010). Movimientos de rebeldia y las culturas que traicionan. *Race/ Ethnicity: Multidisciplinary Global Contexts, 4*(1), 1–7.

Campbell, M. (1973). *Halfbreed*. Toronto: McClelland and Stewart.

Cardinal, T., Highway, T., Johnston, B., King, T., Maracle, B., Marchessault, J., Qitsualik, R. A., & Taylor, D. H. (2004). *Our story: Aboriginal voices on Canada's past*. Toronto: Anchor Canada.

Carlson, N., Steinhauer, K., & Goyette, L. (2013). *Disinherited generations: Our struggle to reclaim treaty rights for First Nations women and their descendants*. Edmonton: University of Alberta Press.

Clutesi, G. *Stand tall, my son*. (1990). Illustrated by the author and Mark Tebbut. Port Alberni, BC: Clutesi Agencies.

Deerchild, R. (2008). *This is a small northern town*. Winnipeg: J. Gordon Shillingford.

Dennis, D. (2005). Tales of an urban Indian. In D. Dennis, *Two Plays* (pp. 35–36). Toronto: Playwrights Canada Press.

Doerfler, J., Sinclair, N. J., & Stark, H. K. (2013). *Centering Anishinaabeg studies: Understanding the world through stories*. East Lansing, MI: Michigan State University.

Dumonet, M. (1996/2015). *A really good brown girl*. London, ON: Brick Books.

French, A. (1992). *The restless nomad*. Winnipeg: Pemmican.

Guthrie, G. (2005). *Indian country: Essays on contemporary Native culture*. Waterloo, ON: Wilfrid University Press.

Highway, T. (1988). *The rez sisters: A play in two acts*. Saskatoon: Fifth House.

Johnson, E. P. (1912/1974). *Flint and feather: The complete poems of E. Pauline Johnson (Tekahionwake)*. Toronto: Hodder and Stoughton.

King, T. (2003). *The truth about stories*. Toronto: House of Anansi.

Manitoba First Nations Education Resource Centre. (2014). *Grassroots Anthology* (Vol. 1, revised ed.). Winnipeg: Manitoba Curriculum Support Centre.

McCall, S., Reder, D., Gaertner, D., & L'Hirondelle Hill, G. (Eds.). (2017). *Read, listen, tell: Indigenous stories from Turtle Island*. Waterloo, ON: Wilfrid Laurier University Press.

McLeod, N. (2007). *Cree narrative memory: From treaties to contemporary times*. Saskatoon: Purich.

Mishenene, R. A., & Toulouse, P. R. (Eds.). (2011). *Strength and struggle: Perspectives from First Nations, Inuit, and Métis peoples in Canada*. Toronto: McGraw-Hill Ryerson.

Morra, L. M., & Reder, D. (2009). *Troubling tricksters: Revisioning critical conversations*. Waterloo, ON: Wilfrid Laurier Press.

Newhouse, D. R., Voyageur, C. J., & Beavon, D. (2005). *Hidden in plain sight: Contributions of Aboriginal Peoples to Canadian identity and culture*. Toronto: University of Toronto Press.

Reder, D., & Morra, L. (2016). *Learn, teach, challenge: Approaching Indigenous literatures*. Waterloo, ON: Wilfrid Laurier Press.

Six Nations of the Grand River Territory. (2019). *GoodMinds.com: First Nations, Métis, Inuit books*. Available from: http://www.goodminds.com/

Sterling, S. (1992). *My name is Seepeetza*. Toronto: Douglas & McIntyre.

Wagamese, R. (1997). *A quality of light*. Toronto: Doubleday Canada.

Wagamese, R. (2008). *Ragged company*. Toronto: Doubleday Canada.

Wheeler, J. (1989). *Brothers in arms*. Winnipeg: Pemmican.

Young, M. I. (2005/2009). *Pimatisiwin—walking in a good way*. Winnipeg: Pemmican.

NOTES

1. I use the term *His/story* to remind myself, and others, that the story of humankind often neglects and dishonours our Mothers and Grandmothers, the women who have given us life. As I was taught history, I was told about all the Great Men who did Great Things. If we don't tell Her/story, and remember the truth about women, we will continue to dishonour them, and disgrace ourselves.

2. I will use the term *Anishinabe*, an Anishinabe/Ojibway word meaning "the Original Peoples of this Land," unless I am referring to a specific Nation.

3. *Terra Nullius*, translated as "land belonging to no one," was incorporated along with the Doctrine of Discovery in the mid-15th century. The conquering nations believed that if the land they came upon was not inhabited by "Christians" then the land was deemed to be empty and could be claimed by those who "discovered" the land, and further, that there were no recognized human beings (those who were not Christian). (http://stage6.pbworks.com/f/The+Doctrine+of+terra+nullius.pdf)

4. And just as a reminder, Canada's North is a proper use of the "possessive." Saying *Canada's Aboriginal Peoples* is NOT an appropriate use of the possessive.

5. See, for example: http://www.constellation-guide.com/big-dipper/

6. See, for example: Classrooms Without Walls (available at https://www.meadowridge.bc.ca/academics/experiential-outdoor-education/classroom-without-walls); Schools Without Walls (available at https://en.wikipedia.org/wiki/School_Without_Walls_(Washington,_D.C.)); and Preschools Without Walls (available at https://www.nytimes.com/2015/12/31/fashion/outdoor-preschool-in-nature.html).

REFERENCES

Benton Banai, E. (1988). *The Mishomis book: The voice of the Ojibway*. Minneapolis: Red School House Press.

Deloria Jr., V. (1992). *God is red: A Native view of religion*. Golden, CO: Fulcrum.

Dumont, J. (2002). Indigenous intelligence: Have we lost our Indigenous mind? *Native Americas, 19*(3–4), 14–16.

Gardner, H. (1983). *Frames of mind: The theory of multiple intelligences.* New York: Basic Books.

Highway, T. (2018). *From oral to written: A celebration of Indigenous literature in Canada, 1980–2010.* Vancouver, BC: Talonbooks.

Illich, I. (1971). *Deschooling society.* London: Calder and Boyers.

Katz, J., & Lamoureux, K. (2018). *Ensouling our schools: A universally designed framework for mental health, well-being, and reconciliation.* Winnipeg, MB: Portage & Main Press.

King, T. (2003). *The truth about stories.* Toronto: House of Anansi.

Meyer, M. A. (2001). Acultural assumptions of empiricism: A Native Hawaiian critique. *Canadian Journal of Native Education, 25*(2), 188–198.

Richmond, C. (2018). The relatedness of people, land, and health: Stories from Anishinabe Elders. In M. Greenwood, S. de Leew, & N. M. Lindsay (Eds.), *Determinants of Indigenous Peoples' Health: Beyond the social* (2nd ed.; pp. 167–186). Toronto: Canadian Scholars Press.

Tagalik, S. (2018). Inuit knowledge systems, Elders, and determinants of health: Harmony, balance, and the role of holistic thinking. In M. Greenwood, S. de Leew, & N. M. Lindsay (Eds.), *Determinants of Indigenous Peoples' health: Beyond the social* (2nd ed.; pp. 93–101). Toronto: Canadian Scholars Press.

Vygotsky, L. (1978). *Mind in society: The development of higher psychological processes.* Cambridge, MA: Harvard University Press.

Wagamese, R. (2011). *One story, one song.* Toronto: Douglas McIntyre.

Conclusion

A Vision of Vibrant Wholeness, Inter-Relatedness, and Meaningful Purpose

Michelle A. Honeyford

As my colleagues in this volume suggest, in the spaces of our classrooms, in our relationships with our students, and in our pedagogical practices as educators and teacher educators, we need literacy theories and practices that are as dynamic, complex, and multiple as our students. We need to understand our students and their literacy practices as intimately connected to the people in their lives, the places they are from, the ways they understand their worlds, and the languages and discourses they use to participate in their day-to-day lives. We need to recognize that literacy is not an academic concept, but a human one.

Our local and global communities are suffering. The cultural, economic, human, and ecological toll of colonialism, racism, and other systemic forms of discrimination, inequity, violence, and injustice affect our students on a daily basis. If we are to engage with one another in truth and reconciliation, we must understand how words like *savage* have been used to dehumanize Indigenous peoples and to justify the cultural genocide of children and youth in educational institutions. We need to acknowledge that the loss of a language is also the loss of cultural identity, the loss of stories and songs that connect us to loved ones, the loss of beauty and poetry and humour, and the loss of ways of understanding who we are and what our purpose is in this world.

The authors of these chapters have provoked, inspired, challenged, and questioned us to think deeply about the future of language and literacy education. They have problematized the unthinking acceptance of educational policy, curriculum, and practice that continue to oppress, ignore, and harm. The chapter authors have taken up the concerns that I know are important to many of us engaged in language and literacy education: ethical concerns about what we teach and how; political concerns about whose interests our courses, programs, and assessments serve; professional concerns about job demands that pull us away from the very reasons we chose this profession: our love for the art of teaching, for our students, and for our subject matter. In the contexts of high school classrooms, alternative programs, faculties of education, afterschool programs, adult education, and international learning experiences, these authors have considered the challenges and opportunities that we are facing. They urge us, in the complexities of our own contexts and locations, to respond.

Transcultural literacies offer a vision for teaching and learning that calls us to be in relationship with one another. It is difficult to build trust in a broken relationship. The Truth and Reconciliation Commission of Canada (2015) called for changes in education to signal a commitment to learning how to live in respectful, responsible relationship. To us, the cover image by Métis artist Christi Belcourt is a vision of relationship. In Haida, Cree, and Anishinabe cultures, the bear is a powerful and sacred guardian. Indeed, the bear is often viewed as an "Elder Kinsman" to be revered and honoured (Kaldera & Krasskova, 2012). There is a close spiritual bond between bears and humans (Newhouse, Voyageur, & Beavon, 2005). Viewed as the protector of the animal kingdom, bears are said to possess miraculous powers to heal their own wounds, despite severe injuries. In many Indigenous cultures, the bear is associated with courage, vitality, and purpose. Kaldera and Krasskova (2012) write that in ancient cultures, "Bear holds the wisdom of how to nurture and care for one's tribe, how to ensure the continuity of a tradition, and how to sustain oneself in the harshest of climates" (p. 155). To re-vision relationships in teaching and learning is a call to listen and respect, to acknowledge the harm that has been done, and to commit to creating a better future together. This requires an openness to re-vision education as a "beautiful risk" to learn anew.

In their book, *Manitowapow*, a collection of "Aboriginal writings from the land of water" (Manitoba), Sinclair and Cariou (2011) discuss how Daphne Odjig's mural, the *Creation Story* (featured in the Manitoba Museum), tells many stories, one of them a story about creating a "respectful and dignified home" (p. 4). For our purposes, we might borrow from their description to consider what it means to create "respectful and dignified" schools, spaces that honour the relationships we wish to build with one another:

> It takes a tremendous amount of constant and tireless work. It involves creating a place full of possibility, built through sustainability and equitable relationships involving people, animals, spirits, and the landscape. It involves being honest with one's history, truth-telling, and talking about the complicated parts—even if that inspires discomfort and disagreement. It involves recognizing and understanding that many have sacrificed much to provide others with opportunities. It involves constant motion, eternal change, and a commitment to balance, cooperation, and

mutual responsibility. It involves acknowledging that life is complex, that it is all around us, and that we are a part of it. (p. 4)

Belcourt's image inspires us to envision what education can be.

Transcultural literacies entangle us with one another, creating a living tapestry of vivid colour, beauty, and strength. In our schools, we need to cultivate literacies of compassion. We need to teach with tenderness and care, acknowledging the hurt and pain that our students are experiencing, and helping one another see beauty and possibility. We need to seed spaces of empathy, acknowledging that if we are asking our students to learn, they will be encountering deep and significant questions. Upon the release of the Canadian National Truth and Reconciliation Commission's Calls to Action (2015), Justice Murray Sinclair argued that education should engage students in answering four key questions: Where do I come from? Who am I? Why am I here? Where am I going? Our classrooms should be places where learners are reading, writing, speaking, listening, viewing, and creating in the process of engaging those questions—in and through literacy practices that tell their own stories. Belcourt's work is a vision of vibrant wholeness, inter-relatedness, and meaningful purpose. That is our vision, too.

REFERENCES

Kaldera, R., & Krasskova, G. (2012). *Neolithic shamanism*. Rochester, NY: Destiny Books.

Newhouse, D. R., Voyageur, C. J., & Beavon, D. (2005). *Hidden in plain sight: Contributions of Aboriginal peoples to Canadian identity and culture*. Toronto: University of Toronto Press.

Sinclair, N. J., & Cariou, W. (Eds.). (2011). *Manitowapow: Aboriginal writings from the land of water*. Winnipeg: Portage & Main Press.

Truth and Reconciliation Commission of Canada. (2015). Calls to Action. Winnipeg: Truth and Reconciliation Commission of Canada. Available at https://nctr.ca/assets/reports/Calls_to_Action_English2.pdf

Contributor Biographies

Dr. David B. Anderson (Wahwahbiginojii) teaches in the Kenanow Faculty of Education, University College of the North, and with the Aanda Wiinjigewin Graduate Program, Seven Generations Education Institute. The Kenanow Learning Model is a traditional Aboriginal educational approach based on the Teachings of the Seven Grandfathers. Translated from the Cree, *Kenanow* means "all of us who are here." The model is based on the kinship system that envisions all things together functioning in an organic system. It teaches identity, belonging, community history, the roles and responsibilities of families and communities, and the process of handing down this knowledge to future generations. His writing shares the vision for education that can be found in Aboriginal teachings—that is, an education that respects children and prepares them to live *Mino Bimadiziwin*, the good life.

Karla Costa is an international PhD student in the Faculty of Education at the University of Manitoba. She holds a master's degree from University of São Paulo (USP). Her research interests focus on teacher development, teaching English as an additional language, critical literacies, and post-colonial studies in education. Karla is an assistant professor at the Federal University of Mato Grosso do Sul in Brazil.

Dr. George J. Sefa Dei (Nana Adusei Sefa Tweneboah) is a professor in the Department of Humanities, Social Sciences, and Social Justice Education at the Ontario Institute for Studies in Education. His teaching, writing, and research interests are in social justice education, the sociology of race and ethnicity, international development, Indigenous knowledges, anti-racist education, and minority schooling. Professor Dei has received numerous awards and distinctions that include: the New Pioneers Award (Skills for Change, 2004); the William P. Hubbard Award for race relations (City of Toronto, 2003); the Community Builder and Community Partnership Award (Toronto Catholic District School Board 2001, 2003); the Ghanaian New Award for education and community development (2000); the ANKH Ann Ramsey Award for Intellectual Initiative and Academic Action (2005); and the Canadian Alliance of Black Educators Award for Excellence in Education and Community Development (2007). Dr. Dei's books include *New Perspectives on Africentric Education* (with Arlo Kempf, 2013), *Removing the Margins* (with Irma Marcia James and Leeno Luke Karumanchery, 2000), and *Inclusive Schooling: A*

Teacher's Companion to Removing the Margins (with Sonia James-Wilson and Jasmin Zine, 2002).

Dr. Michelle A. Honeyford is an associate professor in language and literacy in the Faculty of Education at the University of Manitoba. Her research interests focus on opening up spaces for learning where the cultural identities and ways of knowing of students, teachers, and communities can flourish. Her current research is situated in collaboration with teachers engaged in a professional inquiry community around the teaching of writing, and with teacher candidates designing and leading interest-driven afterschool programs for middle school students. Michelle is the co-director of the Manitoba Writing Project.

Dr. Lloyd Kornelsen is an associate professor in the Faculty of Education and the practicum coordinator for Global College at the University of Winnipeg. His research interests derive from his current work with high school social studies teachers and with international university practicum students; they are grounded in his own 25-year high school teaching career. In 2013, Lloyd was awarded the Manitoba Education Research Network award for outstanding achievement in education research in exploring the intersection of experiential learning, peace education, and global citizenship. His recently published book, *Stories of Transformation: Memories of a Global Citizenship Practicum*, examines the meaning of global citizenship and its most affecting pedagogies.

Marc Kuly is an assistant professor and service-learning coordinator in the Faculty of Education at the University of Winnipeg. Marc works primarily in pre-service teacher education, helping aspiring teachers recognize the operation of power within school systems. His research focuses on the experiences of marginalized students and the utility of narrative approaches to exploring and relating experience.

Dr. Karen M. Magro is a professor of literacy education, adult learning, and applied psychology in the Faculty of Education at the University of Winnipeg. Her teaching and research interests are in refugee and newcomer education, transformative learning theory, creativity, adult literacy, and social justice education. She completed her doctoral studies in education at the Ontario Institute for Studies in Education of the University of Toronto. Karen has been an educator for over 30 years and has taught both nationally and internationally.

Dr. Burcu Yaman Ntelioglou is an assistant professor in the Faculty of Education, Department of Curriculum and Pedagogy at Brandon University. She completed a post-doctoral fellowship and a PhD at the Ontario Institute for Studies in Education, University of Toronto and holds a master's in education from York University. She teaches in both the teacher education and graduate education programs. Her work focuses on the education of linguistically and culturally diverse students in contexts of migration, multiculturalism, and multilingualism; curriculum studies; phenomenology; philosophy in education; literacy education; language maintenance and revitalization; drama education; and the use of collaborative, community-based, participatory, multimodal, and digital methodologies in research.

Dr. Tim Skuce is an assistant professor in the Faculty of Education, Department of Curriculum and Pedagogy at Brandon University. He completed his PhD at the University of Calgary. He is a social studies educator in undergraduate pre-service teacher education and also instructs as part of the graduate studies program. His research interests include philosophical hermeneutics, curriculum theory, and pedagogy.